FRENCH LITERATURE
AND ITS BACKGROUND

1

The Sixteenth Century

FRENCH LITERATURE AND ITS BACKGROUND

EDITED BY

JOHN CRUICKSHANK

1

The Sixteenth Century

OXFORD UNIVERSITY PRESS

LONDON   OXFORD   NEW YORK

1968

Oxford University Press

LONDON OXFORD NEW YORK
GLASGOW TORONTO MELBOURNE WELLINGTON
CAPE TOWN SALISBURY IBADAN NAIROBI LUSAKA ADDIS ABABA
BOMBAY CALCUTTA MADRAS KARACHI LAHORE DACCA
KUALA LUMPUR HONG KONG TOKYO

FIRST PUBLISHED BY
OXFORD UNIVERSITY PRESS, LONDON, 1968

PRINTED IN GREAT BRITAIN

Contents

Introduction

THIS is the first of six volumes under the collective title *French Literature and its Background*. With the exception of one chapter, it has been written by a group of scholars working together in the University of Sussex. The contributors consulted one another regularly and have written a book which deals with what they consider to be the most important and interesting aspects of literature and ideas in France in the sixteenth century. Inevitably, the choice of subjects to be treated in no more than twelve chapters involved an element of arbitrariness but not, we hope, of eccentricity. It has not been our aim to offer the type of exhaustive coverage associated with more traditionally conceived histories of literature. Several writers of the period, whose significance in terms of literary history is clear, were eventually excluded after lengthy discussions in which our own critical preferences, as well as limitations of space, played a part. For example, we debated the relative merits of Marot and d'Aubigné and agreed that, if there was not room for both, we considered d'Aubigné the more important and original poet.

Different kinds of consideration gave rise to other departures from the more familiar 'history of literature' pattern. We decided not to emphasize the programme of the Pléiade, as set out particularly in Du Bellay's *Deffence et Illustration de la Langue Francoyse*, because in practice the Pléiade poets largely ignored it. As is pointed out in the chapter on Louise Labé and Du Bellay, 'the members of the Pléiade were not primarily employed in the fifteen-fifties in writing Pindaric odes and inventing new words. They were writing love sonnets.' Again, we have allowed ourselves some latitude in the treatment of major figures, so that certain chapters offer a distinctly personal interpretation of an important writer's significance (e.g. Rabelais) while others give a more general picture (e.g. Ronsard). Perhaps it is also worth emphasizing that these chapters are complementary so that a single author or theme may be seen from more than one angle in more than one chapter. Important aspects of Ronsard's work are discussed in 'The French Court and its Poetry' as well as in the chapter entitled 'Ronsard'; discussions of Théodore de Bèze will be found in both 'Aspects of the Theatre' and 'The Two Faces of Calvinism'; the Wars of Religion are seen both from the reconciling position of Bodin and the Huguenot militancy of d'Aubigné.

These two chapters on the Wars of Religion indicate, in different ways, something of the historical and religious background of the period. Other more directly 'thematic' chapters are included. Thus the main ideas comprising what is called 'the Renaissance' are approached from the viewpoint of philosophy and theology in 'From Analogy to Scepticism', and in a much more sociological manner in 'Humanists, Reformers, and French Culture'. A somewhat different aspect of the Renaissance—its emphasis on the relationships between the various arts—emerges in 'The French Court and its Poetry'. Thematic chapters of this kind also allow one to see the historical significance, within a given context, of writers who are not of major literary importance (e.g. Des Périers, Jean Lemaire de Belges, etc.). This kind of treatment means, of course, that the Index to the volume should be frequently consulted.

Finally, we have included a 'Chronology'. This presents particular problems for the sixteenth century, since the date of composition of so many works remains speculative. Where a work of the period was not published until the following century, the supposed date of composition is given, and where a firm publication date within the century is known, this has usually been preferred to the date of writing. Generally, the Chronology is designed to serve several purposes: it enables one to relate sixteenth-century French literature to historical events (mainly French), to the literature of England and Italy, to the main European painters and composers of the period, and to major works of ideas, from Brandt's *Ship of Fools* to Hooker's *Laws of Ecclesiastical Polity*, which influenced European intellectual life in the sixteenth century.

JOHN CRUICKSHANK

University of Sussex
April 1967

1. From Analogy to Scepticism

EVERY major sixteenth-century writer is a polemicist, and all attack the same target. Whatever their differences, Erasmus, Luther, Paracelsus, Rabelais, Ramus, and Montaigne all agree on one point: their condemnation of the fifteenth century. It would, however, be a grave mistake to take their polemics at their face value, for there is, of course, no sharp dividing line between the two centuries such as these writers imply. Rather, there is a sudden growth in self-consciousness which gives the illusion of dramatic change. The writers of the sixteenth century seem to be capable of drawing the full consequences from the changes that had been taking place over the previous two hundred years in man's conception of his relation with God and with his fellows, but which had remained for the most part unacknowledged—no matter how unsettling such consequences might be. It is therefore not enough to contrast the sixteenth century with the fifteenth. We need to see both in relation to the thirteenth, for it is the disappearance of the premises on which the culture of the high Middle Ages was based that underlies the intellectual and artistic history of the sixteenth century.

The Middle Ages were centuries of faith, and this faith rested upon a particular view of human character. A fourteenth-century writer expresses it in this way: 'The heavenly Father created all men in his own image. His image is his Son . . . who was before all creation. It is in reference to this eternal image that we have all been created. It is to be found essentially and personally in all men; each man possesses it whole and entire and undivided, and all together have no more than one. In this way we are all one, intimately united in our eternal image, which is the image of God.'

This image was blurred, or, say some writers, shattered into fragments, by the Fall. The Incarnation, however, restored to man the possibility of regaining this lost unity. We all fell with Adam, but with Christ, the second Adam, there is a chance for each of us to undo the effects of the Fall, to put off the old man, as St. Paul said, and put on the new.

Such an attitude takes for granted that there is an analogy between man and God. Not only is man made in God's image; in some way God is in man. 'By the sacrifice of Christ the first man is saved, that man who is in us all', says the Pseudo-Chrysostom; and St. Paul frequently stresses the fact that Christ is within man as well as a historical figure, as when he says, 'But when it pleased God, who separated me from my mother's womb, and called me by his grace, to reveal his Son in me, that I might preach him among the heathens . . .' (Galatians 1: 15). The Incarnation can bring salvation to the individual Christian because Christ, putting on human nature, died as all men have had to die since the Fall, and then *undid* the effects of the Fall by His resurrection. So, as each man had been born to death as a result of the Fall, each man can now be born to life everlasting as a result of the Incarnation.

Individual salvation does not, however, follow automatically from the Incarnation as the blurring or shattering of the image of God followed from the Fall; the Incarnation has only given men back the *possibility* of salvation. The 'new man' is only to be found 'in Christ', but Christ can only be found in the Church which is His Body. No metaphor is implied here: Origen speaks of the Church as 'the real and more perfect body of Christ' in direct comparison with that physical Body which was crucified and rose again, while St. Gregory of Nyssa quite simply says: 'If someone looks at the Church he really looks at Christ.' The Christian enters into and renews his ties with the Church by means of the sacraments, which are thus the means to salvation. Chief among the sacraments is of course the eucharist, instituted by Christ Himself when He broke the bread and poured the wine, asking His disciples to 'do this in remembrance of me'. The eucharist is thus the chief

---

[1] The Greek word *anamnesis* implies much more the notion of 're-enactment' than that of simple remembrance. In a sense the whole mystery lies in this one word.

means of acquiring salvation, and medieval authors are extremely fond of discoursing upon it. St. Cyril of Alexandria, for instance, says:

To melt us all into unity with God and among ourselves, although we each have a distinct individuality, the only Son has invented a marvellous means: with one single body, His own, He sanctifies the faithful in the mystical communion, making them one single body with Him and among themselves. All of us united in the one Christ, through His own body; all of us receiving Him, alone and indivisible, in our bodies, we are the members of that single body, and hence He is for us the bond of unity.

Just as Christ, the second Adam, came down to redeem the world from the effects of the Fall of the first Adam, so each Christian, by partaking of the eucharist, re-enacts Christ's redeeming action.

Today we tend to feel that a man has most completely fulfilled himself when he has been able most sharply to distinguish himself from other men by the development of what is peculiar to himself. The Christians of the Middle Ages felt, on the contrary, that a man most completely fulfilled his human potentiality as he shed what was peculiar to himself and let the image of God, in which he had been made, shine through. It is not just that our view is different from theirs; it is that they thought in terms of the two views together. What I have called the modern view they saw as the denial of man's true nature, but a denial that had been endemic to man since the Fall. To hold on to one's individualizing traits was simply to repeat the sin of pride committed by Lucifer and then by Adam, and to believe that it was possible to live without a recognition of God. But this would be denying something in oneself, since man had first of all been made in God's image. We must not think that the re-enacting of Christ's own action in the eucharist would force men to conform to a given pattern and rob man of his freedom: this kind of straight-jacketing of the personality would only be true if the notion of analogy did not exist, and Christ was seen as someone who must simply be imitated. But the notion of analogy, with its implication that there is a Christ as well as an Adam *in* every man, makes sense of what would otherwise be a contradiction: that only by 'putting on' Christ can man become fully himself.

To help man see where his salvation lies, God has written two books. The first of these is the Book of Scripture, which reveals to those who read it aright the working of God in history. For the Jews the Old Testament was simply the history of their people; for the Gnostics the Bible as a whole was a series of fables which hid a mystical truth. For the Christians it was both history and the revelation of a hidden truth. For the events of the Old Testament foreshadowed or prefigured the events of the New. The sacrifice of Isaac foreshadowed the sacrifice of Christ, the twelve tribes of Israel the twelve apostles, and so on. But in doing this they did not loose their historicity. That was precisely the point. The fact that these events had happened in history, and that they foreshadowed events which were to take place later in history, showed that everything is part of God's design, that every temporal event is fraught with extratemporal significance; the Scriptures were proof that every man's life had meaning, and that history was only the fulfilment of God's design.

The notion that God works through history was reinforced by the notion of God as the author of a second book, the Book of Nature. Hugh of St. Victor presents the metaphor in this way:

> For this whole visible world is as a book written by the finger of God, that is, created by divine power, and individual creatures are as figures, not devised by human will, but instituted by divine authority to show forth the wisdom of the invisible things of God. But just as some illiterate man who sees an open book looks at the figures but does not recognize the letters: just so the foolish and natural man, who does not perceive the things of God, sees outwardly in these visible creatures the appearance, but does not inwardly understand the reason. But he who is spiritual, and can judge all things, while he considers outwardly the beauty of the work, inwardly conceives how marvellous is the wisdom of the Creator.

As God works through history, so He works through the world around us. Hugh has in mind the text of St. Paul which is so fundamental to an understanding of medieval thought and art: 'For the invisible things of Him from the creation of the world are clearly seen, being understood by the things that are made.' Just as God can be seen in man, so He can be seen in history and in nature.

Never has there been such faith in the phenomenal. What guarantees this faith is the Incarnation, for it is the eruption into time of the eternal, into space of the infinite; it is the justification of man's belief that he is made in God's image; it is proof that everywhere behind the natural order is to be found the supernatural, that there is an assured correspondence between appearance and meaning. The 'foolish and natural man' will never see this, but 'he who is spiritual' will. It is not that he will 'read' such meanings into history or nature or other men; rather it is that if he learns to read correctly he will see these things where another had missed them. Thus the task of the medieval artist is quite simple: to teach men to see by the accurate depiction of reality. The didactic and the pleasurable, the interests of the preacher and of the artist, have never been more unified.

The art of the Middle Ages is, above all, an anonymous art. Even when we know the names of the artists the information seems strangely irrelevant. Not only the artists, but their productions, possess this anonymity; the saints, prophets, and sinners who adorn the walls and windows of the churches and cathedrals are stripped of any individualizing traits and distinguished only by a few iconographical motifs which help to identify them. A striking example of this is to be found in the depictions of the life of Christ. Émile Mâle, the great French art historian, comments on this:

All the human, tender, or simply picturesque side of the Gospels does not seem to have touched the medieval artist. He evidently did not see in the New Testament the things which appealed to a Veronese or a Rembrandt. Those aspects of Christ's life are illustrated which are not the most humanly moving, but those connected with the great feasts of the liturgical year: it is the sacramental, not the human aspects of Christ which are stressed. . . . The thirteenth-century artist saw in the Gospels not a collection of picturesque or affecting scenes, but a succession of mysteries.

A fascinating insight into the way the medieval artist worked as well as into the nature of his products emerges from Mâle's discussion of a French illuminated manuscript of the thirteenth century. This manuscript, he says,

contains a collection of the gospels for all the Sundays of the year, and numerous miniatures accompany the text. The book opens with the gospels for Christmas time, which related the stories surrounding the child-hood of Jesus. Faithful to his text, the artist illustrates in turn the Flight into Egypt, the Circumcision, and the Adoration of the Magi. The gospels which refer to the public life follow, and here the artist shows the Baptism, the Marriage at Cana, the Temptation and the Transfiguration. Then suddenly he stops, and half the book is left without illustrations until the work is begun again in Holy Week with the Passion, the Resurrection, and the Appearances of Christ as subjects for the pictures. It is evident that the artist has used pounced tracings of older drawings whose number was strictly determined. Where tradition offered him no model it did not occur to him to invent, he did but what others before him had done and no more.

The artist here obviously conceives his task as akin to that of the musical performer; he is an interpreter rather than an inventor—the master of a particular craft doing to the best of his ability what is given him to do. To invent his own illustrations where the tradition can give him no guidance would certainly seem to him presumptuous—if it ever occurred to him.

The medieval attitude to art and the conceptions of character and analogy upon which it is based emerge even more clearly from the literature of the time. A particularly good example is afforded by the greatest poem of the Middle Ages, Dante's *Divine Comedy*, though it would be just as easy to demonstrate it from the fourteenth-century English *Piers Plowman* or the thirteenth-century French *Quête del Saint Graal*.

The narrator-protagonist of the *Divine Comedy* is Dante himself; but he is also any man who sets out in search of salvation in this life. The journey to salvation involves a descent to the very bottom pit of Hell, and then the arduous climb up Mount Purgatory. Each stage of this ascent is marked by the shedding of another deadly sin by the narrator. At the top of the mountain lies the Garden of Eden, where Beatrice will come in glory to carry him to Heaven. Between Dante and the Garden flows a river—Lethe—the classical river of forgetfulness. Beyond this point Virgil cannot go, and as they emerge from the flames which have cleansed Dante of the last of the deadly sins Virgil, who has guided Dante all the way, turns to him and says:

> Non aspettar mio dir più, né mio cenno.
> libero, dritto e sano è tuo arbitrio,
> e fallo fora non fare a suo senno:
> per ch'io te sovra te corono e mitrio.
>
> (*Purgatorio*, canto 27.)[1]

Cleansed of human imperfections, Dante is ready to enter the Garden where, so long before, Adam had been tempted and had fallen, thus blurring, seemingly for ever, the image of God in which he had been created. The arduous journey travelled by Dante has thus been an undoing of the harm done by the Fall—quite literally a recovery of the image of God. And, as a sign that this is synonymous with the recovery of his own complete personality, Dante is now for the first time addressed by name. It is Beatrice who speaks, rebuking him for weeping at the disappearance of Virgil:

> Dante, perché Virgilio se ne vada
> non pianger anco, non piangere ancora. . . .
>
> (*Purgatorio*, canto 30.)[2]

The structure of the poem is here, as everywhere else, threefold. Virgil and Beatrice and the protagonist are first and foremost characters in Dante's narrative, the first a figure out of history, the second a figure out of Dante's own life. But it is also necessary, since the protagonist is not just Dante but any man who goes in search of salvation, to see Virgil as signifying Reason, and Beatrice Divine Wisdom. Thus the protagonist's literal journey is an analogue to the spiritual journey undergone by the reader. Seen in this focus the poem reminds us that it starts on Good Friday and ends on Easter Sunday, and that Dante's descent into Hell and his ascent to Eden parallel Christ's Passion and Resurrection. As the Christian who partakes of the eucharist re-enacts in himself Christ's redemptive action, so the reader of the poem re-enacts Dante's journey, itself an analogue to the eucharistic action.

But there is a third focus to be considered. We are here asked to

---

[1] 'Do not expect my word or my sign any more. Now is your will free, upright and whole, and it would be a fault not to act as it prompts you: therefore do I crown and mitre you over yourself.'

[2] 'Dante, do not weep yet because Virgil goes away; do not weep yet.'

remember that Virgil was the poet of Augustan Rome, man's most successful attempt to impose a secular peace on earth, as though to prepare men for the Divine order that was about to appear. The river Lethe, which Virgil cannot cross, is here seen as the dividing line of history, marking the point beyond which the purely natural cannot go.

There are thus three different areas of experience in the poem, all co-existing. The literal narrative reveals both the spiritual and the historical one. But we must guard against imagining that it is we who 'put' or 'read' into the poem these three areas of meaning. Rather it is the poem which draws them out and reveals them to the reader. As a foremost Dante scholar, C. S. Singleton, has put it: 'Dante's poem means to be an imitation of reality, mirroring the true nature of the real world wherein there are actual relationships between orders of existence.' In other words, Dante's allegory signifies what it does not because Dante means it to, but because God does. Dante simply asks the reader to look hard, and he will see in history and in the world around him evidence of the working of God. Thus the reader will be transformed from a 'foolish and natural man' to one who is 'spiritual'. Dante does not teach, he merely asks the reader to look; but the reader who looks the right way will come to see what he is and thus will be ready to start out on the path to salvation, which is nothing more than the recovery of that which he is.

The medieval Church can be said to have reached its high-water mark in 1264, when it showed a conscious awareness of its own nature by instituting the feast of Corpus Christi. Although it was not to be decisively challenged until Luther, and although its greatest monuments were to be the products of the next hundred and fifty years, it is possible to trace its decline from this point. Like all decisive changes this one went unnoticed for a long time, but slowly the premisses upon which the medieval analogical synthesis had rested disappeared, to be replaced by others which could not carry such a system. Since it is from these premisses that the sixteenth century launched its attacks on the Middle Ages, it is worth while trying to understand the nature of the change.

The Church had always been aware of the possible misunderstandings of its nature. Formulated heresy it could fight with formulated dogma, crusades, or the Inquisition. More difficult to deal with was that mechanization of Christianity which had to some extent been a problem ever since the mass conversions of the fourth century. It is easy to see how a religion which rests upon the doctrine of the Incarnation is open to such mechanization. It is a small though crucial step from the belief that there can be no salvation except through the sacraments of the Church to the belief that merely to partake of the sacraments is to ensure salvation. The enormous increase in mechanical aids to salvation in the later Middle Ages has many causes: the Black Death which decimated Europe giving rise to the feeling that evil was not simply a denial of good, but a positive force in the world; the economic conditions which resulted from the breakdown of the feudal system and the growth of towns; the abuses within the Church itself. Historians are still debating the causes; the results are indisputable. Pardons, relics, indulgences could all be bought for money, and all were thought capable of conferring spiritual benefits upon their possessors. We hear of a parrot which, being carried away by a kite, uttered the invocation dear to its mistress, 'Sancte Thoma, adjuva me', and was miraculously restored. A merchant of Groningen, having purloined an arm of John the Baptist, grew richer and richer so long as he kept it in his house but was reduced to beggary as soon as his secret was discovered and the relic taken from him. Men invoked saints against the toothache as well as the plague; it was thought to be enough to have looked at an image or statue of St. Christopher to be sure of escaping accidental death.

In reaction to this widespread mechanization of religion a new wave of piety set in during the fourteenth century. This was the movement known as the Devotio Moderna, which sprang up around Gerard Groote in the Netherlands and led to the foundation of the Brethren of the Common Life. The most famous product of the Brethren was *The Imitation of Christ* (*c.* 1418), usually attributed to Thomas à Kempis, and the most popular book of the late Middle Ages. In it one can see very clearly the characteristics of the whole movement: a great emphasis on personal piety and the inner life of the spirit, and a consequent lack of interest in the Church or the sacraments. So intense is the author's concentration on the inner life that he tends to regard all visible symbols and formal acts as entirely without value unless accompanied by strong internal feelings. 'If we esteem our progress in religious life to consist only in some exterior observance,' he remarks, 'our devotion will quickly come to an end.' Even when he does consider the eucharist, it is more as food for the spirit than as the means of salvation.

The notion of human character taken for granted by *The Imitation of Christ* is clearly quite different from that of the medieval Church. What it stresses is not the mystery of the Incarnation but the moral goodness of Christ the man; not his Passion and Resurrection but his parables and teachings. The medieval Church did not talk about an imitation of Christ; rather it held that the eucharistic action was a re-enactment of Christ's own death and resurrection. Man, since he was made in God's image, is, essentially, like Christ already; but, tainted by the Fall, it required Christ's Incarnation to give man back the possibility of realizing what he essentially is. The only kind of imitation envisaged by the Church is the mystical imitation of Christ's action through the eucharistic rite. *The Imitation of Christ*, on the other hand, seems to take it for granted that man is essentially *unlike* Christ, and that only through a studied conformity will he find any salvation. The stress on imitation implies a loss of faith in the phenomenal world and a loss of belief in the idea that man is made in God's image. By advocating imitation in this way the author implicitly dismisses the idea that there is something in man which is not only like Christ, but *is* Christ; and in so doing he sets up morality and freedom in opposition to each other.

It was at about the same time as the appearance of *The Imitation of Christ* in the Netherlands that the artists of the great towns of Italy were themselves beginning to show an interest in the notion of artistic imitation. This was partly the result of the changing situation of the artist within this society, which has been described by Anthony Blunt in the following way: 'The artist was no longer a purveyor of goods which everyone needed and which could be ordered like any other material goods, but an individual facing a public. . . . In this spirit of competition he began to carry out works other than those directly commissioned. We are here at the beginning of those modern ideas which make of the artist a creator who works for himself alone.' What this change meant in practice is shown by a letter sent to Vasari, the great art historian, by one of his patrons: 'My wish to have a notable work by your hand is as much for your fame as for my pleasure, because I would like to show it to certain persons who know you better as a speedy than as a careful painter. Whether you do it fast or slowly I leave to you, because I believe one can be both speedy and good when carried away by passion. . . . As to subject, that too I leave to you. . . .' The contrast of this with the medieval illuminator mentioned by Mâle is striking and absolute. The artist is now free to choose his own subject and to treat it as he wishes. He is no longer an interpreter but an inventor.

As we would expect, the views of the artists themselves reflect the new situation. Leonardo da Vinci, for instance, insists on the artist's following his own inner image, and compares the inventive faculty to the power of God in creating the world: 'That divine power which lies in the knowledge of the painter, transforms the mind of the painter into the likeness of the divine mind, for with a free hand he can produce different beings, animals, plants, fruits, landscapes, open fields, abysses, terrifying and fearful places.' But Leonardo never encourages the artist to give free play to his imagination; what he invents must always be an exact imitation of nature: 'That painting is most to be praised which agrees most exactly with the things imitated', he says. The greater the freedom of the artist to invent, the more he will need to refer himself to external objects. But verisimilitude can never be the sole criterion, for however accurately the artist has imitated nature the question still arises of why he should choose this subject to imitate rather than that. Once the artist feels himself to be free to paint what he likes he also raises the question of the truth and meaning of what he paints. Although at first it looks as if verisimilitude, the exact imitation of nature, would answer this problem, it soon becomes clear that another criterion is needed to justify the choice of subject-matter and the kind of treatment it receives. This does not seem to worry the painters, who stress more and more strongly the self-authenticating power of the artist's imagination as the period progresses, but it does worry such writers of fiction as Rabelais and Cervantes, who raise the question of why one man's inner image should necessarily be considered true or meaningful. In a famous scene Pantagruel visits the sepulchre of his ancestor Geoffroy 'à la grand dent'. He there sees a portrait of Geoffroy which gives him a shock:

car il y est en image comme d'un homme furieux, tirant à demy son grand malchus de la guaine, et demandoit la cause de ce. Les chanoines dudict lieu luy dirent que n'estoit aultre cause sinon que *Pictoribus atque Poetis*, etc.; c'est à dire que les painctres et les poëtes ont liberté de paindre à leur plaisir ce qu'ilz veulent. Mais il ne se contenta pas de leur responce, et dist: 'Il n'est ainsi painct sans cause, et me doubte que à sa mort on luy a faict quelque tort, dont il demande vengeance à ses parens.' (*Pantagruel*, chapter v.)

The monks make use of a well-known Renaissance dictum, which they take to mean that the artist is free to invent what he pleases. That may be so, says Pantagruel, but what does the picture *mean*? The careful imitation of an external reality seems to hide rather than reveal meaning. And if the picture means nothing at all, then what is its worth? The new freedom of the artist seems to go hand in hand with the relegation of art to the superfluous. With the disappearance of the medieval notion of analogy, inner meaning and outer experience no longer seem to reinforce one another. The world, instead of manifesting the 'invisible things' of God, becomes an enigma without a key.

In order to understand Pantagruel's position a little more clearly it is necessary to turn to two men who were to influence the sixteenth century more than any others. Both, interestingly enough, were pupils of the Brethren of the Common Life. They are Luther and Erasmus, and the fact that they both received the same kind of education serves to emphasize that even the bitterest antagonists of the period started from the same premisses: the late medieval pietistic view of character with its strong stress on the opposition between internal worth and external observance.

Although the Reformation is usually regarded as having begun in 1517, when Luther nailed up his ninety-five theses on the church door at Wittenburg, the really decisive break came in 1519, when Luther debated with his Catholic opponents at Leipzig, and in 1520 when he put forward his position in his *Appeal to the German Nobility*. At Leipzig he denied the authority of the Pope and Councils, and in the *Appeal* he claimed that Scripture outranks even the Pope in determining what is right and wrong. The truth is what conscience is compelled to believe on reading Scripture, not what the Pope and Councils say. Now this raised questions of a fundamental kind. As the Catholics were quick to point out, the individual conscience is extremely unreliable and the fact that people have differed about the interpretation of Scriptural passages shows that there is no way of telling what the correct interpretation is without the guidance of the Church. For how is one to tell a perverse interpretation from a sound one without recourse to some external authority? The Reformers retaliated by asking why it should be taken for granted that the Church should always be right? If all men are fallible, ran one extremist argument, except the Pope, then only the Pope can know who is the Pope, and there is no reason for our accepting the judgement of the occupant of the pontifical chair. The Catholic position is in fact open to the same reductionist argument as is that of their opponents. Is there then no possibility of establishing the truth of religious propositions?

Luther's questioning of the criterion of truth seemed to have raised an unanswerable problem. And of course, raised in those terms, there could be no answer. So long as there was a community of belief in the Church as the 'real Body of Christ' the problem of the criterion would not arise in any acute form. But when this belief disappears, with the growing opposition between 'inner feeling' and 'outer observance' which we saw to be characteristic of the later Middle Ages, it is only a matter of time before the problem emerges. When inner and outer are contrasted in this way any institution claiming to be directly in touch with the divine, and arrogating to itself authority for this reason, will inevitably be regarded as either hypocritical and fraudulent, or simply superstitious. Philosophically, the problem of the criterion cannot be solved in the terms of either the Catholics, with their insistence on an external authority, or the Protestants, with their insistence on an internal authority. It requires the medieval analogical view of man and nature to resolve it, and this view rests only on faith. Luther's 1520 pamphlet is a clear indication that such a faith had disappeared.

In reaction to extremists of all kinds, there arose in the sixteenth century an attitude of what a recent historian has called 'mitigated scepticism'. The source of this attitude was Erasmus who had, of course, formed his opinions before Luther's break with Rome, but who came to be seen by many of the more intelligent men as offering a solution to the problems raised by Luther. Erasmus argues that since we cannot in this life know with any certainty what the ultimate truth is, the most sensible course is to accept the traditional solutions offered by the Church, though without committing ourselves to a belief in them. Erasmus regarded extremists with distaste because he felt that what they really desired was to be released from the daily responsibility of exercising their human faculties in a free choice. What he felt to be important was a simple Christian piety, such as the Brethren of the Common Life had advocated, tinged with a healthy scepticism. Such an attitude was to lie behind much that was best in sixteenth- and seventeenth-century culture. But it is easy to see how it could degenerate into an eighteenth-century deism. For the Christ of Erasmus is not very different from Socrates —a good man whom we ought to imitate in order to lead the good life. All notion of the Incarnation as the appearance of the second Adam come to redeem us from the sin of the first has disappeared. As Luther rightly pointed out, Erasmus's position is basically a secular one; it can perfectly well do without God. The natural and the divine have quite parted company. Truth can be defined only in negative terms: that which is not what the extremists take as truth. However hard we look at the world around us it will not yield us its secret. It will only throw back our own reflections.

In the twelfth century, Hugh of St. Victor had been able to talk of the visible world as 'a book written by the finger of God', and of men as 'instituted by divine authority to show forth the wisdom of the invisible things of God'. On this optimistic faith the whole art and thought of the Middle Ages had rested. But events were so to shake this faith that by the end of the sixteenth century Montaigne could write: 'Or, nostre estat accommodant les choses à soy et les transformant selon soy, nous ne sçavons plus quelles sont les choses en verité; car rien ne vient à nous que falsifié et alteré par nos sens... L'incertitude de nos sens rend incertain tout ce qu'ils produisent' (*Apologie de Raimond Sebond*). In such a world the discovery of truth is the prerogative of the scientist who measures rather than of the artist who sees. Whether, when it has been found, this truth is of any value is a question that will sometimes be asked in the following centuries. At the start of the sixteenth, however, such questions do not yet present themselves. The writers of the time turn with tremendous gusto to attack their immediate predecessors. In the course of this attack the last vestiges of the medieval analogical system are destroyed and a new world emerges—our world.

NOTE

Listed below are some of the most important primary and secondary sources which will help to illustrate and explain further the changing attitudes outlined in the above chapter:

Basic texts

DANTE (1265–1321). His *Divine Comedy* was written *c.* 1307–19; a useful modern edition is the three-volume Italian text and English translation by J. D. Sinclair (1939).

THOMAS À KEMPIS (1380–1471). His *Imitation of Christ* was written *c.* 1418; the most convenient modern translation is by Leo Shirley-Price (1952).

LUTHER (1483–1546). *Selections from his Writings* are available in an American paperback edited and translated by J. Dillenberger (1961).

ERASMUS (1466–1536) and LUTHER. *The Free Will* by Erasmus and *The Bondage of the Will* by Luther are translated and edited by E. F. Winter in Erasmus–Luther, *Discourse on Free Will* (1961).

A selection of writings by the Fathers on the concept of man, etc., is included in H. de Lubac, *Catholicisme* (1937).

Criticism

A. Blunt, *Artistic Theory in Italy, 1450–1600* (1940).
C. S. Lewis, *The Discarded Image* (1965).

H. de Lubac, *Catholicisme* (1937).

E. Mâle, *The Gothic Image* (1961 reprint).

R. H. Popkin, *The History of Scepticism from Erasmus to Descartes* (1960).

O. von Simpson, *The Gothic Cathedral* (1956).

C. S. Singleton, *Commedia: Elements of Structure* (1954).

2. Rabelais

READERS of Rabelais tend to fall into two groups. There are those who see him as a great comic writer whose content must not be taken too seriously and hardly needs to be understood, since for much of the time it is deliberate nonsense. And there are those who see him as a sort of Renaissance encyclopedist in whose pages are to be found examples of nearly every aspect of the period, held together by a frivolous and often boring series of anecdotes modelled on the worst medieval romances and included as a sop to a mass audience greedy for such stories. There does not seem to be any way of reconciling the comic form with the serious content, or, to put it in terms which Rabelais himself would have used, of reconciling the pleasurable and the didactic elements of his work.

Such a split in critical reaction is not, of course, confined to Rabelais. It is to be found, in connection with nearly every major Renaissance writer, in the dichotomy between the Romantic stress on the beauty and sensuousness of the language and imagery, and the more recent stress on the argument and themes of these writers. But with Rabelais we have rather a different type of problem because the whole question of critical attitude and mode of interpretation is one of the central *themes* of his work. It is not simply that he lays himself open to two radically different types of interpretation; he is himself concerned with the problem of the status of the work of art and with the possibility of reconciling these two ways of looking at the work. Nor does he simply discuss the problem: his book is in itself a solution to it, an 'éducation intellectuelle' which teaches the reader how to reconcile *delectare* and *prodesse*.

The tone is set in the opening pages of *Gargantua*: 'Et, posé le cas qu'au sens literal vous trouvez matieres joyeuses et bien correspondentes au nom, toutesfois pas demourer là ne fault, comme au chant de Sirenes, ains à plus hault sens interpreter ce que par adventure cuidiez dict en gayeté de cueur' (Prologue to *Gargantua*).[1] Have you ever seen a dog eating a marrow bone? See how carefully he guards it, how he breaks it, with what relish he sucks out the marrow. This is how you must treat this book: 'A l'exemple d'icelluy vous convient estre saiges, pour fleurer, sentir et estimer ces beaulx livres de haulte gresse, legiers au prochaz et hardiz à la rencontre; puis, par curieuse leçon et meditation frequente, rompre l'os et sugcer la sustantificque mouelle . . .' (ibid.). This is a restatement of a critical commonplace which goes back to Plato and the early allegorizers of Homer, is to be found in the Gnostic interpreters of the Bible, and appears everywhere in the Middle Ages in the metaphors of the kernel and the nut, the fruit and the rind, the spirit and the letter. According to this point of view the work of art— or the sacred book—may at first sight appear to be nothing more than a frivolous story, a tale of gods making love to mortal women, or of a man who is the son of God and ends up crucified like a common criminal. But beneath the absurd surface lies hidden a mystical doctrine or a theory of the universe, put there by the author and waiting to be extracted by the initiate. Such an attitude bears more than a passing resemblance to our second group of readers. It is true that they do not dismiss the story or its incidents in favour of a spiritual truth hidden beneath it, and to which the incidents allude allegorically. But they do concentrate their attention on what Rabelais seems to be saying about women, or Luther, or Neoplatonism. Abel Lefranc, one of the pioneers of Rabelais studies, puts this point of view very clearly when he says: 'L'élément réel apparaît sous le mythe. Le fait est si fréquent, ou plutôt si constant, qu'il pourrait être érigé en principe' (*La Navigation de Pantagruel*). Such a reader feels that Rabelais's meaning cannot lie simply in the absurd stories that he tells. To find out what the work is really *about* we have to look beyond these. And the marrow-bone passage seems to sanction just such an approach.

[1] The book is treated as a whole here and as it appears in every modern edition, i.e. with *Gargantua*, written second, preceding *Pantagruel*. All quotations follow the text used by Pierre Jourda in his Classiques Garnier edition of 1962.

But does it? Listening, as we always must with Rabelais, for the *tone* of the argument, we soon realize that he may not be endorsing but burlesquing the allegorical approach; for, he goes on, this way of reading will reveal in the book a 'doctrine plus absconce... laquelle vous revelera de très haultz sacremens et mysteres horrificques, tant en ce que concerne nostre religion que aussi l'estat politicq et vie œconomicque' (ibid.). The book might conceivably have held a 'doctrine plus absconce', but it could not possibly conceal mysteries which concern religion, politics, and socio-economic organization! Rabelais deliberately overstresses so as to burlesque. And in case the reader should have any doubt about his attitude, in the next paragraph he comes out into the open:

Croiez-vous en vostre foy qu'oncques Homere, escrivent l'*Iliade* et *Odyssée*, pensast es allegories lesquelles de luy ont calfreté Plutarche, Heraclides, Ponticq, Eustatie, Phornute, et ce que d'iceulx Politian a desrobé? Si le croiez, vous n'approchez ne de pieds ne de mains à mon opinion, qui decrete icelles aussi peu avoir esté songées d'Homere que d'Ovide en ses *Metamorphoses* les sacremens de l'Evangile, lesquelz un Frere Lubin, vray croque lardon, s'est efforcé démonstrer, si d'adventure il rencontroit gens aussi folz que luy... (ibid.)

Rabelais is not here simply deriding a specific late medieval allegorization of Ovid. He is attacking the general tendency to find a hidden meaning beneath the literal surface, since this too often consists in reading into an author what one wants to find rather than what is there.

Rabelais's book abounds in burlesques of this kind of interpretation. *Gargantua*, for instance, ends with a verse enigma to which various solutions are proposed. The correct answer turns out not to be, as Gargantua maintains, the course and maintenance of divine truth, but a game of tennis! The best examples, however, are to be found in the *Tiers Livre*.

This is the most obviously unified of the five books. Its one subject is Panurge's search for an answer to his double question: should he marry? and, if he does, will he be cuckolded? The fundamental theme of the book is not the 'querelle des femmes', which acts as a mere scaffold, but the questions which are before Rabelais throughout the five books: is there such a thing as absolute truth?

Can we mortals ever find it? Can we ever be sure of it once we appear to have found it?

Right from the start Pantagruel points out to Panurge that it is absurd to expect an answer to his questions:

> Aussi (respondit Pantagruel) en vos propositions tant y a de si et de mais, que je n'y sçaurois rien fonder ne rien resouldre. N'estez vous asceuré de votre vouloir? Le poinct principal y gist: tout le reste est fortuit et dependent des fatales dispositions du ciel... Il se y convient mettre à l'adventure, les œilz bandez, baissant la teste, baisant la terre et se recommandant à Dieu au demourant, puys qu'une foys l'on se y veult mettre. Aultre asceurance ne vous en sçauroys je donner. (III. x)

Panurge, however, is determined to get an answer, and he consults in turn the *sortes virgilianae*, his own dreams, a sybil, a dumb man, a dying poet, a mage, a theologian, a doctor, a philosopher, and a fool. Each of these encounters follows the same pattern. Panurge is never given a straight reply; every time he is confronted with a riddle or an image which he has to interpret. And each time Panurge interprets the evidence so as to make it fit in with his own desires, or when he cannot possibly do this, as in the case of the mage Agrippa, he impugns the integrity of the speaker.

In his dream, for example, Panurge finds his wife sticking horns on his forehead. He interprets these as the horns of abundance and flies into a rage when Pantagruel points out to him that these are the horns traditionally associated with cuckoldry. He is so anxious to get married and so terrified at the prospect of his wife being unfaithful to him that he clutches at anything that seems capable of giving him the answer that he wants. In his interpretation of his dream, as elsewhere in this book, he acts in exactly the same way as the friar of the Prologue to *Gargantua* who saw in Ovid's *Metamorphoses* an allegory of the Gospels.

The contrast with Pantagruel is elaborated throughout the book. Pantagruel is sure that the answer to a question of this type cannot be given, even by those, like the sybil or the mage Cornelius Agrippa, who profess to be in touch with the workings of the universe, because it is not something immutably decreed but rather something that Panurge is free to bring about or keep from occurring. Panurge's attitude, on the other hand, is deterministic and mechanical. He does not believe that the answer to his questions depends on his will at all, but that in some way it already exists. And this attitude leads him to foist his own desires upon an uncertain future and to read it off as though it would inevitably fulfil those desires.

One of the finest ironies in the *Tiers Livre* is that so long as Panurge maintains his mechanistic view of the world and his deterministic view of fate there can be little doubt that he will be cuckolded and beaten by his wife. The answers which he receives are not answers about the future at all; they are answers about the present. To ask the sort of question he does is to think of the future as determined. But to think of it in this way is to think of one's own will as bound. And to do this is to enter a world that is indeed deterministic. There can be no other answer to Panurge's question than that marriage and cuckoldry go together. As Coleridge noted, 'the reason can only give the inevitable conclusion, the syllogistic *ergo*, from the premisses provided by the understanding itself, which puts each case so as of necessity to predetermine the verdict thereon'. It is only, as Pantagruel keeps pointing out, by ceasing to ask this type of question that the possibility will present itself of Panurge marrying without incurring the consequences he dreads.

The belief that there is *an* answer which can be obtained if one employs the right techniques, which can be handed on from one person to another, and which does not depend upon the exercise of judgement or the possibility of error leads, then, to a failure to grasp the likely answer and to a substitution of one's own desires for the truth. This interesting psychological fact is not limited to the interpretation of a picture or an enigma. It extends to the use of language itself. This is the subject of an argument between Panurge and Pantagruel:

Vous doncques [says Panurge] ne croyez ce qu'escript Herodote des deux enfans guardez dedans une case par le vouloir de Psammetic, roy des Aegyptiens, et nourriz en perpetuelle silence, les quelz après certain temps prononcerent ceste parole: *Becus*, laquelle, en langue Phrygienne, signifie pain? — Rien moins, respondit Pantagruel. C'est abus, dire que ayons languaige naturel. Les languaiges sont par institutions arbitraires et convenences des peuples; les voix (comme disent les dialecticiens), ne signifient naturellement, mais à plaisir. (III. xix)

To believe that language is natural is to believe that words correspond directly to reality; that meaning lies buried in language, waiting to be extracted from it; and that this meaning was put into the language by the creator of the world. To believe that language is conventional is to believe that it was invented by man; that there is no necessary connection between words and what they signify, but that words have acquired the meanings they have because men decided that they would; and therefore that it is no use scrutinizing each word in order to make it yield its secret, for words acquire meaning according to the contexts in which they are used.

The views of Panurge and Pantagruel on language, then, correspond to their views on the place and function of man in the universe. And just as it comes about that Panurge's belief that there is an answer to his question leads him to foist his own desires upon an enigmatic world, so his view that language is natural leads him into far more arbitrary use of language than Pantagruel, who accepts its conventional character. The logic of this is dealt with by Rabelais when he discusses the colours of the young Gargantua's livery, early in the first book.

Grandgousier had dressed his son in blue and white, meaning by that to signify celestial joy. But, says Rabelais to the reader, you are bound to sit up at this and tell me that white signifies faith and blue fortitude. But who says so? The author of the *Blason des couleurs*. But who is he? Whoever he was, it was wise of him not to set his name to the book, for I don't know what I admire more about it, its presumption or its folly:

son oultrecuidance, qui, sans raison, sans cause et sans apparence, a ausé prescripre de son autorité privée quelles choses seroient denotées par les couleurs, ce que est l'usance des tyrans qui voulent leur arbitre tenir lieu de raison, non des saiges et sçavans qui par raisons manifestes contentent les lecteurs; sa besterie, qui a existimé que, sans aultres démonstrations et argumens valables, le monde reigleroit ses devises par ses impositions badaudes. (I. ix)

Not only Panurge, but the allegorizers of Homer and Ovid are people of this kind. Rabelais goes on to give an example of a 'natural' use of language: 'En pareilles tenebres sont comprins ces glorieux de court et transporteurs de noms, lesquelz, voulens en leurs divises signifier *espoir*, font protraire une *sphere*... de *l'ancholie* pour *melancholie*... un *lict sans ciel* pour un *licentié*...' (ibid.). With this he contrasts the hieroglyphics of the Egyptians, which were conventionally established symbols. Then, having shown up the folly of taking white to signify faith and blue fortitude, he goes on to explain why they are more likely to signify celestial joy, since in all countries everywhere black signifies grief, and white is the opposite of black as joy is of grief. He concludes: 'Et n'est cette signifiance par imposition humaine institué, mais receue par consentement de tout le monde, que les philosophes nomment *jus gentium*, droict universel, valable par toutes contrées' (I. x). There is thus a threefold distinction to be made. There is a *natural* language, which is an impossibility; to imagine that it exists is to set up a wholly *arbitrary* and personal language; and finally there is *conventional* language, which is arbitrary in so far as it is not natural, but whose arbitrariness is kept in check by convention, the outcome of the agreement of men with one another.

Panurge's attitude rests on the assumption that man is in touch with the workings of the universe, that he can, if he discovers the right techniques or questions the right people, learn what the future has in store for him. But since this is not the case his attempts take on the form of mania. For it is only in a state of madness that man and the world are at one, since the madman makes the world in his own image. If Panurge is not exactly mad, at least he is the victim of his unconscious impulses. Trying to raise himself above his natural condition he falls below it; trying to by-pass the discriminating mind in order to arrive directly at the truth, he is thrown back upon his subjective fantasies.

Pantagruel's view, on the other hand, depends on his acceptance of man's limitations. His attitude to life is well summed up in a passage from the Prologue to the *Tiers Livre* concerning Diogenes: 'S'il avoit quelques imperfections, aussi avez vous, aussi avons nous', says Rabelais. 'Rien n'est, sinon Dieu, perfaict.' Only God can know the answers to the questions Panurge asks, and to pretend to be God is to become a beast. The acceptance of man's condition is exemplified by Judge Bridoye who, for forty years, has been able to pass correct judgement simply by throwing dice. This, however, is not done out of any belief that the dice will reveal to him the true answer if he studies them hard enough, but because he recognizes that all the paraphernalia of a court of law will never yield any certainty about the rights and wrongs of a case, and he prefers to put his trust in God to reveal it. Epistemon[1] explains that the heavens rewarded Bridoye because of his 'simplicité et affection syncere', and because 'soy deffiant de son sçavoir et capacité, congnoissant les antinomies et contrarietez des loix, des edictz, des coustumes et ordonnances... [il] se recommenderoit humblement à Dieu le juste juge...' (III. xliv).

It is in this spirit that Pantagruel himself judges the case of Baisecul and Humevesne, cutting through the tangle of legal jargon and the crazily involved accounts of the two litigants to deliver a sentence, which, amazingly, pleases them both. And it is in this spirit that Gargantua founds the Abbaye de Thélème: 'En leur reigle n'estoit que ceste clause: *FAY CE QUE VOULDRAS*, parce que gens liberes, bien nez, bien instruictz, conversans en compaignies honnestes, ont par nature un instinct et aguillon, qui tousjours les poulse à faictz vertueux et retire de vice, lequel ilz nommoient honneur' (I. lvii). This is a freedom of the will, a freedom to use the mind to make a choice in accordance with the dictates of reason backed by common sense and a sound education. It is exactly contrary to Panurge's kind of freedom, which is an imposition of private fantasy on the world, and thus in reality a complete bondage to his irrational impulses.

It follows naturally from what has been said above of the difference between Pantagruel and Panurge that Rabelais should endorse the views of the former on the subject of language. At the close of the episode of the Limousin scholar he states his position unequivocally: '... il nous convient parler selon le langage usité, et ... il fault eviter les motz espaves en pareille diligence que les patrons des navires evitent les rochiers de mer' (II. vi). This attitude to language coincides in Rabelais with a homely peasant strain which

---

[1] George Kaiser has convincingly argued that this speech should be made by Pantagruel. See *Praisers of Folly*, p. 169, n. 12.

results in a style far richer and more supple than anything the humanists produced. It is a style which reminds one of a rural Villon rather than of Montaigne or Ronsard. We have to wait for Samuel Beckett to find in French a prose style which can compare with Rabelais's for richness of evocation and simplicity of form: '... le vieux bon homme Grandgousier, son pere, qui après souper se chauffe les couiles à un beau, clair et grand feu, et, attendent graisler des chastaines, escript au foyer avec un baston bruslé d'un bout dont on escharbotte le feu, faisant à sa femme et famille de beaulx contes du temps jadis' (I. xxviii).

But here we come to a crucial paradox. As soon as we begin to talk in this way about Rabelais's style we become aware of the fact that passages such as the above form only a very small proportion of the entire work. The greater part of the book reads much more as if it had been written by Panurge than by Pantagruel. This surely is an extremely odd fact if we are right in our analysis of these two characters and of what they stand for. How are we to explain it?

The answer is quite simple. Essentially the work of fiction is no different from the fantasies of a Panurge, a Picrochole, a Dindenault. Chapter 33 of *Gargantua*, for example, presents us with an exact model of the position of the writer of fiction such as Rabelais. Picrochole and his henchman are planning the destruction of Gargantua and the conquest of his territories. But soon their plans grow wilder and less realistic, and they are imagining the conquest of the whole known world:

— Voirons nous (dist Picrochole) Babylone et le Mont Sinay?
— Il n'est (dirent ilz) jà besoing pour ceste heure. N'est ce pas assez tracassé dea avoir transfreté la mer Hircane, chevauché les deux Armenies et les troys Arabies?
— Par ma foy (dist il) nous sommes affolez. Ha, pauvres gens!
— Quoy? dirent ilz.
— Que boyrons nous par ces desers? Car Julian Auguste et tout son oust y moururent de soif, comme l'on dict.
— Nous (dirent ilz) avons jà donné ordre à tout. Par la mer Siriacè vous avez neuf mille quatorze grands naufz, chargées des meilleurs vins du monde; elles arriverent à Japhes... (I. xxxiii)

The words are no sooner spoken than they are taken as describing

an achieved reality. But though they embody the desires of Picrochole and his ministers, they remain nothing but words. In the same
way the work of fiction is made up only of words; the events it
describes do not really take place, but remain pure fantasies on the
part of the author. Most writers of fiction make every effort to lull
the reader into a state of mind where he will accept their imaginings
as the transcript of reality, but Rabelais is unwilling to countenance
such a hoax. On the contrary, he is fully aware of the fact that to take
words on a page for reality in this way is to regress to the world of
Picrochole.

But, it will be argued, no reader of fiction ever really believes that
what he is reading is actually happening. This is true, but there is
a second, more insidious way in which the writer of fiction seduces
the reader. This is to make him believe that, however false or unreal
the story may appear to be, it nevertheless hides a number of truths
which the author wishes to communicate to the discerning reader.
We have met this argument before in connection with the allegorizers
of Homer and Ovid. But, says Rabelais, he has got no truths to
convey, he is not in touch with the workings of the universe, and
there is thus no necessity, no supernatural *reason*, why one event
follows another, or even why one word follows another in his fiction.
The only reason why they do so is because it is his whim that they
should. Right from the start he stresses the extempore and subjective nature of his work. Immediately after the attack on allegorization in the Prologue to *Gargantua* he points out that '... à la
composition de ce livre seigneurial, je ne perdiz ne emploiay oncques
plus, ny aultre temps que celluy qui estoit estably à prendre ma
refection corporelle, sçavoir est beuvant et mangeant'. In the last
chapter of *Pantagruel* he suddenly says that he will bring his
chronicle to a close because 'la teste me faict un peu de mal et [je]
sens bien que les registres de mon cerveau sont quelque peu
brouilléz de ceste purée de septembre'. Rabelais keeps bringing
before the reader the image of the writer engaged in his work
so as to drive home the fact that this is no transcript of reality
but words and scenes which emanate from the head of just one
man.

Rabelais will not allow the reader to settle into a comfortable suspension of disbelief. He keeps interrupting the action with direct remarks to the reader: 'Je me doubte que ne croyez asseurement ceste estrange nativité. Si ne le croyez, je ne m'en soucie, mais un homme de bien, un homme de bon sens, croit tousjours ce qu'on luy dict et qu'il trouve par escript' (I. vi). He makes a show of detaching himself from what he recounts: 'Je n'en scay rien de ma part, et bien peu me soucie ny d'elle ny d'aultre.' In the first two books he even puts on the *persona* of M. Alcofribas, 'Abstracteur de Quinte Essence'—a title which burlesques the alchemists' pretence that they are in touch with the secrets of nature—and takes an occasional part in the action as one of Pantagruel's men.

As well as stressing that what is before the reader is nothing but a book, Rabelais keeps reminding him that the events recorded in it are made up of words, which are subject to such printing errors as the substitution of an 'n' for an 'm' in the word 'asme', or to such misplacement of words as in the chapter entitled 'Comment Epistemon, qui avoit la coupe testé…'. He takes proverbial expressions literally, as in the account of the games played by the young Gargantua or in some of the titles of the Library of St. Victor; or he makes Panurge parade about with a flea in his ear to illustrate the proverbial expression for wanting to get married. This is all very much in the style of the anonymous author of the *Blason des couleurs*, or of the men who exhibited a *sphère* for *espoir*. By burlesquing 'natural' language Rabelais forces the reader to work, translating the terms into conventional discourse, and thereby recognizing that they *are* conventional. By setting up a conflict between two kinds of discourse he makes the reader recognize that there is a gap between the fiction before him and the world outside.

It is the same with the elaborate and minute descriptions in which Rabelais so frequently indulges. Here, for instance, is a typical battle-scene: 'Soubdain après, tyra son dict braquemart et en ferut l'archier qui le tenoit à dextre, luy coupant entierement les venes jugulaires et arteres spagitides du col, avecques le guarguareon, jusques es deux adenes, et, retirant le coup, luy entreouvrit le mouelle spinale entre la seconde et tierce vertebre: là tomba l'archier tout mort' (I. xliv). By focusing very minutely on the event Rabelais makes us aware of the fact that it is not really happening at all. The description becomes an end in itself, no longer the means of apprehending a certain action. Moreover, the precision of detail and the total lack of emotive vocabulary give the whole thing a dreamlike quality, for it is impossible to relate the detail to any larger context of war and death. It would not really surprise us if the dead man were to rise again, as Epistemon does a little later from a similar situation.

One of the things Rabelais is doing here, as in the equally elaborate transcriptions of the sign-contest between Panurge and Thaumaste, is rendering the ludicrousness of the fiction-writer's realistic art. For what will it avail him to describe in detail a series of incidents if he is incapable of giving them any meaning? But to ascribe meaning to them would be to try, like Panurge, to usurp God's function. For no novelist is omniscient, no novelist has been given a special key to unlock the secrets of men's lives. He can describe with as much accuracy as he likes the surfaces of things, but to give them any meaning is to claim transcendental knowledge. The sign-contest is not just an attack on scholastic argument; it is also an attack on the artist's arrogation to himself of universal knowledge—and Rabelais attacks both for the same reason: logic-chopping and minute description make the same error of tackling the minutiae of things without asking into what scheme these minutiae fit.

The great lists, the feasts, the exuberant piling up of words all serve the same purpose: to reveal the impossibility of giving a true and meaningful account of the world. The mock-eulogies also belong here. When Panurge delivers his speech in praise of debt he is not merely parodying Ficino in praise of love. We are meant to recognize that the eulogy is absurd, that it does not in any way correspond to the truth of the matter. Similarly when Dindenault praises his sheep: '— Comment, respondit le marchant, l'entendez vous, nostre amy, mon voisin? Ce sont moutons à la grande laine, Jason y print la toison d'or. L'ordre de la maison de Bourguoigne en feut extraict. Moutons de Levant, moutons de haulte fustaye, moutons de haulte gresse' (IV. vi). These last are exactly the words Rabelais used about his book in the Prologue to *Gargantua*: 'ces beaux livres de haulte gresse', and the intention is just the same. We are meant to recognize that the object does not correspond to the description; thus the description itself becomes the true object.

Everywhere within his book Rabelais sets up mirror images of himself and his own situation as the author. We have seen that Panurge, Picrochole, and Dindenault are all in some ways similar to their creator. But this applies to almost every character in the book. Rabelais always makes us aware of the speaker, throws us back from the words to the utterer. Hence the many harangues which are set in a context of elaborate ritual, as in the case of Ulrich Gallet: 'Les parolles annoncées au roy, ne consentit aulcunement qu'on luy ouvrist la porte, mais se transporta sus le bolevard, et dist à l'embassadeur: "Qu'i a il de nouveau? Que voulez vous dire?" Adoncques l'embassadeur proposua comme s'ensuit: "Plus juste cause de douleur naistre ne peut entre les humains que si, du lieu dont par droicture esperoient grace et benevolence, ilz recepvent ennuy et dommaige..." ' (I. xxx–xxxi). This goes on for three pages. Then: 'A tant se teut le bon homme Gallet.' Instead of an impressive harangue we have a sort of cartoon picture of a little man striking grand poses, the words pouring in unrestrained torrents from his mouth. Once more the end—persuading Picrochole—has been swallowed up by the means, our attention drawn wholly to the intricacies of the language rather than to what it is trying to convey.

It would, however, be wrong to see Rabelais as a sort of Renaissance Mallarmé, engaged in freeing words from their referential content and giving us a pure language. For unlike Picrochole and Dindenault and Panurge and Ulrich Gallet, Rabelais is supremely self-conscious. We feel him inserting himself into every role he parodies, drawing sustenance from it even as he pushes it just far enough to make us realize that he is aware of what he is doing. This is true even of the famous humanist documents, the letters of the giants, the 'contion' (harangue) of Gargantua (I. i). As in the oration of Ulrich Gallet, the slightly over-insistent Ciceronianisms draw our attention to themselves and allow us to glimpse the playful Rabelais behind the serious façade. For if Rabelais is very like Gallet or Panurge, there is one essential difference between them. It is the difference which we register when watching a man who does not know he is on a tightrope stretched between two houses calmly striding along as though he were going to buy a packet of cigarettes, and watching a clown teeter very perilously on a line of chalk he has drawn on the circus ring. We hold our breath at the dangerous situation in which the first finds himself, but we hold it at the brilliance of the performance of the second.

Our laughter at reading Rabelais stems from our recognition of the gap between words and things, fantasy and reality, private expression and public truth. Rabelais's whole effort is directed towards making us aware of this gap. To take his language by itself and to talk of his wonderful comic zest is to blur the distinction between a conscious and an unconscious use of this type of language, between Panurge and Rabelais. We fail then to see the meaning of laughter or the reason for the style. To take the discussions of education and the woman question by themselves is to look for an extractable meaning hidden in the work, which gives the work its value and its *raison d'être*, and which can be separated from the style. But if we read Rabelais as he asks to be read we will take note of both the content and the transformation it undergoes in the interests of playful imitation. To read Rabelais in this way is to be made aware of the gap between our wishes and the world's reality, between human civilization and the state of nature. The difference between Panurge and Pantagruel is that the latter is aware that he is only human, with a man's limitations, and is thus to some extent able to overcome these limitations; while the former, imagining that he is like God, is made into the victim of these limitations. Laughter is the prerogative of Pantagruel, and it can be that of the reader.

Rabelais begins by quoting Aristotle's famous dictum that what differentiates man from the animals is not his intellect, but his capacity for laughter. Rabelais, with his early Franciscan training with its stress on original sin behind him, would perhaps have modified this and said that laughter is not the distinctive feature of man, but of fallen man. In Heaven there is no laughter. But then there is no art either.

NOTE

FRANÇOIS RABELAIS, 1494(?)–1553, was born near Chinon in the Touraine, and appears to have spent his early years as a Franciscan friar. Persecution arising from his interest in the new humanism made him join the less severe Benedictines in 1521. He soon left this order and began to travel round the universities of France studying medicine. In 1531 he caused a sensation by lecturing at Montpellier on Hippocrates and Galen, using the Greek texts. Between 1534 and 1550 Rabelais visited Rome three times as physician to his friend and protector Cardinal Jean du Bellay, and during this period he wrote a number of works, including his masterpiece centred on the adventures of Gargantua and Pantagruel. His satirical attacks on obscurantism aroused the enmity of the Sorbonne and the Paris Parliament, though he received the income from two country livings before his death in Paris in 1553.

Works. The first volume, *Pantagruel*, of Rabelais's great work of prose fiction appeared in 1532; the second, *Gargantua*, in 1534. There followed the *Tiers Livre* in 1546 and the *Quart Livre* in 1549 (an expanded version was published in 1552). The *Cinquissme Livre* appeared posthumously in 1564 and is largely the work of another hand.

Scholarship and modern editions. The bulk of writing on Rabelais is scholarly rather than critical. It can be found in the 'Études rabelaisiennes' series of monographs and in the journal *Bibliothèque d'Humanisme et Renaissance* (known earlier as *La Revue du seizième siècle* and, before that, as *La Revue des études rabelaisiennes*). The great critical edition of the *Œuvres*—begun in 1912 and now almost complete—is edited by Lefranc, Plattard, Clouzot, Sainéan, and others. More manageable are the Pléiade (ed. J. Boulenger) and Garnier (ed. P. Jourda) editions.

Criticism. The standard general work remains J. Plattard, *La Vie et l'œuvre de Rabelais* (1932). Other useful studies include M. A. Screech, *The Rabelaisian Marriage* (1958), A. J. Krailsheimer, *Rabelais and the Franciscans* (1963), M. Tetel, *Étude sur le comique de Rabelais* (1964) and *Rabelais* (1967), and G. Kaiser, *Praisers of Folly* (1964). The best single essay is probably chapter 11 of E. Auerbach, *Mimesis* (1953). Relevant to this kind of fiction are Coleridge's essay 'On the Distinction of the Witty, the Droll, the Odd and the Humorous' and the sections in Northrop Frye's *Anatomy of Criticism* (1957) dealing with Menippean satire.

3. Humanists, Reformers, and French Culture

In 1532 Gargantua wrote to his son Pantagruel:

Par la bonté divine, la lumière et dignité a esté de mon eage rendue es lettres, et y voy tel amendement que, de present, à difficulté seroys je receu en la premiere classe des petitz grimaulx, qui, en mon eage virile, estoys (non à tord) reputé le plus sçavant dudict siecle... Je voy les brigans, les boureaulx, les avanturiers, les palefreniers, de maintenant, plus doctes que les docteurs et prescheurs de mon temps.

Not only fictional characters believed in this restoration. From the later fifteenth century onwards the idea began to spread in France, as elsewhere, that the 'age of darkness' was over and that a new age had begun. In the mid sixteenth century, this new beginning is referred to as a *restitution* or *renaissance des lettres*. What made the age new was, above all, the revival of poetry and oratory, the renewed study of Greek and Hebrew, and the invention of printing.

In many ways, as modern historians like to point out, the age was not new at all. France in 1500 had much in common with the France of 1400 and even with the France of 1200. Society was still in many ways 'feudal', dominated by a military aristocracy which was based on the 'land'—that is, on the labours of the peasantry. The lesser nobles were still often dependent on the greater, on 'overmighty subjects' like the Constable Charles de Bourbon in the first half of the sixteenth century, or the Dukes of Guise in the second. Bayard, pattern of knighthood and 'adopted son of Dame Courtesy', did not die until 1524. François Ier had had himself knighted by Bayard on the battlefield of Marignano in 1515 in the best medieval manner.

Tournaments and jousts were still fashionable, and Henri II was to be killed in a joust in 1559.

Most educated men were still clerics in 1500, as they had been in that period soon to become known as the Middle Ages. In the sixteenth century, at certain stages in their lives, Rabelais and Bodin were friars, Amyot and Pontus de Tyard were bishops. Men's values—or at least their ideals—were still predominantly otherworldly, centred on the after-life. Death played a leading role in the European imagination at this time. Pictures of the *Danse macabre* were common; a famous series of woodcuts on this subject was published in Paris in 1485. Books on the *ars moriendi*, or how to make a good death, were a popular literary genre, with illustrations of skulls and scythes, devils and crucifixes.

Education was largely traditional. If a Parisian scholastic philosopher of about 1200 could have revisited his university three hundred years later, he would have felt at home in many ways. The basic method of instruction and examination was still the disputation, the formal Latin debate. The vocabulary of scholasticism was still current coin. Bricot, Mair, and Tartaret, the leading philosophers of the day, had much in common with Abélard and his opponents.

Literature too was traditional. Romances of chivalry, the descendants of the *roman courtois* of the twelfth century, remained popular throughout the sixteenth: favourites were *Les Quatre Fils Aymon* and a translation from the Spanish, *Amadis de Gaule*. Medieval mystery, miracle, and morality plays continued to flourish in France during the first half of the sixteenth century. Marguerite de Navarre wrote some, and her brother François Ier went to see them on occasion. The famous thirteenth-century allegorical poem the *Roman de la Rose*, with its complex personifications like Doux Regard and Bel Accueil, continued to be reprinted frequently until the end of the 1530s. Didactic poems, full of personifications and allegorical in form, continued to be written. An example from about 1516 is Pierre Gringore's *Mère Sotte*. This poem consists in large part of tales taken from the fourteenth-century compilation, the *Gesta Romanorum*—tales of Roman history which Gringore interprets as allegories of Christian doctrine. For example, there is a story about a king's daughter who is guarded by five soldiers but elopes with a duke; later she returns to her father and is forgiven. For Gringore, the king is a symbol of God; his daughter, of the soul; the five soldiers, of the five senses; the duke, of the devil.

These remarks are not meant to imply that contemporaries were completely wrong about the new age which they thought they saw coming to birth. We are better placed than they for seeing the similarities between the sixteenth century and the centuries before it, but they were better placed than we for seeing the differences. There were important changes around the year 1500. There was a revival of classical learning, and, still more important, though not openly stated by contemporaries, there was a shift in the values implicit in French culture. This revival and this shift were preconditions essential for the 'take-off' of French literature into modernity in the 1530s, the decade with which this account of French literature truly begins; and so the years 1470–1530 may be seen (with conscious retrospection and from a literary point of view) as a period of preparation, a *Prérenaissance*.

The revival of classical learning and the shift in values are connected movements, and it is convenient to describe both of them as the rise of 'humanism'. Humanism in the first of these two senses is the study of the *disciplinae humanae*, as they were called in the sixteenth century. These disciplines were grammar, rhetoric, history, poetry, and ethics. These subjects had been studied in the Middle Ages too, but more emphasis had been placed on logic and on theology. Besides the change in emphasis, there was a change in the method of study. Now there was a 'return to the sources', that is, to reading certain Greek and Roman writers. Studying rhetoric meant studying Cicero; studying poetry meant studying Virgil, Horace, and Ovid; studying ethics meant studying Aristotle. Before this revival, studying had meant reading texts less and commentaries more; and even reading commentaries on commentaries, like Tartaret's commentary on Peter of Spain's commentary on Porphyry's commentary on the logical works of Aristotle.

But why call these disciplines 'human'? The answer that contemporaries would probably have given is 'because the study of these classical authors teaches us how to be human, how to live the

good life': 'bien et honorablement vivre', as the French humanist
Budé put it. These authors were guides in the quest for new ideals,
because the values implicit in their culture were different from the
values implicit in medieval European culture, and different in the
right way; that is, they expressed values towards which Europeans
were already moving. The classical writers were more worldly, in
the sense of fundamentally accepting life on earth instead of trying
to escape from it or reject it. They were not irreligious, but tended
to see religion as a means to bettering the human condition or to
think of it as simply the good life. Their values may thus be described
as man-centred rather than God-centred, and in this sense 'humanist'.
Ancients and humanists both tended to emphasize reason rather
than faith; the natural goodness and the powers and dignity of man
—not original sin. Humanists liked to quote the Delphic oracle,
'know thyself': or Protagoras on man 'the measure of all things'; or
the Psalmist on man as 'little lower than the angels'. Pope Innocent
III had written in the twelfth century a book about the misery of the
human condition; in the fifteenth century the Italian humanist Pico
della Mirandola wrote an *Oration on the Dignity of Man*. Ancients
and humanists also emphasized the power of the word. Man is
human, they argue, man differs from animals principally because he
has reason, and this is shown by his power of speech and writing.
To quote Budé again, 'il nya rien parquoy lhomme differe tant des
bestes brutes, que par parler fonde en science'. This is to make
literature tremendously important. In fact, the study of *disciplinae
humanae*, or *humana philosophia*, is also referred to as the study of
bonae litterae, or *bonnes lettres*. In other words, the rise of modern
French literature was immediately preceded by a shift in values
which made literature more important than before.

It is not surprising to discover that the period 1470–1530 was
important for the editing and translating of Greek and Latin
literature. Ovid and Virgil were translated into French, and so were
Caesar and Sallust, Thucydides and Xenophon. Cicero's essay *On
Duties* and Aristotle's *Ethics* were both published in French translation at this time. This recovery and diffusion of the classics was
a development big with consequences for both literary form and
literary content. In content, French literature for much of the

sixteenth century expresses humanist values, as later essays in this volume will show; but in form too. There is at this time a new interest in classical metres, in classical figures of rhetoric, and in classical literary genres—the epistle, the epigram, the epic, the ode. From studying these genres men move on to imitating them, first in Latin and then in French. In this period one French humanist wrote a Latin epic about Jeanne d'Arc; later in the century Ronsard was to write his *Franciade*. Jean Lemaire de Belges (1473–c. 1520), a poet in the service of Margaret of Austria, wrote the *Épîtres de l'amant vert* (1505), letters to his mistress in the name of her pet parrot. The parrot claims to have died for love of her by allowing itself to be killed by the dog while she was away. The playful tone of these pieces is unlike late medieval literature but like Ovid, whose *Amores* contain an elegy for a parrot, and whose *Heroides* are letters written in the name of famous lovers, like Ariadne and Penelope. In general, this imitation of classical genres had an important function. Late medieval literature tended to lack structure; it tended to ramble. Classical literature, on the other hand, tended to be well articulated, to obey certain rules of form, and these rules were not imitated. The epistle, for example, as Lemaire and Marot write it, has the standard form of ten-syllable lines rhyming *aabb*. So the French humanists discovered antiquity at a time when French literature had much to learn from it, and the recovery of the classics is immediately followed by the rise of modern French literature. An age of scholars preceded—and perhaps had to precede—an age of writers.

The most famous of these scholars is, of course, Erasmus (*c.* 1466–1536), who came to Paris about 1495, made his intellectual début there, and published there the first editions of both his *Adages* (1500) and his *Praise of Folly* (1511). But there were humanists in Paris before Erasmus. The greatest of them was Jacques Lefèvre d'Étaples (*c.* 1450–1536), or Faber Stapulensis, as he was known in the world of humanism. Until he was about forty, Lefèvre seems to have been a conventional Paris scholastic philosopher, with leanings towards nominalism;[1] but about 1490 his intellectual life took a new

---

[1] *Nominalism* is the doctrine that 'universals' (abstractions like 'man', 'table', and so on) are just empty sounds, in contrast to *realism*, the doctrine that universals are more real than individual men or tables.

direction. He learned Greek. He went to Italy. He abandoned
scholasticism; and he began to publish. Lefèvre was not greatly
interested in literature. He disapproved of Catullus, Ovid, Terence,
and Lucian, on moral grounds. His own Latin style was not elegant.
His interest in antiquity was an interest, above all, in Greek philosophy, in Aristotle and in Plato. It was to meet the Italian students
of Greek philosophy that he went to Italy; to see the 'triumvirate' of
Marsilio Ficino, the Platonist; Ermolao Barbaro, the Aristotelian;
and Pico della Mirandola, who tried to harmonize both philosophical
traditions. Lefèvre returned to France to teach what he had learned.
He edited Aristotle paying more attention than his predecessors had
done to what Aristotle had actually said, establishing a better text. In
his commentaries he was at pains to avoid the vocabulary of
scholasticism. He preferred to elucidate Aristotle by quoting Homer,
Virgil, and Horace. He did not edit Plato, but he did edit various
neoplatonic treatises such as those by a fifth-century writer (then
believed to be St. Paul's contemporary, Dionysius the Areopagite)[1]
and some second-century writings (then believed to be by the god
Hermes Trismegistus himself).

Lefèvre was an intellectually timid man and more of an editor than
a writer. It is in the writings of his friends and disciples that one has
to look for the changes in ideas and values at this time—the writings
of Clichtove, Bouelles, Budé, and Champier.

Josse Clichtove (c. 1472–1543) made a contribution to the traditional literature on the 'art of dying' with his How to Die (De doctrina
moriendi, 1520), but his emphasis was a new one. He does not stress
the horrors of dying like his predecessors, but suggests that the
death of the body is not to be feared. He is even more untraditional
in the way in which he supports his argument, with frequent quotations from Roman writers—Horace, Virgil, Ovid, Seneca, and,
above all, Cicero, who is given a chapter to himself.

Charles de Bouelles (c. 1481–1553), in his The Wise Man (De
sapiente, 1510) developed the ideas of man's dignity and powers to
be found in Pico's famous Oration. Bouelles discusses four levels of
existence. Something may simply exist, like a stone (esse). It may live,

---

[1] It was also believed at this time that this Dionysius was identical with St. Denis,
patron saint of France.

like a tree (*vivere*). It may perceive, like a horse (*sentire*). At the
highest level, only a man can understand (*intelligere*). The slothful
man is no better than a stone; the gluttonous man no better than
a tree; the sensual man no better than a horse. Only the *sapiens*, the
studiosus, in other words the humanist sitting at his desk, is truly
human. He possesses two kinds of knowledge: knowledge of the
outside world, and knowledge of himself. His knowledge of the world
sets him at its centre, makes him its judge; but he also follows the
command of the Delphic oracle, 'know thyself'. The proper study
of mankind is man.

Guillaume Budé (1468–1540), François Ier's librarian, was the
greatest scholar of them all, much more critical than Lefèvre. One of
his most famous works was *The As and its Parts* (*De Asse et partibus
eius*, 1515), a study of Roman coinage which developed in the direction of the as yet unknown historical genre, economic history. Some
of the digressions in this book may be of interest to the literary critic,
because Budé applies his learning to disproving the then common
view of the unaptness of the French for literature. He quotes Strabo
on the Gauls to show that this was not the case then, and (writing
in Latin himself) anticipates some of the arguments of Du Bellay's
more famous defence of the French language. Budé also wrote in the
vernacular, for example the *Institution du Prince* (1516), one of the
many Renaissance treatises on the qualities of the perfect prince,
addressed to the young François Ier at the same time that Erasmus
was writing a similar treatise for the benefit of the young Charles V.
In this work Budé defends absolute monarchy, not yet established in
France. He also tells François, as a humanist would, that to achieve
fame he needs to acquire *sapience*, and that this is done by the study
of the Bible and the classics. The prince must study oratory, to
make men do his will more easily. He must also patronize the arts,
as Augustus and Maecenas did; if there are no patrons, there will
be no poets. Echoing Martial, he writes: '... dit on aujourduy que
par faulte de mécénates il n'est plus de Virgiles ne de Horaces.' It
was in fact thanks to Budé's (protracted) efforts that François did
eventually found the *lecteurs royaux* to teach Greek and Hebrew
(1530). This was the beginning of the present Collège de France.

Symphorien Champier (*c.* 1472–*c.* 1540) was a doctor of Lyons, an enthusiast for Plato. Like Pico, he tried to harmonize Plato and Aristotle, throwing in Galen and Hippocrates for good measure in his *Symphonia* (1516), which has a woodcut on the title-page showing his four authors playing a string quartet. He wrote an apologia for humanism in which he quotes from the Fathers of the Church to show that a Christian may read Plato and Hermes Trismegistus with a good conscience. In the vernacular he wrote, among other works, the *Nef des dames* (1503), a book in praise of women with which the neoplatonic theory of love enters French literature. After having listed all the gifted women he can think of, including Minerva, Penelope, Medusa, Eve, Judith, and the Virgin Mary, Champier goes on to treat of *vraie amour*. Quoting Plato's *Symposium*, he sings the praises of love. Love is a god. Love is a circle, with *bonté* at the centre and *beauté* at the circumference. Love makes the world go round. The moral: 'O dames aimes et ensuives amour comme chose divine. Et de tout votre pouvoir soies serventes en amour, car amour est en toutes choses et va à toutes créatures et est créateur de toutes choses et la maîtresse de toutes créatures.'

There had been enthusiasm for Plato in France before Champier, but his real impact on French literature came after Champier's death. It was in the 1540s and 1550s that the dialogues began to appear in French: the *Apology*, *Phaedo*, *Symposium*, *Timaeus*, and *Io* among them. At the same time came French translations of Italian neoplatonists like Ficino and Bembo. The poetry of the Pléiade is part of this wave. The high value placed on love in French culture from the time of the troubadours and the *roman courtois* now received a philosophical justification, and poets writing about love received a free gift of Platonic images—the Ladder, the Chariot of the soul, the Torches.

Not all humanists were members of Lefèvre's circle. An example of one who was not is the merchant, sea-captain, and poet Jean Parmentier of Dieppe (1494–1530). Michelet defined the Renaissance as 'la découverte du monde, la découverte de l'homme'. Charles de Bouelles illustrates this two-pronged definition by his insistence that the wise man look both outward and inward, but Parmentier illustrates it even more vividly. He led an expedition to Sumatra, in the course of which he died. On this last voyage he wrote a poem,

Merveilles de Dieu et dignité de l'homme, in which he approaches God by contemplating the marvels of Nature and the nature of Man. As he tells God:

> ... bien pres d'angelique haultesse
> Il a attainct en son esprit noblesse
> Par la vertu que luy as dispensée...
> Tu l'as esleu souveraine admiral,
> Grand capitaine et grand chef general,
> En mer, en terre, et mesme en my l'air.

Parmentier also illustrates the common enthusiasm for antiquity. He translated Sallust into French.

It has often been observed that Renaissance and Reformation had important common characteristics. Both humanists and reformers desired to advance by going back, whether to classical antiquity or to the primitive Church. Both opposed what they thought of as the sterile subtleties of the schoolmen. Both took a great interest in the inner life, almost as if the Renaissance were simply the secular expression and the Reformation the religious expression of a general psychological change, an increasing self-consciousness or 'individualism'. Both humanists and reformers have great faith in the power of the word, written or spoken, and place great emphasis on texts: the classics, the Bible. Both Renaissance and Reformation have important literary consequences; humanists taught French literature classical discipline, and reformers, through their interest in a vernacular Bible and a vernacular liturgy, helped, unintentionally, the development of French as a literary language. For a time, some men were active both as humanists and as reformers; the obvious example is Erasmus. He edited the Bible and the Fathers. He wrote a guide to the spiritual life, the *Handbook of a Christian Soldier.* His Latin dialogues, the *Colloquies,* often discuss religious subjects. He criticized the Church for its superstitions, for its emphasis on exterior religion, 'Judaic ceremonies' as he called them. We should not venerate the relics of the saints so much as follow their example.

However, Renaissance and Reformation did not move in quite the same direction, and the conflicts between humanists and reformers,

or inside the men who tried to be both, became more acute as time
passed, especially after about 1520. The clash between Erasmus and
Luther will serve to illustrate this. For Erasmus, reason and faith
were allies; for Luther, they were enemies, and reason was wrong.
Erasmus stressed the freedom of man's will, like Pico and other
humanist writers on the dignity of man; Luther, in his *The Bondage
of the Will* (1525), attacked Erasmus head on. Erasmus passionately
admired the ancients. In one of his *Colloquies*, the speakers say that
they cannot believe that Virgil and Horace and Cicero are not among
the saved: 'Saint Socrates, pray for us.' Luther rejected the ancients.
For him they were simply 'pagans', and he did not think Aristotle's
Ethics worth reading.

Lefèvre holds a position somewhere between the two. He believed
in a religious 'renaissance', the restoration of the Church to the likeness of the primitive Church, and the restoration of 'the light of the
Gospel' thanks to the revival of Greek and Hebrew studies. Like
Erasmus he believed that the best of the pagan writers and philosophers would be saved. Like Erasmus he criticized the cult of
relics and the trust in stereotyped prayers; for him too, religion was
not ritual but a way of life. But Lefèvre criticized Erasmus for his
dislike of dogma and his pride in knowledge, in terms reminiscent of
Calvin's later attack on the humanists (below, pp. 49–50.) Lefèvre had
a mystical side which Erasmus lacked; his God was less accessible to
reason. One illustration of the difference between them is their contrasting attitudes to the passage from Psalm 8 which Saint Paul quotes
in his *Epistle to the Hebrews* (ch. 2, vv. 6–7): 'What is man, that thou
art mindful of him? . . . Thou madest him a little lower than the
angels.' Erasmus took this passage literally, as one might expect a
humanist to do; Lefèvre gave it a mystical interpretation.

In the 1520s Lefèvre moved further away from Erasmus than
before. He gave up producing scholarly Latin editions and began
to translate the Bible into French for a wider public. He moved
towards accepting the Lutheran doctrine of justification by faith.
His circle was no longer composed of humanists like Bouelles or
Champier, but of the 'Luthériens' or 'Bibliens' as they were called,
a circle which centred on Guillaume Briçonnet and his bishopric
of Meaux. Briçonnet in fact opposed Luther, but he did hold

untraditional views; for example, he thought preaching more important than the administration of the sacraments.

The patron of the Meaux group was the king's sister, Marguerite de Navarre (1492–1549). In many ways she was a woman of the Renaissance: interested in philosophy, a patron of authors (Rabelais dedicated his *Tiers Livre* to her), and herself the author of poems, plays, and stories. Her interest in neoplatonism comes out even in the way in which she asked Briçonnet to become her spiritual director: 'Puisqu'il plaît au grand organiste vouloir la faiblesse des petits tuyaux être confortée par la force des grands.' However, in some ways she was anti-humanist. Like Lefèvre she criticized Erasmus for his spiritual pride:

> ... un cuider hautain
> De trop savoir conduisant plume et main.

In her religious poetry Marguerite comes out against 'mondaine raison'; and she welcomes death, 'o douce mort'. Her cross-pressures are expressed in the poem, *Discord estant en l'homme par la contrariete de l'esprit et la chair*, where Man describes himself as follows:

> Noble d'esprit et serf suis de nature,
> Extraict du ciel, et vile geniture,
> Siege de Dieu, vaisseau d'iniquite,
> Immortel suis, tendant à pourriture.

The contradictions are reconciled at the end of the poem 'par vie spirituelle', but one is left with the impression that they are stated more forcefully than they are resolved.

Another aspect of Marguerite's religious sensibility is that it is sentimental. In this respect it is very much in the main line of fourteenth-, fifteenth-, and sixteenth-century trends, whether they are called declining Middle Ages, Renaissance, or Reformation; parallels could be made with Thomas à Kempis, with Erasmus, with Luther. For Marguerite, prayers are only of value if they come straight from the heart. Good works are simply 'le bon cœur'. In a famous poem, *Le Miroir de l'âme pecherresse* (1531)—translated into English by Queen Elizabeth I—she calls Christ her father, her brother, her husband, her son, even (here taking over the vocabulary of courtly love) her 'parfait ami'.

A more entertaining expression of reformed ideas is provided
by the *Farce des Theologastres*, performed by the students of the
University of Paris in 1523. The occasion of the performance was
the release from prison of Louis de Berquin, translator of Luther
and Erasmus, and the farce may have been written by him. The
theme is a common one in satirical literature of the Reformation
(see below, p. 57, the *Pape malade*). Dame Foi is ill. She has
caught 'mal Sorbonnique' (or 'passion sophistique'). One character,
Theologastres, offers her a decretal (a papal ruling in canon law) but
she refuses it. Another character, Fratrez, representing the friars,
offers her a 'sermonnaire' (a collection of sermons) but she refuses
this too. Theologastres offers her Lucian, Ovid, or Virgil; she refuses again. Even humanism will not cure her. What she wants is
medicine from Germany, and it is brought by Berquin, who cures
her by means of 'le texte de sainte écriture'. In the course of the
play there is much incidental mockery of the clergy; of 'Sorbon-
nistes', 'Holcotistes', and 'Bricotistes' (the Sorbonne being the
Faculty of Theology at Paris, Holcot and Bricot late scholastics);
and of allegorical interpretations of the Bible. For example, Texte
complains that she has been so much interpreted, anagogically,
tropologically, and allegorically, that she does not know where she is.

In its mixture of new ideas and old forms, the farce is very much
a work of the 1520s. It is a kind of miracle-play, and the miraculous
cure of Dame Foi does take place as a result of touching her
with a text. The personifications—Foi, Raison, Texte—are in
the medieval tradition. But the farce praises Erasmus, 'grand
textuaire', and criticizes exterior religion as nothing but 'Judaïque
cérémonie'.

More important than the clashes between humanists and reformers
in the 1520s was the conflict between the new ideas on one side, and
the forces of tradition on the other. The University of Paris came to
have 'two heads', as a contemporary put it. It came to be divided
into two parties, as Oxford was into the humanist 'Greeks' and the
anti-humanist 'Trojans'. Hence Budé's insistence on the foundation
of the *lecteurs royaux*, a centre of humanism which was separate
from the rest of the university, under special royal protection. This
division was already clear at the time that the Reuchlin affair caused

an international stir in the university world. Johann Reuchlin was a German scholar, a pioneer in the study of the Hebrew language and of Jewish religious texts. In 1513 he was summoned for trial by the inquisitor of Cologne on a heresy charge. The underlying issue was whether it was permissible to study the Bible like other texts, by a return to the sources to find out the meaning intended by the original writers. It was not just Reuchlin who was on trial; it was humanism. In 1514 a committee was appointed by the Sorbonne to consider the case; its verdict went against Reuchlin although Lefèvre, a member of the committee, was on his side. In 1521 the Sorbonne censured both Erasmus and Lefèvre. In 1526 Lefèvre was attacked as a disciple of Wyclif and a teacher of Luther, and forty-eight propositions of his were condemned by the Sorbonne. They could do more than condemn propositions. Berquin was arrested three times, and the intervention of Marguerite de Navarre and even of the king on his behalf did not prevent his being burned in 1529. It is not surprising that Lefèvre chose to publish his translation of the Bible anonymously at Antwerp (1530). The Sorbonne even tried to prohibit Marguerite's *Miroir*, but the king would not stand for that. It was in this atmosphere that the new ideas were disseminated. Small wonder that some men were crypto-reformers and that historians cannot discover how many Frenchmen supported humanism and reform.

It remains to account for the appearance and the spread of these new ideas at this time. Humanism has often been seen as an 'import' from Italy, the Reformation as an 'import' from Germany; and the 'influence' of Ficino, Erasmus, Luther, and others has been traced. It does indeed seem that Lefèvre's first visit to Italy was crucial for his intellectual development, as perhaps for Rabelais and Du Bellay later. In the later fifteenth century a number of Italians (including Pico) visited Paris or taught there, spreading an interest in humanism as Primaticcio and Leonardo spread the taste for Renaissance art. Lyons was an important centre for the diffusion of Renaissance ideas, because it was near the Italian border, just as Strasbourg was an important centre for the diffusion of Reformation ideas because of its contacts with both France and the empire.

However, this is only the beginning of the problem. Why did people want to import these ideas? The answer seems to be, because French values were already changing. In so far as there was a gradual shift during the fourteenth and fifteenth centuries, a more rapid shift thereafter, it seems reasonable to stress the role of a technological factor, printing. The first French press was established in 1470, but at Lyons in 1515 there were already more than a hundred printing houses. Some printers were enthusiasts for the Renaissance, as were Badius, the Estiennes, and Tory; Badius and Tory both studied in Italy. Tory had his own ideas about the reform of typography and the vernacular, which he set out in his *Champfleury* (1529).

The development of printing seems to have speeded up the shift in values which made men talk of a 'new age'. But what started the shift? The Renaissance and the Reformation may both be described as in some sense movements of 'secularization', and this provides a clue as to why they happened. They are important stages in a much larger movement—the rise of an educated laity, which began in the twelfth century and has not stopped yet. In the sixteenth century, the reading public and the narrower circle of writers, both predominantly clerical in the past, widened to include gentlemen, ladies, and even members of the third estate. As methods of warfare changed and their military usefulness declined, the French nobility began to define themselves more in terms of their manners and education, to change from *chevaliers* into *gentilshommes* (a word that first came into general use in the sixteenth century). Some of them even wrote books: most of the Pléiade are gentlemen, so is Montaigne. Ladies too began to take more interest in literature. Marguerite de Navarre, Pernette de Guillet, Louise Labé, and others wrote and even published. So did members of the third estate. The humanist Budé and the reforming bishop Briçonnet both came from commercial-financial families, and Louise Labé was a ropemaker's daughter. Behind the rise of modern French literature lies a movement of social change.

NOTE

Some of the most useful and important primary and secondary sources for further study of the main ideas in this chapter are as follows:

Basic texts

Works by two of the leading humanist scholars have recently been republished. Guillaume Budé, *L'Institution du Prince*, is printed in C. Bontems and others, *Le Prince dans la France* (1965); J. Lefèvre d'Étaples, *Épistres et Évangiles*, is edited by M. A. Screech (1964). An important work by the great *rhétoriqueur* Jean Lemaire de Belges is his *Épîtres de l'amant vert*, edited by J. Frappier (1948).

Criticism

(*a*) *General background.* L. Bradner, 'From Petrarch to Shakespeare', in W. K. Ferguson and others, *The Renaissance: Six Essays* (1962); J. Huizinga, *The Waning of the Middle Ages* (1965 reprint); A. Tenenti, *La Vie et la mort à travers l'art du XV*ᵉ *siècle* (1952); H. Weber, *La Création poétique au XVI*ᵉ *siècle en France de Maurice Scève à Agrippa d'Aubigné* (1956: 2 vols.).

(*b*) *Humanism.* P. O. Kristeller, *Renaissance Thought* (1961); A. Renaudet, *Préréforme et humanisme à Paris pendant les premières guerres d'Italie (1494–1517)* (1953 reprint); A. Renaudet, 'Paris de 1494 à 1517', in Renaudet and others, *Courants religieux et humanisme* (1959).

(*c*) *Reformation.* J. Delumeau, *Naissance et affirmation de la réforme* (1965: esp. chapter 1); A. G. Dickens, *Reformation and Society in Sixteenth Century Europe* (1966: esp. chapters 1–5); L. Febvre, *Au Cœur religieux du XVI*ᵉ *siècle* (1957: esp. the classic essay entitled: 'Les Origines de la réforme française').

4. The Two Faces of Calvinism

ONE of the many forms of Protestant propaganda in the sixteenth century was the striking of satirical medals. These medals often bear the head of a pope or cardinal, but turn the medal round, and there is another face. The pope's neck becomes the devil's horns, or the fool's cap and bells.

'Calvinism' (to use a term which sixteenth-century followers of Calvin disliked) also had two faces. The better-known one is that of Calvin the hammer of the humanists. The other side of the medal is the humanist face of Calvin and Calvinism.

Since the revival of antiquity began, there had always been tension between humanism and Christianity. Firstly, because the admired ancients were not Christians; the attempt to fuse the two systems of belief and speak of 'Saint Socrates' did not satisfy everyone. Secondly, because the humanist faith in the powers of man seemed to others like spiritual pride. After about 1530 this tension increased; humanism and reformation began to pull away from one another. This split can be seen in part as a natural result of the assumptions of the two movements. They had always agreed more in methods than in aims, and, as the aims came near to realization, a split was inevitable. Erasmus and Lefèvre d'Étaples, who did not want such a split, died in 1536. Now it was the turn of a younger generation, that of Jean Calvin. Calvin was virtually born into the Reformation. Born in 1509, he was still a child when Luther was excommunicated. It was easier for a man of his age to think that the Reformation had not yet gone far enough.

Another reason for the split between humanism and reformation was political. Their common enemies, the supporters of tradition and the Sorbonne, were growing more frightened, and consequently persecuting more harshly after 1530 than before. To meet this persecution the reformers needed discipline and organization. In the 1540s their situation worsened with the deaths of François Ier and Marguerite de Navarre, who had so often protected men accused of heresy. In the same decade the protection and the discipline which the reformers needed were provided by Calvin, who from 1541 till his death in 1564 organized a French-speaking reformed church over the French border, at Geneva.

Calvin's world-view was quite explicitly God-centred, not man-centred: 'C'est chose notoire que l'homme ne parvient jamais à la pure cognoissance de soy-mesme jusques à ce qu'il ait contemplé la face de Dieu, et que, du regard d'icelle, il descende à regarder à soy.' Where the humanists stressed the dignity of man, Calvin stressed his corruption. They placed high value on reason; he repudiated it. They were optimists; he was a pessimist. Man had once been little less than the angels, but Calvin never forgot that that was before the Fall: 'Nous disons que tous les désirs et appétis des hommes sont mauvais, et les condamnons de péché... il ne peut rien procéder pur ny entier de nostre nature vitieuse et soillée.' Where the humanists believed in free will, Calvin believed in determinism—'predestination', he called it: 'Nous appelons Prédestination: le conseil éternel de Dieu, par lequel il a déterminé ce qu'il vouloit faire d'un chacun homme. Car il ne les crée pas tous en pareille condition: mais ordonne les uns à la vie éternelle, les autres à éternelle damnation.' Only a few men were predestined to eternal life; Calvin believed in a *porte étroite*. His God was not so much the loving and suffering Jesus of Erasmian piety as a distant, severe, majestic king or father. Many of Calvin's sermons end with this sentence: 'Nous nous prosternerons devant la maiesté de nostre bon Dieu en cognoissance de nos fautes.'

This world-view, so different from that of Pico della Mirandola or Erasmus, was well adapted to the harsh conditions of the mid-century, wars and persecutions. A Calvinist learned to be harsh with others and with himself, to expect little but suffering in this life, to channel his hopes into the inevitable future victory of the elect. He had little time for learning or for literature unless they served the cause. Learning for its own sake was simply vain curiosity—even theological learning. The printers' device of the Estienne family at

Geneva summed up the Calvinist attitude. There was a picture of the tree of knowledge, with the motto: *noli Altum sapere*, *sed time*: do not try to know God—fear Him. Calvin's assumptions are reflected in his vocabulary. For him *plaire* and *jouer* are words of disapproval like *vain* and *frivole*, to be contrasted with approval-words like *utile* and *solide*.

Calvin did not simply differ from the humanists; he attacked them. His *Excuse aux Nicodemites* (1544), for example, is a pamphlet against all those who are in favour of reformed religion but lukewarm in its support; fellow-travellers with the Reformation, we might say. Calvin calls them 'Nicodemites' after Nicodemus the Pharisee, because he came to see Jesus by night. He spits them out of his mouth. He includes among the Nicodemites people who sound much like the humanists surrounding Marguerite de Navarre. He writes against 'ceux qui convertissent à demy la Chrestienté en philosophie ...il y en a une partie d'eux, qui imaginent des idées Platoniques en leurs testes, touchant la façon de servir Dieu, et ainsi excusent la pluspart des folles superstitions qui sont en la papauté... ceste bande est quasi toute de gens de lettres'. Calvin goes on to make a general point against humanism as a distraction and temptation: 'J'aimerois mieux que toutes les sciences humaines fussent exterminées de la terre, que si elles estoyent cause de refroidir ainsi le zele des Chrestiens et les destourner de Dieu.'

Again, the *Avertissement contre l'astrologie* (1549), however 'modern' an attack on astrology it may appear, was a criticism of the vain curiosity of the humanists, and in particular of a book lately published by the poet Mellin de Saint-Gelais. A year later, in his *Des Scandales* (1550), Calvin attacked the humanists still more directly, in some cases by name. They find the 'langage grossier et simple' of the Bible a stumbling-block: 'ceux... qui ont esté instruits aux sciences humaines, et sont accoustumez à un style pur et elegant, rejettent ou mesprisent ceste façon de parler, comme trop rude et mal polie.' So much the worse for them. Similarly, Calvin recognizes the existence of the humanist objection to his doctrine of predestination, but he has no patience with it, explaining it by the weakness of the flesh: 'C'estoit chose odieuse d'anéantir totalement l'homme, et cela repugne au jugement commun de la chair. Ces bons personnages

cherchent un moyen plus conforme au sens humain, c'est de con-
ceder je ne say quoy au franc arbitre, et laisser quelque vertu
naturelle aux hommes: mais cependant la pureté de la doctrine est
profanée.' There is worse to come. There are some men (Dolet, Des
Périers, and Rabelais are among the names mentioned) who blas-
pheme against God and wish to destroy all reverence for Him. They
believe 'que toutes religions ont esté forgees au cerveau des hommes:
que nous tenons qu'il est quelque Dieu, pource qu'il nous plaist de
le croire ainsi: que l'esperance de la vie éternelle est pour amuser les
idiots: que tout ce qu'on dit d'enfer est pour espouvanter les petits
enfans'.

The difference of opinion between Calvin and these three humanists was in fact not so simple as that. It is both complicated and important and deserves, for both reasons, to be examined in some detail.
Étienne Dolet (1509–46) was a man of Calvin's generation who had
studied at the University of Padua (famous for its freedom of
thought) and had become a printer at Lyons. He was a considerable
classical scholar, and a passionate admirer of Cicero. He refused to
use Latin words which Cicero had not used, and wrote religious
poems in Latin which do not mention Christ but only Jupiter or
'superi' (those who are above). Some thought him a pagan, others,
like Calvin, an atheist. All that is clear is that he disapproved of disputes about doctrine; discussion of the mysteries of religion breeds
contempt, he thought. Silence was better. He seems to have interpreted the doctrine of the immortality of the soul as referring to the
fame that lives on when a great man dies. Dolet was burned as a
heretic, perhaps for his views on immortality, perhaps—puzzling and
ironic as this would be—for distributing Calvinist propaganda.

Bonaventure Des Périers (1498/1510—c. 1544) also frequented
Lyons and at one time collaborated with Dolet. He is the probable
author of the *Cymbalum Mundi* (1537), a little book containing four
dialogues, 'fort ... joyeux et facetieux', as the title-page declares.
They are brilliantly written and full of remarkable and disturbing
ideas, expressed so ambiguously that we shall never know quite
what Des Périers really thought, although not expressed ambiguously enough to save the book from condemnation and virtually
complete destruction—only three copies survive. Like the *Colloquies*

of Erasmus, the *Cymbalum* owes a great deal to the dialogues of the Greek satirist Lucian; but Des Périers is much more radical than Erasmus. His second dialogue, for example, shows Mercury on a visit to earth. He finds the philosophers searching for the 'pierre philosophale' which he had broken up and hidden in the sand. None of them has found any of it, 'mais il n'y a celuy qui ne se vante qu'il en a grande quantité, tellement que si tout ce qu'ilz en monstrent estoit amassé ensemble, il seroit dix foys plus gros que n'estoit la pierre en son entier'. Each of them has his own opinion about what must be done to find it: 'L'un dict que pour en trouver des pieces, il se fault vestir de rouge et vert. L'aultre dict qu'il vauldroit mieux estre vestu de jaune et bleu. L'ung est d'opinion qu'il ne fault manger que six fois le jour avec certaine diette. L'aultre tient que le dormir avec les femmes n'y est pas bon.'

The sterile disputes of the philosophers had been fair humanist game since before 1500; the Erasmian mocking of fasting and celibacy was more dangerous in the 1530s than before, but nothing new. However, it is not likely that the author intended to strike a blow for the Reformation either; among the philosophers who quarrel like children over the stone are 'Rhetulus' (an anagram for 'Lutherus'), 'Cubercus' (a near-anagram for 'Bucerus', another reformed theologian), and 'Drarig', who bears a disconcerting resemblance to Erasmus. So Erasmus and Luther are as bad as the Sorbonne. No one has a monopoly of the truth. It looks as if Des Périers, like Dolet, thinks silence best. It is not surprising that Calvin, whether he was in the author's mind or no (the first edition of his *Institutes* appeared the year before the *Cymbalum*), was not amused by the book and thought Des Périers a blaspheming dog. Des Périers does seem to want to sail very near the wind of blasphemy; what is the reader to make of Mercury, who is at once the son of God, sent to earth, and the father of lies?

Next to the *Cymbalum*, the mockeries of Rabelais seem almost timid. But then Rabelais belongs to an older generation. He was born around 1490, some twenty years before Calvin and Dolet, and in 1550 he was (as Raymond Lebègue says) 'the last of the French Erasmians'. It was not very perceptive of Calvin to put him with Des Périers, although it is not difficult to understand Calvin's dislike for the abbey of Thélème, home of free will, and for 'ce diable qui s'est nommé Pantagruel'. Rabelais made his riposte in his Fourth Book, when he included in the list of monsters brought forth by Anti-Nature 'des ... démoniacles Calvins imposteurs de Genève'.

What Dolet and Des Périers and Rabelais have in common is that they are all humanists. The younger men are more pessimistic, but they have similar ideals, even if they have less hope. These humanist ideals—the value of classical antiquity, the dignity and powers of man, the importance of literature—are all under general attack in the 1530s and 1540s, and not only by Calvin. The humanists were caught between two fires: militant Protestantism on one side, the Counter-Reformation Church on the other. There was great pressure on them to choose sides, and many did so. Those who did not choose found themselves attacked both by Rome and by Geneva; the works of Rabelais were put on the Index at much the same time as Calvin wrote against him. Opinions turned into parties, and the religious wars began. The value of literature was questioned, unless it was a weapon in the struggle. 'Pure' literature was a waste of time, or worse. When Théodore de Bèze (1519–1605) was converted to Calvinism he repented having written Latin epigrams. In the preface to his play *Abraham sacrifiant* (1550) he addressed himself to the 'bons esprits' he knew in France, telling them that they would do better to sing a canticle 'que de petrarquiser un sonnet, et faire l'amoureux transi, digne d'avoir un chaperon à sonnettes: ou de contrefaire ces fureurs poétiques à l'antique...'. This reads something like a reply to Du Bellay's *Deffense*, which had appeared the year before. It must not be thought that all contemporaries approved of the Pléiade.

Calvin's own attitude to literature—as one might have expected—was a utilitarian one. This appears in the preface he wrote to some satirical dialogues by his colleague Pierre Viret (1511–71). For Calvin, the way in which a book is written ought not to matter at all: 'La seule doctrine, quand nous la congnoissons bonne et utile, nous devroit bien suffire, pour nous inciter à lire voulentiers un livre.' To write in a pleasing manner is to make a concession to human weakness, necessary as that concession may be. Books which contain neither good doctrine nor evil are not things indifferent, but positively bad: 'Ceux qui s'occupent à composer livres de passetemps vain et frivole, et amusent le monde à les lire, sont à vituperer, encore qu'il n'y eust nulle corruption.' In this spirit he had the romance of chivalry, *Amadis de Gaule*, banned from Geneva; it might corrupt young people, and anyway it was fiction, nothing but 'mensonge et rêverie'.

It is amusing to see Calvin rushing to Viret's defence against the possible charge that his intention was to give pleasure: 'Ce serait un labeur trop maigre, et une peine mal employée à un homme de tel esprit et savoir.' It is not that Calvin could not laugh, as his enemies made out; but he could only enjoy a joke if he had persuaded himself in advance that it was not 'just' a joke.

For all his hostility to literature, Calvin had a humanist side too. He could not entirely escape the Renaissance ideals in which he had been trained, however hard he struggled in later life. When he studied at the University of Paris, one of his teachers was the humanist Mathurin Cordier. When the *lecteurs royaux* were founded and the regular teaching of Greek began at Paris, the young Calvin was one of the first to take advantage of this opportunity. At Bourges he went to the law lectures of the famous Italian humanist Alciati. His first book was a commentary on a 'pagan' work—on Seneca's treatise *On Clemency*. In this book Calvin praised Seneca both for his style, or eloquence, and for his views on ethics. He also paid tribute to the great humanists of the day; Erasmus, who had already edited Seneca, and Budé, from whose books Calvin had learned a great deal about Rome in Seneca's day.

After his conversion (*c.* 1533) Calvin did not change all his ideas and ideals. There are links between the Seneca commentary and his later works. He went on to write commentaries on the *Epistles* of St. Paul and on other parts of the Bible. His famous *Institutes* was also (in its original version) organized in the form of a commentary —on the Apostles' Creed, the Ten Commandments, and the Our Father.

Calvin inherited more from his humanist days than the habit of writing commentaries. He did not so much deny the humanists' picture of man as put brackets round it; before the Fall, Calvin admitted, man was 'un chef d'œuvre'. Even after the Fall some sparks continue to shine in the nature of man, which prove him to be a rational creature. Calvin never turned completely against classical antiquity, pagan though it was, but continued to admire both Seneca and Plato. Seneca is favourably noticed in the *Institutes*, and it is tempting to see in the doctrine of predestination an adaptation to Christian use of the stoic idea of *fatum*. Plato also appears in the *Institutes*, and the quotations and references increase in successive editions, until by 1560 there are eighteen of them. Plato, says Calvin, is the only ancient philosopher to realize that 'le souverain bien de l'homme est d'estre conioinct à Dieu'. Some themes which are important for Plato are echoed by Calvin. There is the theme of the prison of the body—'qu'est-ce aultre chose de ce corps qu'une prison?' There is the theme of the two worlds, the *transitoire* and the *céleste*, and the doctrine that the world of ideas is more real than the world of experience. Calvin believes in the Idea of the Church, which 'peut consister sans apparence visible'.

If, as is often said, medieval thought means Aristotle and Renaissance thought means Plato, it is possible to make something of a Renaissance figure out of Calvin. He does have something important in common with his contemporary Dorat, the tutor of the Pléiade. Of course, Calvin cannot help admiring Plato because he admires Augustine, and Augustine is a kind of Platonist; if there are eighteen references to Plato in the *Institutes*, there are 204 to Augustine. But from Petrarch's time on, there has been nothing 'anti-Renaissance' about admiring Augustine. It is true that Calvin's Plato is above all the late Plato of the *Phaedo*, while the Pléiade's Plato was rather the Plato of the *Symposium*—but these works do share important common themes.

It is tempting to see Calvin as the philosopher-king of Geneva, and even his opposition to poetry as Platonic. Like Plato and Augustine, he feared literature because he was aware of its power and, again like them, he took pains to write well himself—both in Latin and in French. Even Bossuet had to admit that Calvin deserved the credit for having 'aussi bien écrit qu'homme de son siècle'. A voluminous writer (his collected works fill fifty-nine volumes), Calvin was careful to revise what he wrote. He produced five Latin versions of the

Institutes, and four French ones. Some of these revisions were due to developments in his ideas; predestination, for example, is stressed much more in the late Calvin. But some of these revisions were stylistic, and show his interest in the craft of writing. He abandoned his treatise *Des Scandales* for a time because, he wrote, 'le style ne coulait pas de source'. In French he wrote an extremely personal prose, concise—by sixteenth-century standards—clear, plain, colloquial, forceful, enlivened by irony. He recognized that his spare style was a personal characteristic: 'Peut-estre ma brieveté est-elle parfois une concision excessive... mais je suis mon naturel.' At the same time, characteristically, Calvin thought that even in this respect he was doing God's will: 'La langue est créée de Dieu pour exprimer la cogitation... pourtant, c'est pervertir l'ordre de Dieu... de circuir par embages à l'entour du pot.'[1] He used a colloquial style in his French works because he was writing for an unlearned audience; the learned could always read him in Latin. What he thought his vernacular public wanted can be seen clearly from the alterations he made to the *Institutes* when turning them into French. Greek words and references to Aristotle disappeared, explanations, proverbs, and colloquial phrases were added. In doing this, Calvin made an important contribution to the *illustration* of the French tongue, to the development of the vernacular as an instrument for argument. This contribution was all the more important because Calvin—like Montaigne soon afterwards—seems to have written as he spoke, *picardismes* included. In his pamphlet against the Nicodemites, he echoes them mockingly before undertaking to refute them: 'Maintenant il m'est avis que je les oy; qu'on ne nous parle plus de Calvin; c'est un homme trop inhumain.'

When he wanted to exploit it, Calvin possessed a formidable satiric vein. He compared the Nicodemites to 'cureurs de retrets': 'Car comme un maistre Fifi, apres avoir longtemps exercé le mestier de remuer l'ordure, ne sent plus la mauvaise odeur, parce qu'il est devenu tout punetz, et se moque de ceux qui bouchent leur nez; pareillement ceux-cy, s'éstans par accoutumance endurcis à demeurer en leur ordure, pensent estre entre des roses.' His *Traité des reliques*

---

[1] *pourtant*, as often in sixteenth-century French, means 'therefore'. *embages* (from Latin *ambages*) means 'digression'.

(1543) pokes more traditional fun by suggesting that 'tout y est si brouillé et confus, qu'on ne sauroit adorer les os d'un martyr qu'on ne soit en danger d'adorer les os de quelque Brigand ou Larron, ou bien d'un asne, ou d'un chien, ou d'un cheval'. This satirical writing is of literary importance. In France in the early sixteenth century there were two satiric traditions. One was Latin and international: Erasmus's *Praise of Folly* is an important example of the genre. The second tradition was that of popular vernacular satire, and this was much more crude, as a reading of *Theologastres* (above, p. 43) shows. In mid-century come the first attempts to bridge this gap, to extend the satiric dimensions of the vernacular. There are the epistles of Marot ('du coq à l'âne'), the dialogues of Des Périers, and the pamphlets of Calvin. Calvin lacks the light touch of the other two; his humour, compared with that of Des Périers, is as heavy as that of Karl Marx compared with Kierkegaard. On the other hand, he was probably the most widely read of the three. His satire was continued by two of his disciples, Théodore de Bèze and Pierre Viret. Bèze's most famous satire is the *Épître de Benoît Passavant* (1553), written in Latin but in macaronic or joke-Latin full of vernacularisms. It concerns the adventures of a servant of Calvin's adversary Lizet, who is sent in disguise to Geneva, and is full of what a modern reader is likely to think of as schoolboy jokes about Lizet's red nose—but this is the sort of thing which sixteenth-century adults found amusing, even educated ones, just as they found midgets amusing.

Viret's satires are written in French. They are not pure entertainment; like Calvin, Viret thought that 'profane' (secular) literature should serve sacred. However, he recognized the problem of the literature of his day; there were pious books and there were amusing books, but the pious books were not amusing, and the amusing books were not pious. He set out to remedy this situation by writing satiric dialogues, as if to beat Des Périers with his own weapons. He consciously wrote for the uneducated, and often slipped into his native Vaudois. His level of humour—again, it may seem schoolboy humour to the modern reader—is to call Purgatory *Purge-bourse* or *Pagatoire*, and in his *Physique Papale* to prolong the life of a medical metaphor for the whole length of a dialogue; priests are 'médecins et apothecaires des âmes', their drugs are masses, relics, holy water, and so on, and their methods are as unscrupulous as those of worldly doctors.

An obvious way to appeal to the uneducated was to write plays. Calvin himself did not approve of plays, even religious ones; *jouer* was for him a pejorative term. In 1546 a troupe of actors came to Geneva and asked permission to play the *Acts of the Apostles*. Calvin was consulted and made his disapproval clear, although he did not actually forbid the performance. Similarly, the Calvinist synod held at Nîmes in 1572 denounced all plays, even Biblical ones, arguing that the Bible 'ne nous a pas été donnée pour nous servir de passe-temps'.

Not all Calvinists agreed with such sweeping condemnations. One of those who did not was Bèze, whose *Abraham sacrifiant* (1550)[1] is the first surviving original tragedy in French. Bèze, like Calvin, had had a humanist education, and like a good humanist he went to a classical source. To dramatize the story of Abraham and Isaac he borrowed from Euripides, from *Iphigenia at Aulis*, the play in which King Agamemnon sacrifices his daughter. Biblical and classical elements are skilfully blended; the *angelus ex machina* is extremely effective. Anti-catholic propaganda provides the light relief—Satan 'en habit de moine', for example. Bèze began a Calvinist tradition of Biblical drama, which soon came to include a cycle of three plays about David by Louis Des Masures, and Jean de la Taille's *Saül le furieux* (1572),[2] another blend of Biblical and classical elements—which come this time from the *Hercules Furens* of Seneca.

More remarkable still, the printer Conrad Badius wrote a comedy which he managed to stage in Geneva in Calvin's own lifetime. This was the *Comédie du pape malade* (1561). At the première, Conrad played the Pope himself. The play is much like a stage version of one of Viret's dialogues (in fact the two men often collaborated), except for the allegorical characters like *Église* or *Vérité*, who recall miracle-plays or *Theologastres*. Again we see the medical metaphor and the schoolboy humour; the Pope vomits on stage, and out come errors, cardinals, bulls, and nuns. The prologue makes the point that to be

[1] See further below, chapter 9, pp. 136-7.
[2] The trilogy of Des Masures and *Saül le furieux* are also discussed in chapter 9, pp. 137-8 and 142-3.

a Calvinist it is not necessary to have a 'maigre et triste face'; it is interesting to speculate whether the myth of the inhuman Calvin who never laughed was bad for conversions, and whether such a consideration led to the relaxing of Calvinist opposition to the drama, at least on this occasion. It is a pity that English puritans did not take the lesson of the *Comédie* to heart, and write their own comedies instead of attacking Shakespeare's.

Calvinists were suspicious of poetry as of drama. Secular poetry was, for Calvin, a vain and frivolous pastime. He felt its attraction all the same and confessed that by nature he was very much inclined to poetry. One may take leave to doubt the 'very much', but it is significant that the inclination existed. He channelled it into Biblical poetry—into the Psalms. He translated some of them himself into French verse, he wrote a preface for Marot's versions, and he encouraged those of Bèze. In the early sixteenth century the Psalms had been the special love of Lefèvre, of Marguerite, and of their circle, perhaps because these poems are easily compatible with a mystical, neoplatonic Christianity. It was probably at Marguerite's suggestion that Marot made his versions. In the course of the century, they became associated with the Calvinists. Huguenot composers such as Louis Bourgeois and Claude Goudimel set them to music. Huguenot martyrs sang them as they died, and Huguenot soldiers sang them going into battle, especially Psalm 68, the Psalm of Battles (later called the 'Huguenot Marseillaise'). Bèze's version of Psalm 68 begins like this:

Que Dieu se monstre seulement
Et on verra soudainement
Abandonner la place
Le camp des ennemis épars
Et ses haineux de toutes parts
Fuir devant sa face.

Dieu les fera tous s'enfuir,
Ainsi qu'on voit s'évanouir
Un amas de fumée.
Comme la cire auprès du feu,
Ainsi des méchants devant Dieu
La force est consummée.

In Bèze's case, even more than in Calvin's, it is clear that he was not so much against poetry as cross-pressured about it. He admitted this himself: 'Je confesse que de mon naturel j'ai toujours pris plaisir à la poésie, et ne m'en puis encore repentir: mais bien ai-je regret d'avoir employé ce peu de grace que Dieu m'a donné en cet endroit, en choses desquelles la seule souvenance me fait maintenant rougir.' Appropriately enough, the word *grace* can be taken in two senses in this passage. Before his conversion Bèze had written Latin poems imitating Catullus, Ovid, and Virgil. Afterwards, he turned to the Psalms, and also published a book of emblems with verses below. One of these emblems is an anti-poetic one; Bèze contrasts the Lamb of God with the Golden Fleece, about which 'maint poète discourt de sa bouche menteuse'. Yet the implication of the whole collection of verses is that a man can be a good poet and a good Calvinist at the same time, provided that he writes the right kind of poetry, that is, religious poetry. This is what the Calvinist lady Georgette de Montenay did in her *Emblèmes Chrétiens*. It is also the solution adopted by poets greater than she or Bèze, poets such as d'Aubigné and Sponde.

Jean de Sponde (1557–95) was nearly fifty years younger than Calvin, and forty years younger than Bèze, which whom he was acquainted. The desire to write poetry came upon him suddenly. Significantly, for a man of Calvinist background, it happened while he was reading the Psalms. Later he wrote prose meditations on the Psalms, as did his fellow Huguenots Duplessis-Mornay and d'Aubigné (who died with Psalm 118, in Marot's version, on his lips —*La voici l'heureuse journée*).

The examples of Sponde and d'Aubigné[1] prompt one to ask whether they wrote a particular kind of poetry because they were Calvinists, whether one can say anything in general about the effect of Calvinism upon literature. It is unlikely that anything very precise or anything very certain can be said; it is possible to learn this much from the example of those sociologists and historians who have undertaken to discuss the effect of Calvinism upon the rise of capitalism and upon the scientific revolution. But in this case, as

[1] The poetry of Sponde is discussed at length in chapter 6 below, and that of d'Aubigné in chapter 10.

in those others, it may be possible to say something uncertain and imprecise, but helpful all the same.

There are many ways in which Calvinism touched literature. It encouraged certain genres, like satire, and discouraged others, like plays and poems, though it can be seen that this discouragement was not entirely successful. It encouraged the choice of religious subjects in all genres, and inhibited the choice of secular ones. However, two possible connections stand out. First, the contribution of Calvinism to the general rise of vernacular literature. Second, its contribution to the rise of classicism in particular.

Calvinism, like other forms of Protestantism, laid great emphasis on popular education. The people must read the Word of God: so translations of the Bible must be made accessible. The people must understand the Word of God: so there must be commentaries too, and Calvinists must consciously write for the people. Unlike Erasmus, but like Luther, Calvin, a scholar with a good command of Latin, wrote many of his works in French so as to be understood by ordinary people. Bèze, in his *Abraham*, did his best to avoid words which might 'épouvanter les simples gens'. Conrad Badius turned from publishing Latin books in Paris to publishing French ones in Geneva with the comment: 'Si je ne puis plaire aux savants, il me suffit de profiter aux ignorants.' Calvinism is not the only force behind the rise of the French vernacular in the sixteenth century, but it is likely to have added something to that rise all the same. From a social point of view, both Calvinism and the rise of the vernacular look like responses to the widening of the literate class.

More interesting still is the possibility that Calvin contributed something to classicism as well as to capitalism and science; that (as M. Wencelius puts it) '... il y a quelque chose de calvinien dans l'idéal des lettres du siècle de Louis XIV'. In the sixteenth century a concise, plain style was relatively rare; in the seventeenth century it was much more common, and in the eighteenth century more common still. Calvin's style was the style of the future. Like Pascal, he believed that 'la vraie éloquence se moque de l'éloquence'. He disliked the allegorical interpretation of the Bible, which he thought of as 'playing' with the simplicity of the text; and such interpretations were gradually to decline.

Calvin's love of method was also to be taken up by posterity. The later editions of the *Institutes* are divided into books, the books into chapters, and the chapters into sections, so that each argument has its place, like a stone in some vast building. Calvin loved this: 'Que nous sachions réduire les choses en leur ordre et qu'il n'y ait nulle confusion.' The great methodizer of the sixteenth century was also a Frenchman, Pierre de la Ramée or Ramus (1515–72), and he was in fact a Calvinist. His books on logic and rhetoric had a wide circulation. His preoccupation with method makes him a link between Calvin and Descartes, and so between Calvin and the *Grand Siècle*.

It is easy to slip into arguing that Calvin himself was a classicist, that his love of simplicity and order, white walls, and unaccompanied singing was a conscious aesthetic attitude. Perhaps it was, perhaps Calvin was a conscious member of the anti-Ciceronian movement of the sixteenth century, the international movement for simple or 'Attic' prose. But it is necessary to add that Calvin did not see the point of literature which was not didactic, that he believed that the pleasure given by literature and music was a temptation of the devil, and that style could not be important because God's own style, in the Bible, was not always very elegant. Thus Renaissance humanists stressed aesthetic values but did not stress simplicity; Calvin stressed simplicity, but did not stress aesthetic values. Classicism, in which simplicity itself became an aesthetic value, should be seen as a synthesis of the two.

NOTE

Basic texts

There are several modern editions of Calvin's *Institution de la religion chrétienne* (referred to in English as his *Institutes*). The 1541 text was re-edited by A. Lefranc and others in 1911 and there is a recent five-volume edition (1957–63) by J. D. Benoît. Among Calvin's more accessible shorter works are the *Avertissement contre l'astrologie* and the *Traité des reliques* published together, with Théodore de Bèze's 'Discours sur la vie et la mort de Maître Jean Calvin', in 1962. Other texts relevant to this chapter include: Bonaventure Des Périers, *Cymbalum Mundi*, edited by P. H. Nurse (1958); Clément Marot, *Œuvres satiriques*, edited by C. A. Mayer (1962); Ramus (Pierre de la Ramée), *Dialectique*, edited by M. Dassonville (1964).

Secondary works

J. Boisset, *Sagesse et sainteté dans la pensée de Jean Calvin* (1959). Important on Calvin's humanism.

L. Febvre, *Le Problème de l'incroyance au XVIe siècle: la religion de Rabelais* (1942; reprint 1962).

L. Febvre, *Origène et Des Périers* (1942).

L. Febvre, 'Dolet propagateur de l'Évangile' and 'Crayon de Jean Calvin' in his *Au Cœur religieux du XVIe siècle* (1957).

P. F. Geisendorf, *Théodore de Bèze* (1949).

F. M. Higman, *The Style of John Calvin in his French Polemical Treatises* (1967).

A. Lefranc, *Calvin et l'éloquence française* (1934).

W. J. Ong, *Ramus* (1958).

A. M. Schmidt, *Jean Calvin et la tradition calvinienne* (1957.)

F. Wendel, *Calvin* (1950. English translation, 1963).

L. Wencelius, *L'Esthétique de Calvin* (1937).

5. The French Court and its Poetry

'MAROT était un poète et un poète de cour, ce caractère est à peu près incompatible avec le grand mérite.' This terse condemnation by a late seventeenth-century critic (Jurieu), and at a time when Marot was held in great esteem by writers such as La Fontaine and La Bruyère, prompts several questions. It does so all the more since the majority of works of literature and art in the sixteenth century were created in response to the specific demands of rich patrons, or in the hope of attracting the attention of such patrons. In a sense, then, most literary creation at this time could be termed 'production de cour'. If this is so, and if Jurieu's criticism is fair, all sixteenth-century artists were born to work in conditions which could cramp their natural genius. This chapter is concerned to explore the nature of the limits imposed upon the artist's activity—in particular that of the poet—by patronage, and especially royal patronage. It also seeks to show how the demands of the Court, the sixteenth-century idea of kingship, and the personal taste of particular monarchs could both use and preserve traditional literary forms, and also encourage the exploration and invention of new forms of art.

Any study of the relationship which exists between artists and kings is complicated. Kings, through their conditioning, expect flattery. Gifted artists have ideas of themselves which stretch out beyond any normal assessment of the individual's achievements and, correspondingly, they have strange expectations and make great demands—those of Benvenuto Cellini or Ronsard, for example. The artist's view of the Court is most often clouded by the popularity he enjoys, the recompense he expects or has already received.

So, Ronsard can praise the courts of Henri II and Charles IX, but describe that of Henri III as

> ... cette Cour fastueuse, odieuse et remplie
> D'erreurs, d'opinions, de troubles et d'envie.

The financial and temperamental needs of the artist as well as those of his monarch must be taken into account.

Precisely how complex the relationship between poet and monarch can be will emerge from a discussion of Clément Marot's 'Au Roy, pour avoir esté desrobé', *Épître*, xxv (1531). Marot was in the personal employ of François Ier and by virtue of his poetic gifts enjoyed the title of 'valet de chambre du roi'. For this office he received a much coveted royal pension. In this *Épître* he requests the king's aid since some villain, having robbed him of his royal earnings, has left him cold, ill, destitute, and near starvation. His demands are made in a light, bantering tone which aims to please, and by giving pleasure he expects to be reimbursed of his loss. Such half-humorous, half-serious intention points to an easy-going understanding between monarch and poet and, furthermore, assumes certain rights on the part of the poet. Marot, however, ventures beyond these limits; imagining himself prosperous, with all the possessions prosperity brings, he creates place-names out of his own name, and claims moneys to pay for the building costs of the establishments he imagines he has had built there. With this joking reminder to a king who from his own experience with the royal palace at Fontainebleau would know all about the extortionate demands of builders and architects, Marot threatens to end his poem:

> Vous sçavez tout, il n'y fault plus rien mettre.

Then, as though he has suddenly realized that such rude and obvious expectancy is out of place, Marot adds a deliberately pointed and splendid song of praise in honour of François Ier:

> Rien mettre? Las! Certes, et si feray,
> Et ce faisant, mon stile j'enfleray,
> Disant: O Roy, amoureux des neufz Muses,
> Roy en qui sont leurs sciences infuses,
> Roy plus que Mars d'honneur environné,
> Roy le plus Roy qui fut oncq couronné,

> Dieu tout puissant te doint (pour t'estrener)
> Les quatre Coings du Monde gouverner,
> Tant pour le bien de la ronde Machine,
> Que pour autant que sur tous en es digne.

Thus he publicly acknowledges the duty of a poet to his king. The praise is, however, discriminating; it reminds the king what he owes to the Muses as well as congratulating him on his generosity towards them. We are made to understand that it is precisely such liberality which especially recommends the king as a worthy governor of the world. Never does Marot allow his monarch to forget that however dependent for their livelihood his artists might be upon his purse, he—the king—depends upon them for his reputation and immortality.

It was indeed part of the sixteenth-century conception of kingly greatness that each prince should employ a train of poets, painters, and musicians, charged to present to the world at large the most impressive and prestigious view of their master. They were the guardians of his reputation, the recorders of his personal achievements to which the whole country must pay homage. It naturally followed from such a conception that the reigning prince was always the greatest prince; inevitably, in view of this, there is a certain stamp of monotony on all the literature and art of this period. Monotony of intention and theme, however, does not of necessity bring about the kind of poetry Jurieu suggests in his criticism. Most themes in poetry are traditional, yet their expression can—and did— find infinite variety, particularly at a time when new ideas and new forms proliferated, resurrected from Ancient writers and resulting from literary experiments and technical discoveries.

From the beginning of the century François Ier and his Court had been the source of inspiration for scholars and artists, and throughout the century until the advent of Henri IV, the Court remained the main centre of artistic pursuits in France. (The same pattern was repeated throughout Europe.) It had not always been so, as the count in Baldassare Castiglione's *The Courtier* implies when he praises Frenchmen for their skill at arms and criticizes their ignorance in letters. Until the time of François Ier, the French Court had been a masculine, itinerant body, wandering from one hunting lodge to another, sometimes at war, rarely indulging in the leisure that learning and literature demand. Gradually many artistic, social, and political factors combined to stabilize the Court: the influence of François's learned sister Marguerite de Navarre, who did much to introduce platonic ideas on love and literature into France; the king's own artistic ambitions (there still exists a volume of light verse composed by him); his desires for personal aggrandizement, and his own experience of the splendour of the Italian and English courts; finally, the mounting clamour of scholars and artists who, convinced of the moral and political importance of their skills, saw their role as being no longer subservient to the whims and fancies of their patrons but as dominating political and artistic events.

In 1520 when François Ier met the equally ambitious Henry VIII at the Field of the Cloth of Gold, ostensibly to make an international show of peace, the French king was determined not to be outdone by his extravagant rival since wild stories of Henry's splendour had preceded the English king across the Channel. In the eyes of their contemporaries, abundance, riches, display regardless of expense were synonymous with power and glory; and to *appear* great was to *be* great. On this occasion, therefore, the French ensured that the world would remember their king's magnificence by printing several official accounts of the meeting, in French and in Latin.

Unparalleled magnificence continued to be characteristic of François Ier's Court, in spite of the financial exigencies of war. Moreover, the French king saw other ways of enhancing his glory. Encouraged by the scholarly Guillaume Budé, who was called by Erasmus 'le prodige de la France', he founded the Collège de France (1530), designed to foster the cause of learning, since not only did learning bring honour and glory to a man but it was necessary for all princes 'de savoir les bonnes lettres tant Grecques que Latines pour bien commander à leurs Royaumes'.

Apart from the splendour of international Court occasions such as the 1520 interview at the Field of the Cloth of Gold, there is no better way of making manifest to the world one's consciousness of the power one wields than by erecting architectural monuments. For the direction of the building operations at his royal palace of Fontainebleau, 'la plus belle maison de la Chrestienté' (Brantôme), which was to stand as witness both to the monarch's greatness and to artistic aspiration and achievement, François Ier retained a French master mason, Gilles le Breton. The decoration of the palace, however, as in many other palaces and castles built during François's reign (Blois and Chenonceaux, for example), was the work of Italians: Giovanni Battista Rosso and Francesco Primaticcio. And it is in the decoration of the gallery, now called the Galerie François Ier, that we can still see recorded the extravagant intentions of the artists and their king.

The gallery was intended to give a complete and honest record of François's main achievements. Its ceiling, almost obscured by countless designs of the Arms of France, was interspersed with representations of the Salamander—François's personal device— which immediately focuses attention on the king. Fourteen paintings, set around the walls, explore mythological subjects appropriate to the king. They narrate, as the seventeenth-century historian Pierre Dan tells us, 'toutes les principales actions de la vie du grand Roy François, telles qu'estoit son inclination aux Sciences et aux Arts, sa fierté, son courage, son adresse, ses amours, ses victoires'. The battle of Centaurs and Lapithae (picture no. 7) records the French victory at Cérizoles in 1543. Semele caught by the fires of Jupiter's love (no. 11) recalls the intensity of François's own amorous exploits. Since the artists aimed at completeness, even the king's military failures find a place on these walls, represented in a glorious shipwreck (no. 10).

For such feats of kingship François earned the title which has since been coupled with his name: 'grand restaurateur des lettres et des arts'. And yet, his main claim to such a title rests almost exclusively, as far as concrete achievement is concerned, on two facts: his encouragement of learning and his love of architecture. For in spite of his own poetic works, his amused toleration of the humorous compositions of Marot, and of the ingenious, flattering 'mignardises' of Mellin de Saint-Gelais, 'qui couraient de fois à autres par les mains des Courtisans et Dames de Cour' (Pasquier), poetry and music had hardly begun to expand their domains. Poets could not yet claim that they would make the king 'plus vivant que maison ny peinture' (Ronsard, *Odes*, III. i). Nevertheless, François's royal encouragement created an atmosphere, set the pattern for his successors, and laid the foundations for great advances in imaginative literature which would not be exhausted until well into the eighteenth century.

Contemporary romance literature, still clinging to its tradition, shows a rather different and idealized picture of life at Court. For example, the tremendously popular *Amadis de Gaule* (first published in French in 1540) still stresses the qualities of the noble warrior who by power of arms successfully defends moral and political right against barbarians, enchantresses, tyrants, and the like. Such a view contrasts considerably with the civilized, peace-loving, all knowledgeable courtier of Castiglione whose work, we like to imagine, conveyed the prevailing view of the sixteenth century. Not only do the terrors of the Wars of Religion remind us constantly of the contrary, we must also remember that for all his attachment to the arts, François Ier considered it an honour to be dubbed 'knight' by the 'chevalier sans peur et sans reproche, le gentil seigneur de Bayard'; that Ronsard, for all his gifts and claims for poetry, put the value of arms above that of letters; and that Montaigne, though he abhorred the excesses of the Civil Wars, praised unequivocally the qualities of the ardent warrior and, by contrast, showed up the barbarisms of the so-called civilized man of letters.

No one realized this dual aspiration towards skill at arms and letters more clearly than Catherine de Médicis (married in 1533 to the second son of François, later Henri II). From her early years in Florence she had been accustomed to lavish Court festivals, designed both to entertain and mirror political power and to occupy nobles often anxious for war. This early experience proved decisive as far as Catherine's attitude towards artists was concerned. She encouraged their grand view of their skills, gave them ample opportunities to explore and to increase their powers of expression, and encouraged them particularly to underline the moral and political implications of their works. These implications were no longer to be restricted to poems in praise of a king or a particular political event, such as Marot's poem on the French victory at Cérizoles in 1543, reworked and perfected by the arrogance of Ronsard with 'un art plus laborieux'. They were to be expanded, on a much more elaborate scale, using multiple forms.

In an attempt to reconcile the turbulent Protestant and Catholic factions at Court she organized the most elaboraté series of festivities at Fontainebleau in 1564: ballets, chivalric combats, a pastoral by Ronsard, a tragi-comedy, *Belle Genievre*, imitated from Ariosto with *intermèdes* by Ronsard; all sought to distract the powerful Guise and Coligny families from their warlike designs. Similarly at Bayonne, a year later, Baïf, Ronsard, Jodelle, and others strove, by their inventions, both to impress their Spanish visitors and to content the French nobles who were unhappy about the marriage of Philip II of Spain to Elizabeth, eldest daughter of Catherine and Henri II of France. The massacre of Saint Bartholomew (1572) was preceded by the splendid entry of Charles IX into Paris, organized by Dorat and Ronsard, and the sumptuous marriage ceremonies of Henri de Navarre and Marguerite de Valois. Some jaundiced contemporaries even maintained that the wedding festivities were deliberately engineered as a rehearsal for the massacre: 'Masques, bagues, ballets ne s'épargnent; purgatoire, enfer, representés en Bourbon [the 'salle de théâtre' of the Louvre] où sont envoyés les Huguenots après un combat de barrière, présage de leur malheur' (Gaspar de Saulx, sieur de Tavannes); hardly a wise precaution, one would have thought. In any event, it is clear that in Catherine's eyes political intentions could, and should, be closely bound up with the activities of her Court artists. Her sons Charles IX and Henri III inherited her attitude, though as we shall see their particular gifts orientated the literature of the Court in somewhat different directions. No expense was spared in the elaboration of these artistic and political designs, and although there were protests that the money could have been better employed, 'la reine disait qu'elle le faisait pour montrer à l'étranger que la France n'était pas si totalement ruinée et pauvre, à cause des guerres passées, comme il l'estimait', and she added that as a consequence of such festivities 'la France serait mieux estimée et redoutée' (Brantôme). Brantôme also insists on the civilizing effects of these Court activities. As a result of Catherine's influence, her Court had become 'un vrai paradis du monde, et école de toute honnêteté, de vertu, l'ornement de la France, ainsi que le savaient les étrangers quand ils y venaient'.

In addition, her presence at Court had done much to accelerate the spread of certain Italian influences on French literature and art. Poets admired and imitated the love poetry of Serafino, Bembo, and Trissino; they read avidly the works of Petrarch, borrowed from his many conceits, and copied his paradoxical themes. Saint-Gelais and Marot were well versed in the Italian manner—Saint-Gelais's picture of Woman, for example, was similarly idealized—but their compositions lacked the metaphysical dimension which neoplatonism had given the poetry of Maurice Scève. Neoplatonism encouraged and gave wide currency to the image of Love seen as a gateway to the Spiritual World, to the theory of Poetry as Divine Inspiration, and to the conviction that the poet was a prophet endowed with extraordinary powers. All these ideas served Catherine's later purpose, for the greater the power of expressivity allowed to poetry, the greater was its effectiveness as a political tool.

Her first royal entry into Lyons in 1548 gives some idea of the extent to which entertainments organized for Court occasions or specifically commissioned by the Court encouraged artists to explore the new realms opened up for them by earlier humanists, to create new forms of art which they thought were closely modelled on Greek and Roman forms, and which consequently and automatically would acquire an increased power of expressivity and persuasion. Maurice Scève was selected by the town councillors to be chief organizer of the whole series of festivities on this occasion. He followed the time-honoured pattern of having triumphal arches and *tableaux vivants* arranged along the royal route, and for these he composed learned Latin inscriptions, intended to explain the significance of each monument and spectacle. Once the public cavalcade had finished its journey, and once Henri II's warlike tendencies had been satisfied by a splendid 'naumachia' (or mock naval battle) on the Rhône, Catherine could enjoy a spectacle which left tradition far behind and introduced an entirely new dimension to the theatre in France. This was a representation of Bernardo Bibbiena's comedy *La Calandria* (imitated from Plautus's *Menaechmi*) and performed in Italian style, that is to say accompanied by a magnificent 'mise en scène' and with interludes concerning gods and goddesses, separating the acts of the play and specifically designed to praise Catherine and her king. Brantôme, who was present, comments that the spectators witnessed 'choses que l'on n'avait encore veu, et rare en France'. He was no doubt thinking of the elaborate stage settings, the cloud machines, the use of perspective (probably for the first time in France)—all technical advances made possible by Italian researches into the principles of architecture of the Ancients. Also, he probably had in mind the mingling of music and poetry together in the interludes. All these elements, still unknown to the French secular theatre, were soon to play an important role in a new orientation of interest in the theatre of the Ancients and in the invention of composite art forms.

A production like *La Calandria* inevitably and immediately served to intensify French activity in the same field. So far, interest in Latin and Greek theatre had hardly extended beyond the confines of the colleges, and scholarly editions and translations, but it was not long before Jodelle had produced his own version of the story of the Argonauts (composed for Henri II's enjoyment in 1558), and Saint-Gelais had composed *Sophonisbe* (Blois, 1559), said to have been better than Trissino's own version.

The coming of Charles IX to effective power in 1563 gave a further impetus to such experimentation, although it changed its direction. He was especially interested in the arts of poetry and music and, like François Ier, had poetic aspirations of his own. Often Ronsard was called upon to make delicate pronouncements on the quality of the king's compositions, and to receive the signal honour of having verses dedicated to him by His Majesty. Since the poet's power is thus acknowledged, it is not surprising that Ronsard frequently adopts such a lofty tone when addressing the king; statements such as 'Par mon noble travail ils sont devenus Dieux' are mainly a compliment to himself. Of Charles IX we are also told that 'bien souvent (il) passait une grande partie de la nuit à lire ou faire réciter ses vers'. For such nocturnal revels, apart from the inevitable Ronsard, Amadis Jamyn, Adrian le Roy, and Roland de Lassus were the king's favourite companions—the last two being famous throughout Europe for the quality of their song.

The blending together of poetry and music had long been one of the sixteenth-century artistic aims. Poets, and Ronsard first among them, thought that their work had diminished expressive power unless it was wrought in musical harmonies. 'La poésie, sans les instruments, ou sans la grace d'une seule, ou plusieurs voix, n'est nullement agréable', stated Ronsard most emphatically in his *Abrégé de l'Art poétique français* (1565). In fact, nearly all his early poems, for example the *Odes* and the first *Amours de Cassandre*, were composed to be set to music, and to be heard by scholars and courtiers alike. Now, with the active encouragement of Charles IX, artists could expand upon such theories. Baïf even went as far as to

> Réformer à la mode antique
> Les vers mesurés inventer.

It so happened that this practice of blending poetry and music together coincided with other more large-scale explorations. These were attempts to recapture old dramatic forms thought to have had a power to express and to persuade beyond any form the sixteenth century had yet discovered.

The imitation and translations of Latin and Greek plays, tried out by Saint-Gelais and others, showed admirable and enthusiastic devotion to scholarly Renaissance demands, but they had proved an inadequate and constraining means of expression for most poets. Artists felt that if they were really going to be able to rival the Golden Age of letters, as evidenced by the writings of the Ancients —and this aim constantly haunted their imaginations—then they must find a form of art capable of total expression. Their questionings led them towards the creation of composite art forms which not only mixed poetry and music, but introduced the art of dancing into a splendid décor, made possible by the developments of theatre technicians, painters, and sculptors.

Although all the major French poets of the century were involved in such experiments, Jean Antoine de Baïf, the fellow pupil of Ronsard at the Collège de Coqueret, is mainly responsible for the implementation of such ambitious schemes which anticipated the dreams of Wagner. With Antoine de Courville he founded the Académie de

Poésie et de Musique in 1571, and one of the first results of its work seems to have been the elaborate *Ballet des Polonais*, 'le plus beau ballet qui fut jamais fait au monde' (Brantôme), invented by Baïf in 1573 to entertain the Polish ambassadors who had come to Paris to offer their throne to Henri d'Anjou (later Henri III). Jean Dorat composed the Latin verses for the occasion which were sung in the French translations of Ronsard and Amadis Jamyn.

Such artistic attempts naturally posed problems for all involved— new problems which would inevitably arise from collaboration. Baïf, in a sonnet addressed to the musician Costeley and probably written in the early 1570s, is aware that such a problem exists, but he is too full of idealism to do anything other than assume that the problem of collaboration will solve itself, by virtue of the fact that the artist will be a total artist—poet, musician, sage, all rolled into one:

> Iadis Musiciens, et Poètes, et sages
> Furent mesmes auteurs: mais la suite des âges
> Par le temps qui tout change a séparé les trois.
> Puissions nous d'entreprise heureusement hardie,
> Du bon siecle amenant la coustume abolie,
> Joindre les trois en un sous la faveur des Rois.

The spectacles demanded by the Court, however, since they imposed necessary time limits on the artist's activity, remained works of collaboration. Usually the poet designed the general framework of the festivities, controlled and directed the activities of a multitude of painters, sculptors, musicians, and so on. This was the case for Charles IX's entry into Paris in 1571, organized by Ronsard and Dorat, who showed themselves good, even erudite humanists, by using the newly translated *Dionysiaques* of Nonnus (published in Antwerp in 1569) for the main themes of the entry, and who then dictated ideas and themes to painters of the calibre of Niccolò Dell'Abbate.

This was also the pattern in the festivities arranged at Fontaine-bleau in 1564 and for which Ronsard composed one of his most extended works (1,100 lines), *Bergerie dédiée à la Majesté de la Royne d'Ecosse*; a work which offered guide lines to the musician and choreographer, and which through its theme dictated the setting for its performance. It is a strange work in many ways, embroidering upon the traditions of the eclogue as handled by Marot, borrowing almost literally from Virgil, Sannazar, and Propertius, and from the *Amadis de Gaule*, to produce a composite art form which mingled poetry and music and dancing against the beautiful, natural décor of the royal gardens and forest of Fontainebleau.

As Charles and his vast suite of courtiers wandered around the gardens, sirens from the many fountains and canals accompanied their steps with songs praising the king's person and encouraging his political enterprises. Suddenly the progress of the company was arrested by the appearance of two strange caverns which skilful artists had secretly built to blend into the natural scenery of the place. From these caverns were to emerge, dancing and singing, bands of nymphs and shepherds, royal actors, players of lutes and lyres—all performers in Ronsard's *Bergerie* which was to keep the Court amused, flattered, and thoughtful, for an hour or more.

The work has clearly defined political intentions, as can be seen both from Ronsard's remarks in his preface, where he says that it was specifically composed 'par le commandement de sa Majesté [Catherine] pour joindre et unir davantage, par tel artifice de plaisir, noz Princes de France qui étaient aucunement en discord', and from the names of the characters of the Pastoral: royal actors, Orléantin (duc d'Orléans, later duc d'Anjou, and then Henri III), Angelot (François, duc d'Anjou), Navarrin (Henri de Navarre, later Henri IV), Guisin (Henri, duc de Guise—assassinated in 1588). The work not only seeks to reconcile the interests of these warring nobles by making them play out their quarrels before the Court, it tries to present the pleasures of peace (only recently achieved—the first Wars of Religion having ended in March 1563), and, in particular, to praise the successful political manœuvres of Catherine de Médicis:

> Si nous voyons le Siècle d'or refait,
> C'est du bienfait
> De la bergere Catherine...

It is the calm, prosperous atmosphere of the Golden Age which Ronsard tries to recreate in this lengthy work, more remarkable for its lyrical than its dramatic power, although it is not without structural merit. Propaganda for the French Court, praise for its virtues and its victories, even detailed comment on contemporary political events do not seem in any way to restrict Ronsard's imagination. On the contrary, they seem to encourage him, allowing his imagination to describe an ideal state of things, an Arcadia rendered more beautiful by the memory of the horrors of war. The more delightful, the more convincing Ronsard can make his picture of Nature, simple and uncoloured by artifice, the more persuasive a political tool his work will prove.

The context of the Festivities is already made attractive enough by Ronsard's ability to evoke particular natural pleasures and give them life and movement:

> Icy diversement s'emaille la prairie,
> Icy la tendre vigne aux ormeaux se marie,
> Icy l'ombrage frais va ses fueilles mouvant,
> Errantes, çà et là sous l'haleine du vent...

Against this background the royal characters—Orléantin, Angelot, Navarrin, and Guisin—sing of the delights of the country, their minds, divested of the pomp and ceremony of Court life, escaping into the simple world of shepherds where thoughts of love, of friendship, of the beauties of nature dominate. Yet, very soon, the poet reminds them that they are playing; that they are indeed in Arcadia, in an ideal world, an unreal world which only exists through the magical power of the poet's art. The real world lies barren and neglected, destroyed by the ravages of war for which they are, in part, responsible. Gradually, they are made to realize that there does exist a means of attaining that state of life which their imagination now enjoys: their young king Charles IX and his virtuous mother (Catherine de Médicis) can and will, through their efforts, bring about a new era of peace and prosperity when once again

> Les vignes n'auront peur de sentir les faucilles,
> De leur gré les sommetz des arbres bien fertilles
> Noirciront de raisins...
> Bref tout sera changé et le monde, difforme
> Des vices du jourd'huy, prendra nouvelle forme...

This detailed example (of only one of the entertainments organized by Catherine at Fontainebleau in 1564) suggests that if the poet is given control of such an enterprise, the demands of the Court, far from hampering or limiting his art, actually encourage him to experiment with old forms (the political intentions here necessitating a transformation of the eclogue), and allow him to develop the work along lines particularly suited to his genius.

It would also be possible to argue that this particular example gives only one view, and that the poet was often not given such scope and powers of organization. There are many forms of poetry written for particular Court entertainments which underwent virtually no change throughout the sixteenth century: these are the dialogues and 'chansons' (often in sonnet form) of the mascarades, the 'cartels' or letters offered by knights at the beginning of tournaments. (Perhaps it was specifically to this kind of writing that Jurieu referred when criticizing Marot's poems.) Not only was their form tightly controlled by convention; their content was also limited by their context. For the most part they are love poems, designed either to sing the bearer's qualities or to describe the happy or disappointed nature of his love. The poet's task was often a subordinate one, dictated by the theme of combat in the case of tournaments, where skill at arms and splendour in dress outweighed all else in importance; or controlled by the subject of the mascarade—a light dramatic indoor entertainment which laid special stress on music, ability to dance well, and above all on a magnificent display in costume. The work of the embroiderers, jewellers, musicians, and choreographers was often thought more able to capture the attention of Court ladies than were the harmonies of the poet. His role was not to attempt to explore feeling, but merely to state it in the cleverest manner possible. Ingenuity and variety, the twin gods of such compositions, are so frequently met with that they each acquire an air of monotony. There is no very great distance, for example, from the playful poem of Marot on 'la chienne de la Royne Elienor' to Saint-Gelais's use of the ephemeral nature of 'arcs de triomphe' to describe the promises of the Emperor Charles V:

> Si chose faible a eu peu de durée:
> L'Estoffe fut à la foi mesurée;

no great distance either to the precious compliments of Philippe Desportes at the end of the century. All these poets depend for the power of their effect upon a wit which does not disturb, but simply amuses.

The demands of the social environment in which they worked is no doubt partially responsible for the kind of poetry they write; but it must also be remembered that well-established traditions and forms are not easy to break away from, and that not every poet had the versatility and prolific gifts of Ronsard. And yet the same environment is also responsible for remarkable innovations in form.

Le Ballet comique de la Reine (1581), a product of this same environment, is the spectacular culminating point of all earlier endeavours to create a composite form of art, and an effective political tool. It was composed by Balthasar Beaujoyeulx as Queen Catherine's contribution to the series of entertainments organized at Court to celebrate the marriage of Henri III's favourite the Duc de Joyeuse. In his preface Beaujoyeulx explains that this new protean form can not only carry moral, political, and philosophical lessons (which are expounded at length in the printed programme of this entertainment); it can even, he claims to the king, 'servir de vraie et infallible marque de bon et solide établissement de votre Royaume'; in other words, bring about political stability. This was a vain hope, but apparently a serious one, for all those who contributed. The story of Circe's magical transformation of Ulysses and his companions into beasts gives a theme and structure to the work. Gods and goddesses walk, ride, and fly about the stage in a concerted effort to give back to man (as represented by Ulysses) his reason. Huge consorts of musical instruments and choirs, complicated geometrical ballets intended to imitate the movements of the heavenly spheres, sung dialogues, long and complaining speeches, with mobile stage machines, were all dexterously controlled, so Beaujoyeulx claims, in a performance which kept the entire Court awake and alert for five hours, and cost hundreds of thousands of *écus*. No artistic undertaking as ambitious or as costly was ever again attempted in the sixteenth century.

However sceptically we might view Beaujoyeulx's intentions and claims, his *Ballet comique* not only sums up many of the political and artistic aspirations of the century; it also anticipates the splendours of Louis XIV's Court at Versailles, pointing the way to the development of ballet and opera. Finally, it offers a splendid illustration of the extent to which the demands of the Court could stimulate artists, perhaps not always to produce great works of literature, but at least to have a new conception of the possibilities of art and to prepare the ground for a future generation.

NOTE

The subject-matter of this chapter was largely provided by sixteenth-century *Mémoires* (e.g. Brantôme, Castelnau, Marguerite de Valois, Tavannes, etc.). These are published in the *Société de l'histoire de France* series. H. Chamard, *Histoire de la Pléiade* (1939–40: 4 vols.) was one of the first to explore the approach to sixteenth-century French poetry which is adopted here. More recent attempts to see art forms operating in their historical and social context are:

J. Jacquot (ed.), *Les Fêtes de la Renaissance* (1955 and 1960:2 vols.).

J. Jacquot (ed.), *Le Lieu théâtral à la Renaissance* (1964).

G. Kernodle, *From Art to Theatre: Form and Convention in the Renaissance* (1944).

M. M. McGowan, *L'Art de ballet de cour en France* (1963).

J. Rousset, *La Littérature de l'âge baroque en France* (1954).

Various, *Musique et poésie au XVIe siècle* (Colloques internationaux du C.N.R.S., Paris, 1953).

F. A. Yates, *The Valois Tapestries* (1959).

6. The Poetry of Scève and Sponde

CERTAIN expectations and values dictate our response to the poetry of any generation; we expect to be interested and intrigued, to be moved and delighted; we value the articulation of emotions we know but cannot ourselves express; we admire speed of impact and economy of expression; we demand a sense of authenticity and we desire to be convinced. At moments in literary history particular factors intervene to direct this general response to poetry towards admiration for one kind of poetry rather than another, for one period of literature rather than another.

French sixteenth-century poetry has always been considered to be one of the high points of literary creation in France. Until some few years ago, however, critics (with scarcely an exception) extolled the poetry of Ronsard and the Pléiade to the exclusion of everything else. The names of Maurice Scève and Jean de Sponde had hardly been heard of. A particular view of poetry, and a response to new ways of writing it, were needed to open our eyes to the nature and quality of these poets' achievement. T. S. Eliot, through his own poetic practice and his critical discovery of the English metaphysical poets, constitutes perhaps the greatest single force in drawing other critics' attention to the work of Scève and Sponde. These critics were deliberately looking for French poets who displayed the same qualities which characterize the difficult poetry of Eliot and the Metaphysicals; poetry which appealed primarily to the intellect of readers; a poetry of strange syntax, a complex intermingling of abstractions and colloquialisms; a poetry which concentrated thought and emotion into tiny frameworks calling forth considerable interpretative and analytical powers from the reader; and above all, a poetry which brought together great passion and deep thought, and from this fusion could produce the most piercing expression and exploration of human emotions and predicaments. The *Délie* of Maurice Scève, together with the two sonnet series of Sponde (rediscovered by Professor Boase in 1930), fulfilled all these complex anticipations of the critics.

Scève's *Délie* is the first of the many cycles of love poems which were written in French in the sixteenth century, on the model of Petrarch and his Italian imitators such as Serafino. Published in Lyons, that most Italianate of towns, in 1544, the cycle is made up of 449 *dixains*. These are separated off into groups of ten, each group ornamented by a picture—there are fifty in all—which provides the main theme of the poems in that section and often furnishes the final image of the first poem of the section. Superficially, the poems of the *Délie* tell the history of Scève's love, describing its birth, its joy, and its tears; its progress towards death and spiritual immortality. And yet this is not any normal love story, although a real love for the gifted poetess Pernette du Guillet inspired these poems. Almost immediately Délie becomes an ideal, a model, an object of meditation, a focal point for self-exploration, for inner debate and analysis, and finally for self-revelation.

Nearly half a century later Sponde composed his two cycles of sonnets: the first, variations on the theme of love; the second, twelve sonnets written around the theme of death. The twenty-six sonnets on love explore the nature of the poet's affection for an unknown woman. They also analyse the roles of reason and emotion and strive especially to maintain the strength of the bonds which link his life to that of another. He fears most of all to lose his love, realizing the dangers which beset even faithful lovers, dangers which come from absence, from great sensitivity to beauty, from false thoughts, suspicions, or apprehensions. Nature, history, cosmology, and science all provide material on which the poet can exercise his thoughts, examine his fears, and give full scope to the intensity and extent of his feelings. Meditation upon human love not only involves Sponde in an examination of his own inner feelings and physical reactions; it leads him to considerations upon the fate of man generally. There is therefore a natural progression from thoughts on love, on the attraction of the world, to ponderings upon the inevitability of death, and the attractions of life after death. The twelve sonnets written on this theme are twelve distinct variations, seeming almost designed to exhaust the possible ways of presenting such a theme.

It may seem strange to link together in one discussion two poets so separated in time, yet this is no haphazard or arbitrary coupling. Their preoccupations and their manner of exploring them are astonishingly similar. In their love poems, both Scève and Sponde explore the antithetical themes of absence and presence, constancy and inconstancy, confidence and insecurity, themes certainly common enough to all debtors of Petrarch but used by Scève and Sponde to state the complex nature of their predicament, to tell of complicated depths of feeling. Antithesis allows these poets to set side by side ambiguities of thought, to give an unresolved tenseness to what they express, and this naturally heightens the emotional power of the poetry. Their expression always goes beyond the mere juxtaposition of witty antitheses, so often found in early Pléiade poets and in the work of Philippe Desportes (1546–1606). Even when at a first reading one might be inclined to dismiss as an artful pun Sponde's lines:

> ... qu'un superbe dessein
> Fondé dessus le vent, il faut en fin qu'il fonde
> (*Sonnets d'Amour*, xv)

closer inspection reveals that the poet is making an ironical point. He directs our thoughts straight at the city of Carthage and its fate, contrasts this image with the lasting, burning nature of his own love, and thus gives these lines a dimension of irony; in this way it is through the play on words that the true tone of the poem is discovered, together with a hint at the depth of the poet's feeling. A similar intensity is achieved in Scève's line:

> [Espoir] Est Calamyte a mes calamitez

which ends *dixain* 190. Scève has used the two meanings of the word 'Calamyte'—a magnet and a calamity—to sum up in the most concentrated way possible the magnetic pull of hope at moments of deepest despair.

Power of concentrating thought and feeling, fusing the two together, also distinguishes these two poets from other sixteenth-century poets. Ronsard and his fellow poets handle emotion as though it were at some distance from them, providing them, as any other theme might do, with a means of expressing at some length their view of beauty in the world, whereas for Scève and Sponde, what they feel is all they want to express, and the intensity of their feeling makes its sharpest impact through a language which demands full participation from the reader. We are made to ponder long on their concise statements and involve ourselves in them, whereas the poets of the Pléiade seek our admiration and often remain at a remote distance from us.

Most often this concentrative power is expressed through images which linger in the memory long after the other lines of the poem are forgotten; the final image of *dixain* 148, for example:

> Mon An se frise en son Avril superbe

which sums up a prolonged antithesis between Scève's cold winter of age and impotence and Délie's splendid spring with all its power of beauty and renewal. The stark juxtaposition of abstract and concrete terms reveals, with the greatest possible economy, both the despair of the poet acknowledging his decrepitude, and his sense of joy at the renewed vigour he gains from intellectual contact with Délie. Sponde sums up his own torn feelings in the metaphor:

> Je suis cet Actéon de ses chiens deschiré
> (*Sonnets d'Amour*, v)

which he places at the climax of his poem—the moment of revelation. It had been preceded by perplexed wonderings, by emotions so strange, so difficult to define, and so powerful that the sensations of dying and breathing are indistinguishable:

> ... je ne sçay que je suis,
> Si j'empire du tout ou bien si je respire.

The simplicity of these remarks helps to underline the physical content of the image when it comes. To produce the same kind of effect, in the opening lines of the sonnet, Sponde had used his

favourite disrupting technique—that of disturbing the normal syntactical order of the phrase, of piling up the parenthesis, deliberately
giving his poem an unexpected rhythm:

> Je meurs, et les soucis qui sortent du martyre
> Que me donne l'absence, et les jours et les nuicts,
> Font tant, qu'à tous momens...

Such halting phrases, parentheses, often giving the impression of
the poet feeling his way through an emotion or a thought, are part of
a larger technique which Sponde and Scève share—a technique
which has often led critics to describe their poetry as 'rough'. It is
true that one rarely finds a long, flowing musical phrase in their
work (though both poets can produce a sustained lyrical line—
Sponde's 'Stances de la Mort', for example, or *dixains* 6 and 7 of
Scève). Music, in fact, is the last word which comes to mind when
one tries to describe the impact their verse makes on the ear; Scève's

> Ma face, angoisse a quiconques la voit
> (*dixain* 45)

is designed to arrest our attention immediately. It places the words
in order of importance, regardless of normal syntax, regardless of
rhythm even—or rather, knowing the reader's expectations, Scève
turns them inside out in order to strike with the maximum force.

A superabundance of argumentative words 'Mais', 'pour', 'car',
'Doncques' (*dixain* 3), 'Mais', 'tant que', 'toutefois', 'lorsque', 'car'
(*dixain* 10), 'Que', 'que', 'car', 'pour affin que', 'pour' (*dixain* 13),
pin down our minds, and never allow poet or reader to relax. Unremittingly, they draw our attention to a structure which seems
awkward, but the apparent clumsiness is a measure of the tentative,
exploratory nature of the poet's investigations. They are signs of an
attitude of mind, determined to examine and argue out feeling,
thereby increasing its intensity, and revealing its paradoxes and its
complexities. Music and lyricism seem to need exuberant confidence,
a certain basic unconcern, lacking in the temperament of both Scève
and Sponde. Both write their love poems from a position of conscious weakness, with a knowledge of the ultimate unattainability
of their desires. Nevertheless, behind all their emotional insecurity

lies a very real sense of the stability of their moral and spiritual worlds. This allows Scève to move naturally from inner debate to Platonic considerations about the moral worth of love and beauty, and permits Sponde to pass just as easily from analyses of love to meditations upon death.

The highly complex nature of what Délie means to Scève is outlined in *dixain* 22, which also gives some indication of the extent to which Scève's thoughts rely on images capable of carrying multiple layers of meaning:

> Comme Hecaté tu me feras errer
> Et vif, et mort cent ans parmy les Umbres:
> Comme Diane au Ciel me resserrer,
> D'ou descendis en ces mortelz encombres:
> Comme regnante aux infernalles umbres
> Amoindriras, ou accroistras mes peines.
>   Mais comme Lune infuse dans mes veines
> Celle tu fus, es, et seras DELIE,
> Qu'amour a joinct à mes pensées vaines
> Si fort, que Mort jamais ne l'en deslie.

The name "Délie" contains Hecate, Diana, and the Moon with all their aspects. Délie is as variable and as harmful as the infernal Hecate, possessing all her powerful charms, and the power to condemn her lover; she offers him the constant, chaste face of queenly Diana, reserving for herself the power to give him celestial life and supreme joy. Both Hecate and Diana are brought together in the symbol of the Moon since, in sixteenth-century mythology, the Moon is often thought of as a kind of Sun commanding over the other planets and appropriate to the figure of Diana, and since the moon possesses the uncertain, unreliable, tormenting qualities of Hecate. All these elements are unified in the name "Délie", the source of a love which stretches over time,

> ... tu fus, es, et seras DELIE.

In the early poems of the cycle Scève describes, in various ways, the surprise of love, which in *dixain* 1 instantly penetrates into the innermost part of his being—'L'ame de mon ame' as he says with his gift for abstraction. A slow, much more insidious approach of love is given in *dixain* 42:

> Si doulcement le venin de tes yeulx
> Par mesme lieu aux fonz du cœur entra,
> Que sans douleur le desir soucyeux
> De liberté tout seul il rencontra.
> Mais l'occupant, peu a peu, penetra,
> Ou l'Ame libre en grant seurté vivoit.

The domination of love steals quietly, confidently over him, taking possession of his entire being, directing his physical reactions, totally absorbing him, revealing with every flicker of a movement the power of his love which he vainly tries to hide.

Already there have been hints of the pain the poet endures as his love grows within him. As the poems grow in number, so he becomes more convinced of the equivocal nature of his situation *vis-à-vis* Délie. He recognizes his own age and ugliness, and her youth and beauty, and yet he cannot help hoping, desiring, indulging in well nigh impossible, incredible dreams of possession. This rather paradoxical state is given clear expression and expansion through the image of the popinjay who flies all the way from the Orient to join with the black crows (*dixain* 247), braving the most terrible dangers of storm and seas. The fact of such a journey is incredible, but it is none the less a fact. This translates exactly Scève's position; it gives the idea of unrealizability, but retains the fantastic sweep of the dream.

Awareness of the reality of his situation never makes Scève falter in his love; paradoxically, it seems to increase through the power of his imaginings. The picture he paints of love in the *Délie* is based on the torments it brings to its victims. He knows that desire for ever remains unsatisfied, that cravings are always disappointed, yet he nourishes them both in a world of make-believe which somehow never manages to forget the real facts. Indeed, it is the realization of this gap between reality and illusion which allows Scève his most powerful and tense poetic expression. In *dixain* 396 he observes in the real world the Labourer returning at night to the merited warmth of his home, the Pilgrim safe and at peace from his long journey. He continues:

> Et toy, ô Rhosne, en fureur, et grand ire
> Tu viens courant des Alpes roidement
> Vers celle là, qui t'attend froidement,
> Pour en son sein tant doulx te recevoir.

Here is a series of facts, but it is also a list of Scève's hopes and desires for deserved warmth, for peace of mind and soul, for tempestuous union with his Délie. Observable fact and inner desire coexist in the images Scève has selected from life and nature. His own weariness, his consciousness of effort, his longing for peace, and the urgency of his love are also conveyed through the statements about the Labourer and the Pilgrim and then through the expanded movement, vigorous and uncontrolled, of the waters of the Rhône as they rush forward to empty themselves into the calm of the Saône. Fact and desire fall apart in the final words of the *dixain*—economical, simple words, which concentrate and intensify his sense of loss and injustice:

> Et moy suant a ma fin grandement,
> Ne puis ne paix, ne repos d'elle avoir.

Such a degree of emotion often finds its expression in the elaboration of a single image. Just as the Royal Salamander lives without hurt in fire, feeds on its flames, so Scève imagines the queenly Délie nourished by the fire of his love:

> Sans lesion le Serpent Royal vit
> Dedans le chault de la flamme luisante:
> Et en l'ardeur, qui a toy me ravit,
> Tu te nourris sans offense cuisante:
> Et bien que soit sa qualité nuisante
> Tu t'y complais, comme en ta nourriture.

A sense of reality is established in the first six lines of the *dixain* where Scève conveys the feeling of Délie's enjoyment and his own satisfaction. It is the role of the image to draw the unattainable closer, indeed to create the illusion of possession. The exclamation

'O fusses tu' of the seventh line, however, shows how illusory these imaginings really are. Having lulled himself through the expansion of the image of the Salamander into believing real what is only desire, the sudden irruption of actual reality makes his suffering even more poignant:

> O fusses tu par ta froide nature
> La Salemendre en mon feu residente:
> Tu y aurois delectable pasture,
> Et estaindrois ma passion ardente.

This recognition of the distance between desire and the real state of affairs changes his handling and the nature of the image. The first six lines had stressed all the fire attributes of the Salamander. Now Délie's real nature, 'ta froide nature', stresses the Salamander's ability to extinguish fire, and thus the source of the poet's torment becomes a potential remedy. Once again, Scève's preoccupations turn away from reality to the realm of make-believe—he moves away from reality in order to provide a medicine to temper the suffering which awareness of reality brings.

Very occasionally Scève experiences moments of simple joy, unspoilt by thoughts of inadequacy or insecurity. When, after a period of disregard, Délie looks at him with calm kindness, Scève's mood gradually rises to intense joy (*dixain* 58); first only tentatively: 'Je commençay a eslever la teste'; then, as his confidence grows, sudden joy overflows his whole being, and the climax of excitement is reached in the illumination of the final image:

> Dont mes pensers guidez par leurs Montjoyes,
> Se paonnoient tous en leur hault Paradis

where the mere thought of a sympathetic look is registered almost as the parading of some physical satisfaction. The excessive nature of the image matches the intense excitement of the poet.

This rapid setting on fire of the poet's desires and imagination, this sudden leap from quiet resignation to extreme joy, are characteristic of Scève's presentation of love, whose sudden bursts are so often caught in final images intended to shock the reader into feeling intensity of desire and adoration. It is as though we discover the

moment of revelation at the same instant as the poet, when he leads
us through the world of his imagination, searching for comfort
from his powers of invention, 'Je me nourris de si doulce mensonge'
(*dixain* 143), and finally says:

> En mon penser soubdain il te regarde
> Comme au desert son Serpent eslevé.

Far from being a source of anguish as she is presented in the early
part of this poem, forcing the poet to seek refuge in a private world
of make-believe, Délie, through a kind of sudden mental illumination, becomes an object of adoration and assumes the same healing
power and divine qualities as did Moses' staff which, by the power
of God, brought food to his people starving in the desert.

Awakening to the power of love is not always such a speedy process:

> L'Aulbe estaingnoit Estoilles a foison,
> Tirant le jour des regions infimes,
> Quand Apollo montant sur l'Orison
> Des montz cornuz doroit les haultes cymes.
> Lors du profond des tenebreux Abysmes,
> Ou mon penser par ses fascheux ennuyz
> Me fait souvent percer les longues nuictz,
> Je revoquay a moy l'ame ravie:
> Qui, dessechant mes larmoyantz conduictz,
> Me feit cler veoir le Soleil de ma vie.
>   (*dixain* 79)

For once Scève allows himself the luxury of contemplating the
beauty of the rising sun. Its magnificence held up in the highest
point of the firmament is contrasted with the poet's mental state,
full of torment from his wakeful night, itself significant of despair
and melancholy. As the sunlight steals over him, changing night
into day, so a corresponding transformation takes place inside the
poet, and his mind sees the face of Délie, 'le Soleil de ma vie'. It is
rare, however, that Scève finds pleasure in his bed; a more typical
view stresses its physical comfort as a place of mental misery:

> L'oysiveté des delicates plumes,
> Lict coustumier, non point de mon repos,
> Mais du travail...   (*dixain* 100)

Here the unexpected contradictions between physical and mental states are forcefully translated through a combination of concrete and abstract terms.

If Délie's presence constantly reminds Scève of his torments and inadequacies, then her absence serves to deprive him altogether of any sense of life—except the nagging, absorbing remembrance that she is not there. He waits for her return:

> Comme le Lievre accroppy en son giste,
> Je tendz l'oreille, oyant un bruyt confus,
> Tout esperdu aux tenebres d'Egypte...
> (*dixain* 129)

Shivering with apprehension, strained and on the alert in the profoundest darkness, totally bereft of mental or physical movement, Scève confusedly waits and desires her return, yet fears what it might bring. At other moments he manages to break away from such stunned inactivity; but then, desire and imaginative power carry him to paroxysms of jealousy. He sees her, knows her to be in bed with her husband, while he plagues himself with the detail of such knowledge:

> Seul avec moy, elle avec sa partie:
> Moy en ma peine, elle en sa molle couche,
> Couvert d'ennuy je me voultre en l'Ortie,
> Et elle nue entre ses bras se couche.
> Hà (luy indigne) il la tient, il la touche:
> Elle le souffre... (*dixain* 161)

As his work progresses Scève seems to be more and more preoccupied not so much with the analysis and communication of the myriad emotions and reactions love provokes in man, but rather with love's consolations. In our discussion of final images (*dixains* 58, 79, 143) we have already noted moments when a sudden vision of Délie has aroused simultaneously both his love and a recognition of her healing power. Images baldly stated at the beginning of a poem often have the function of separating off the suffering which love of Délie brings and stressing her ability to heal such torment. *Dixain* 372, for instance, opens with the fusion of Délie with the image of the cedar, traditionally accepted as representing the power of healing:

> Tu m'es le Cedre encontre le venin
> De ce Serpent en moy continuel.

She has the power to combat the constant torture, the 'venin... continuel' of the poem, she who was the cause of it.

Délie's powers, however, are not limited to matters of human medicine. As the sub-title of the entire work indicates, Délie is 'L'Object de plus haulte vertu', and it is through her virtue and through her renown that Scève can conquer his suffering and attain the ultimate consolation by triumphing over death. For, as Scève reaches the end of his long exploration, more than ever he feels the physical ravages of time, not only on his own self, but also on Délie:

> Tu te verras ton yvoire cresper
> Par l'oultrageuse, et tardive vieillesse.
> (*dixain* 310)

And from an instrument of delicious torture, Délie becomes the sole means of immortality:

> Tu me seras la Myrrhe incorruptible
> Contre les vers de ma mortalité.

Thus he strikingly concludes *dixain* 378, once again choosing an image which draws together abstract and concrete to express maximum intensity of feeling and intention. These two brief lines not only sum up the precise situation of this poem where Délie's power of granting eternal life is seen as greater than the power of his soul triumphing over death; they also provide a summary of Scève's method generally. Tightly argued poems, moving rapidly from an isolated detail of personal experience to a general abstract expression of emotion, find the general and the particular often fused together in an image which stretches over the physical and intellectual worlds.

In the sonnets of Jean de Sponde there seems to be a basic sense of constancy (whether constancy in love, or certitude in faith) which would suggest exploration in an opposite direction from the weaknesses investigated by Scève. And yet, it is the awareness of such a virtue and the attempt to maintain it, together with the fear of not being able to, which produces the tension and drama of Sponde's verse. Only in the last sonnet of the second sequence is certitude explicitly stated. The assurance which he constantly assumes, but does not yet state, allows him to speak from a great height of generality:

> Je voy ces vermisseaux bastir dedans leurs plaines
> Les monts de leurs desseins...
> (*Sonnets de la Mort*, iii)

Such certitude hardly seems surprising in one who has just been converted to Catholicism, and who is ready to deny the value of all human activities however great their attraction. It is less usual from a lover. Nevertheless, it is on this very general plane that Sponde's discussion often operates:

> Qui seroit dans les cieux, et baisseroit sa veuë
> Sur le large pourpris de ce sec element,
> Il ne croiroit le Tout rienqu'un poinct seulement,
> Un poinct encor caché du voile d'une nuë:
>
> Mais s'il contemple apres ceste courtine bluë,
> Ce cercle de cristal, ce doré firmament,
> Il juge que son tour est grand infiniment,
> Et que cette grandeur nous est toute incognuë.
>
> Ainsi de ce grand ciel, où l'amour m'a guidé,
> De ce grand ciel d'Amour où mon œil est bandé,
> Si je relasche un peu la pointe aigue au reste,
>
> Au reste des amours, je vois sous une nuit
> Le monde d'Epicure en atomes reduit,
> Leur amour tout de terre, et le mien tout celeste.
> (*Sonnets d'Amour*, iii)

Only a great cosmology seems big enough to contain the size of Sponde's love. The manner of conveying intensity is to equate exactly the 'ciel' of the quatrains with his own 'grand ciel d'Amour' of the tercets. Such a parallelism allows him also to stress the durability and quality of his own love as opposed to the finite, earth-bound love of most men.

As one reads this poem and remembers the tight, concentrated structures of Scève's *dixains*, it seems that the sonnet form can permit greater looseness of approach, allow repetitions of words: 'point', 'ciel', 'au reste', of ideas: 'ceste courtine bluë', 'Ce cercle de cristal', 'ce doré firmament', and make room for a much more explicit handling of the subject. And yet, if one considers the detail of the language the two poets use, similarity again is at once apparent. The abstract description of Achilles' state of mind:

> Son oisive douleur, sa vengeance de juge
> (*Sonnets d'Amour*, xiv)

by its unusual juxtapositions and its concision makes the same kind of intellectual appeal as did Scève.

Like Scève, Sponde extends this appeal to his use of the image. The larger form of the sonnet also allows a greater complexity of image-making than was possible in the *dixain*, where Scève relied on careful placing at the beginning or end of his poem. In the sonnet beginning 'Hélas! contez vos jours' (*Sonnets de la Mort*, v), we encounter a series of images already well known to us: 'Aurore' used metaphorically, desires given concrete existence, Death personified, 'Flots', 'escueils', 'butin' used traditionally. And yet the manner of their intertwining is so involved, their meaning at first so obscured by repetitions and strange juxtapositions, their impact held back by the constant see-saw movement of the poem, that they acquire a new status. They no longer seem conventional when we realize how they are being used: to reflect the complex, and often paradoxical, conditions which confront man, to show him that the greatest danger to himself lies in his inability to see clearly into his own motives and those of others:

> Hélas! contez vos jours: les jours qui sont passez
> Sont desja morts pour vous, ceux qui viennent encore
> Mourront tous sur le point de leur naissante Aurore,
> Et moitié de la vie est moitié du decez.

> Ces desirs orgueilleux pesle mesle entassez,
> Ce cœur outrecuidé que vostre bras implore,

Cest indomptable bras que vostre cœur adore,
La Mort les met en geine, et leur fait le procez.

Mille flots, mille escueils, font teste à vostre route,
Vous rompez à travers, mais à la fin, sans doute,
Vous serez le butin des escueils, et des flots.

Une heure vous attend, un moment vous espie,
Bourreaux desnaturez de vostre propre vie,
Qui vit avec la peine, et meurt sans le repos.

(Sonnets de la Mort, v)

An added power is given to the images from the fact that they are
placed side by side with their natural opposites; death drawn close
to birth in the line: 'Mourront tous sur le point de leur naissante
Aurore', for example. Embedded in the centre of this array of
images are the concise lines:

Ce cœur outrecuidé que vostre bras implore,
Cest indomptable bras que vostre cœur adore,...

Their meaning is not immediately obvious, and this difficulty comes
from the criss-cross use of the nouns 'cœur' and 'bras', and of the
demonstrative adjectives 'ce' and 'vostre', together with the play of
concrete and abstract terms. In fact, these lines summarize the tenor
of the whole sonnet: 'Ce cœur outrecuidé' represents the vaunting
conquerors ready to reject supplication, 'Cest indomptable bras'
stands for the display of force which seduces all who see it. They
prove how influenced we are by the show of unreliable appearances.
They also prepare us for the final turn of the poem: the discovery
that we are our own murderers. This point is made absolutely clear
by the transformation of the abstract personification of 'La Mort'
(line 8) which becomes the emphatic, pointed statement 'Bourreaux
desnaturez' (line 13). Death is no abstract force but lives within us.
The full impact of the images finally emerges through the general
pattern and argument of the sonnet.

There are times when Sponde, seduced by the power of concision
which images allow him, seems to throw them down, unexplained,
on the page. The refusal to explain helps him to keep a fine balance
between what he knows is fact and how man reacts to such fact. The
sonnet 'Mais, si faut-il mourir' (*Sonnets de la Mort*, ii) is made up in

this way, with a series of images such as 'ceste ampoule venteuse',
'ce beau flambeau qui lance une flamme fumeuse', whose significance
(they stand as statements on the attractions and the brevity of life
on earth) is only made clear by a process of accumulation and by the
context. Sponde never tells us exactly what they mean, although he
has made it easy enough for us to guess. The fact of inevitable death,
baldly stated at the beginning, is restated emphatically at the end.
These clear statements are obviously intended to direct our interpretation of the images which lie in between. In spite of its circular
movement (the poem begins and ends on the very same phrase:
'Mais, si faut-il mourir'), there is something extraordinarily abrupt
about this sonnet. It is an abruptness which disturbs the reader, and
keeps us constantly on the alert, aware of the equal pull of death and
life in the poem. It goes beyond the awkward rhythms and argumen-
tation of Scève's poetry since Sponde relies for his effects and
power of persuasion on our continual disturbance. The lyrical
opening of *Sonnets d'Amour*, xix:

> Je contemplois un jour le dormant de ce fleuve...

is an astonishing exception to his main stylistic intentions. Most
often, through a variety of means, Sponde holds us in a state of
extreme tension, for he sees clearly enough the spiritual goal he
strives after, but the ability to attain such a goal is tempered by an
equally clear vision of his own human weaknesses. He uses frequent
repetition; the second quatrain of *Sonnets de la Mort*, i, provides
a good instance:

> Vous qui voyant de morts leur mort entresuivie,
> N'avez point de maisons que les maisons des morts,
> Et ne sentez pourtant de la mort un remors,
> D'où vient qu'au souvenir son souvenir s'oublie?

He employs unexpected juxtapositions: 'ces beaux amas de poudre'
(*Sonnets de la Mort*, iii); abundant antitheses: 'le dernier desespoir
sera son esperance' (*Sonnets d'Amour*, xx); skilful play on words:
'Mon feu ne sçauroit mourir si je ne meurs' (*Sonnets d'Amour*, xi).
Above all he taxes our vigilance through parentheses and qualifying

clauses which hold up the argument, through broken rhythms, clashing sounds, questions, and exclamations.

In addition, these elements all serve to give an impression of spontaneity, of great activity and directness to his verse; and in spite of the difficulties arising from his conciseness and use of imagery, he seems to speak his thoughts aloud, feeling his way through an emotion or argument, trying to reconcile thought and emotion. He startles our minds into play with colloquial questions, 'Pour qui tant de travaux? pour vous?' (opening of *Sonnets de la Mort*, iv), or the first line of the final tercet: 'Mais pourquoi ce souci? mais pourquoi cest effort?' In the early sonnets of the series on death this incessant questioning is directed on a very general level. Gradually, however, we grasp that the warning note and the incipient didactic tone stem from Sponde's clear-sighted view of his own fate. He is concerned to persuade himself as well as to communicate his own experience for the good of others.

This concern culminates in the virtuoso, repetitive statements of the final sonnet. Sponde realizes that it is as difficult for other men to accept his arguments of the earlier sonnets as it is for himself to do so. In these final words he not only demonstrates this awareness but tries to help solve others' difficulties by a pointedly personal exposition of the problems involved:

> Tout s'enfle contre moy, tout m'assaut, tout me tente,
> Et le monde et la Chair, et l'Ange revolté,
> Dont l'onde, dont l'effort, dont le charme inventé
> Et m'abisme, Seigneur, et m'esbranle, et m'enchante.

An inner battlefield is evoked, with strong verbs piling up one after another, recalling the same sense of tempest and torture as the clash of weapons of war imitated through verbs in the sonnet which begins:

> Je sens dedans mon ame une guerre civile...
> (*Sonnets d'Amour*, xvii)

Behind this precarious emotional state, however, lies an inner conviction that with God's help we can overcome temptation whatever its force and magnetism. This conviction is pronounced in the exact parallelism of the final lines of the poem:

> Mais ton Temple pourtant, ta main, ta voix sera
> La nef, l'appuy, l'oreille, où ce charme perdra,
> Où mourra cest effort, où se perdra ceste onde.

Although certitude is here projected into the future, it is stated unequivocally, and has, in retrospect, a curious weakening effect on the force of the opening lines. On a second reading the verbs lose their physical penetration, they seem now part of an intellectual demonstration of belief and the power of faith, uttered in long lyrical alexandrines which flow on with their triple runs of verbs and nouns, released from their original drama. Far from being a statement of inner conflict, these lines are transformed into a song, praising the power of God. A Christian means of salvation thus replaces the pagan medicine of Délie, as one would expect after the Wars of Religion.

The confidence which ends Sponde's collection of sonnets on death is the mood which will dominate Jean de la Ceppède's meditations on the Passion of Our Lord in Le Livre des Théorèmes (first part published 1613) and Jean Baptiste Chassignet's consolations on death (published 1594). Although they too will use the sonnet, it proves too tight a form to contain their lyrical effusions which flow over from one poem to the next. Their sense of conviction is absolute. Consequently, there are none of the tremors, the strain or the tension, the consciousness of weakness and fear which beset Sponde. So often he seems to be trying to persuade himself as well as to convince us. Irresolution is everywhere apparent in the antitheses, the strange coupling of words, the images, the tentative colloquialisms he sets before us. Only in the last sonnet does faith overcome such trepidations.

Both Scève and Sponde, lucidly aware of the complexities of the human situation, of the interaction of thought and emotion, employ poetic techniques which have an unquestionably modern look. This no doubt explains their present increasing popularity. Poetry, for them, does not 'dress up' emotions to make them beautiful that they might delight the eye. It does not compose songs of consolation or joy to beguile the ear. Essentially, it is concerned with argument. To feel profoundly we must be made to think. The poems of Scève and Sponde ensure that we do both.

NOTE

MAURICE SCÈVE, *c.* 1500–*c.* 1560, friend of the humanist Étienne Dolet and the poet Clément Marot, admired by Du Bellay and Ronsard, eventually studied at an Italian university—perhaps Pavia or Bologna. 1530–3 found him in Avignon studying and searching for the tomb of Petrarch's Laura. By 1536 he was back in Lyons, active in its Italianate literary circles, in love with Pernette du Guillet who inspired *Délie* (1544). After a retreat in the country Scève returned in 1548 to prepare Henri II's entry into Lyons. He devoted the rest of his life to study, to literary discussions with Louise Labé and Pontus de Tyard, and to the composition of his long philosophical poem *Microcosme*, published, probably after his death, in 1562.

Modern editions. A new authoritative edition (1965) of the *Délie* by I. Macfarlane replaces that of E. Parturier. The complete *Blasons* are published in A. M. Schmidt, *Poètes du XVIe siècle* (1953). Other minor works, *Le opere minori*, are edited by E. Giudici (1958) and *La Saulsaye* in photographic reproduction by M. Françon (1959). *Le Microcosme* was edited and introduced by Valéry Larbaud (1929).

Criticism. V. L. Saulnier, *Maurice Scève* (1949: 2 vols.) is the weighty standard work, though the very detailed information is not always easy to locate. Useful analyses of the *Délie* can be found in H. Weber, *La Création poétique au XVIe siècle* (1956: 2 vols.), O. de Mourgues, *Metaphysical, Baroque and Précieux Poetry* (1954), A. M. Boase, *The Poetry of France* (vol. i, 1964). For analyses of individual poems and Scève's use of imagery see articles by D. Coleman (*Studi francesi*, vol. xxiii, 1964; *French Studies*, vol. xiv, 1960; and *Modern Language Review*, vol. lviii, 1963).

JEAN DE SPONDE, 1557–94, a Protestant born in the Pyrenees. He was first known as a scholar, publishing an annotated *Homer* in Basle in 1583. He played a significant role in public affairs as governor of La Rochelle (1587–92), knew prominent Protestant leaders and supporters such as Théodore de Bèze and the historian Auguste de Thou. In the last years of his life he was converted to Roman Catholicism, wrote a long theological apology and probably composed most of his religious poems.

Modern editions. The *Poésies* are edited by A. M. Boase and F. Ruchon (1949) and the *Méditations* by A. M. Boase (1954).

Criticism. Analyses of Sponde's poems and a penetrating discussion of the quality and nature of his poetry by A. M. Boase can be found in the second part of the Introduction to the edition of the *Poésies* mentioned above.

7. The Uses of the Sonnet: Louise Labé and Du Bellay

'SONNE moy ces beaux sonnetz, non moins docte que plaisante invention Italienne.' Of all the injunctions to aspiring French poets in Du Bellay's *Deffence et Illustration de la Langue Francoyse* (1549), none was more tirelessly obeyed than this. Indeed the history of sixteenth-century poetry is in large measure the history of the rise in dignity and serviceability of the sonnet—still qualified in Sebillet's *Art poétique* of 1548 as a variant of the epigram. The *Deffence* itself had a much more ambitious scope: it outlined a whole programme by which French poets could raise their still undistinguished art to be something more worthy of the spiritual descendants of Greece and Rome. The proposals included both advice on the cultivation of the nobler poetic genres of antiquity, such as the ode and the epic, and detailed instructions on the enrichment of the literary language through the use of archaisms, neologisms, technical terms, 'graves sentences' and 'rare érudition', figures of speech, and unusual grammatical constructions: infinitives, for instance, should be used as nouns and adjectives as adverbs, and the poet would do well to imitate the rhetoricians who, instead of 'depuis l'Orient à l'Occident', write 'depuis ceux qui voyent premiers rougir l'Aurore jusque la ou Thetis recoit en ses undes le filz d'Hyperion'.

Though Ronsard's work came near to fulfilling the spirit of the manifesto, most of the other members of the Pléiade, rightly perhaps in view of the daunting nature of some of the individual recommendations, lowered their sights somewhat from the start. Thus, in the same year as he published the *Deffence*, Du Bellay brought out his sonnet sequence *L'Olive*, clearly modelled on Petrarch's *canzoniere*;

and the highly combative preface to the second edition seems to claim it as a successful exemplification of his theories. The imitation of antiquity, which was the keystone of the Pléiade's programme, has been diluted into the imitation of Italy, and particularly the cultivation of one completely non-classical form which—as their enemies were quick to point out—has little more inherent dignity than the other sorts of short poem of which members of the Pléiade were so scornful. One reason, then, for not studying the work of the period through its famous theory is that the poets in many respects ignored it themselves. The members of the Pléiade were not primarily employed in the fifteen-fifties in writing Pindaric odes and inventing new words. They were writing love sonnets. Petrarch and his Italian followers were the presiding models; and when, in a later satire, Du Bellay says that he has 'oublié l'art de Petrarquizer' he can only be disparaging the very work which he had previously put forward as the first milestone of the new poetry. The *Deffence*, in fact, is a symptom of an already growing spirit as much as an effective aesthetic; the poets were caught up in a very broad cultural movement of which figures like Scève, whom they sometimes in their innovating enthusiasm regarded as inferior or different in kind, were very much a part.

The love poetry of the minor members of the Pléiade is by no means lacking in originality, but they inevitably work under the shadow of Ronsard; and perhaps the intensive output, the sense of collaborative enterprise, were not wholly propitious to the flowering of individuality. It is perhaps not surprising in the circumstances that the most distinctive voices of the fifties are those of two poets who, while remaining faithful to the sonnet, stand outside the main Pléiade undertaking in its now somewhat modified form. Louise Labé, whose poetic work (*Euvres*, 1555) consists of a mere three elegies and two dozen sonnets probably addressed to Olivier de Magny, seems to have had no extensive contact with the Pléiade. Du Bellay's *Regrets* (1558) represent both a reaction against the practice of his fellow poets ('Ne lira-lon jamais que ce Dieu rigoureux?' he asks in a bantering sonnet to Ronsard) and at the same time a formal abdication of the Pléiade's original declared aims and beliefs. The early sonnets of the *Regrets* state his position: he no longer claims the rank of a semi-divine interpreter of nature ('Je ne veulx point fouiller au sein de la nature'); he will no longer 'fueilleter les exemplaires Grecs' or vie with 'la voix d'un Ronsard'. Louise Labé ignores the Pléiade. Du Bellay rejects its theory and practice, though its programme remains a vital term in his work—he makes poetry not by fulfilling it but by writing *about* it, using it as a measure of his private tragedy. Each poet has a very personal aim— but each uses means a little different from those the modern reader might expect.

For Louise Labé, in spite of her independence and individuality, is still working broadly within the Petrarchan tradition. She knows its techniques, and on occasion competes with her contemporaries in reproducing its worst excesses and conventionalities. The opening sonnet of the series is portentously bad. Written in Italian, as if to emphasize the notion of poetry as a learned and derivative exercise, it opens with the sage Ulysses in the unaccustomed role of connoisseur of emotional disasters, then shamelessly strings together the most hackneyed commonplaces of Petrarchism—the wounds of love, the remedy sought in the disease itself, the scorpion, the appeal to cruel fate. The poem may seem an ill-judged advertisement for what follows. But it is an interesting reminder, not only of public expectation, but also of the willingness even of quite independent poets to put their names to the stalest reworkings, to coast along unselfcritically within a convention, only dimly aware of their moments of true originality, or of the vast discrepancies of value within their work. This myopia, however, is understandable: the masterpieces of the sonnet are more often achieved through the personalizing of a conventional form than by total departure from convention; and when we come to try to characterize their value we can sometimes avoid the dangers both of effusiveness and of anachronism by approaching them with this in mind.

Nowhere else in the series does Louise Labé sink to the level of banality of the first sonnet, though we may feel that VIII ('Je vis je meurs; je me brule et me noye') is a dispensable rhetorical exercise, and that IV ('Depuis qu'Amour cruel empoisonna') and XI ('O dous regars, ô yeus pleins de beauté') add little to the by now well-documented theme of the mechanics of love. With II, however, we are in the presence of something very much more powerful and distinctive:

> O beaus yeus bruns, ô regars destournez,
> O chaus soupirs, ô larmes espandues,
> O noires nuits vainement atendues,
> O jours luisans vainement retournez:
>
> O tristes pleins, ô desirs obstinez,
> O tems perdu, ô peines despendues,
> O mile morts en mile rets tendues,
> O pires maus contre moy destinez.
>
> O ris, ô front, cheveus, bras, mains et doits,
> O lut pleintif, viole, archet et vois:
> Tant de flambeaus pour ardre une femmelle!
>
> De toy me plein, que tant de feux portant,
> En tant d'endrois d'iceus mon cœur tatant,
> N'en est sur toy volé quelque estincelle.

The technique is of enumeration, but the effect is of bewildered incantation; the lack of syntax, the random shifts from the loved one's appearance to the lover's sufferings and the cruelty of fate convey the plight of one unable to control her own thoughts or analyse her experience, able only to record the volume of suffering and the irresistibility (conveyed by the speeding up of the ninth and tenth lines?) of the obsessive images which crowd her consciousness. The force of the evocation legitimates the final tercet in a way which would not seem possible if one took it out of its context. The 'tant de feus' now seems a discreet shorthand, an understatement even, for a reality which cannot otherwise easily be faced; and the lover's complaint not an aggressive conceit, but a muted statement of wounded surprise, a way of containing the proven enormity of the injustice rather than of exaggerating it. The sonnet is not a great poem, but one only has to look at other representatives of the tradition, like Ronsard's 'O traiz fichez dans le but de mon ame' and its sources in Petrarch and Gesualdo, to appreciate Louise Labé's very individual achievement. Ronsard is lured by the rhetorical form away from the personal to the routine invocation of earth, sky, demons, and spirits to witness 'quelle peine je porte'; Louise Labé moves towards greater concentration and drama, and concludes not with the proud public challenge of the professional lover and sonnet-writer, but with an intensely personal comment whose succinctness is dictated not by epigrammatic ambition but by the force of the evidence itself.

A similar transformation can be seen in III ('O longs desirs, O esperances vaines'), the only poem of Louise Labé's which can be identified as a direct imitation. The original, by the Neapolitan Petrarchan Sannazaro, was fairly closely imitated by Olivier de Magny:

> Inutille desir, interditte esperance,
> Cauteleuse pensée et vouloir aveuglé,
> Larmes, plainctes, souspirs et tourment dereiglé,
> Donnez ou paix ou tresve à ma longue souffrance.
>
> Et s'au mal le dedain ny l'oubly n'a puissance,
> Et que je doive ainsi sans fin estre comblé
> De tant et tant d'ennuy dans mon ame assemblé
> Face la mort sur moy sa noire violence:
>
> Ou le ciel promptement me foudroie le chef,
> Car je n'ay point de peur de nul mortel meschef,
> Pourveu qu'en trespassant ma peine ne me suive.
>
> Sus donc Amour, va-ten, retire toy, a dieu,
> Ta force en mon endroit demeure ores oisive,
> Puis que nouvelle playe en moy n'a plus de lieu.

Louise Labé eliminates the ratiocination of lines 5–11 and prolongs the invocation for the whole of the first eight lines, building up an atmosphere of desperate incantation similar to that of the sonnet already studied. The final conceit is retained, indeed expanded: but the closing line is led up to not by a sprightly injunction to love to look elsewhere, but by a weary challenge to test her further:

> Qu'encor Amour sur moy son arc essaie,
> Que nouveaus feus me gette et nouveaus dars:
> Qu'il se despite et pis qu'il pourra face:

Thus the final lines, which in Sannazaro and Magny risk evoking the image of the lover as a sort of cluttered dartboard, here seem to translate quite naturally the battered self-knowledge of the victim, certain that a greater degree of suffering is impossible:

> tant navree en toutes pars
> Que plus en moy une nouvelle playe
> Pour m'empirer ne pourroit trouver place.

Technique and convention, then, are almost always made to subserve the poetic personality.

And it is a personality whose chief elements are unintellectual— plangent elegy, direct supplication, imagined ecstasy. Not every poem has the immediacy of the astonishing XVIII ('Baise m'encor, rebaise moy et baise'); but she rarely writes a poem in which emotion is played with or argued about or used to illustrate a general truth in the way which the sonnet, with its tradition of the final *pointe*, encourages. She may begin in sententious, vaguely platonizing language:

> On voit mourir toute chose animee
> Lors que du corps l'ame sutile part:
>
> (VII)

But this is not the starting-point, as it has some appearance of being, for a 'metaphysical' elaboration. It leads to a plea of the utmost simplicity:

> Je suis le corps, toy la meilleure part:
> Ou es tu donq, ô âme bien aymee?
>
> . . .
>
> Las, ne mets point ton corps en ce hazart;
> Rens lui sa part et moitié estimee.

The opening statement turns out to have been only part of a technique of persuasion; but a persuasion not theoretical or juridical in tone; reminiscent, rather, of the flattering but ingenuous urgency of a child. The yearning injunction to give 'le corps', which then becomes 'ton corps', its due establishes a tone from which it is clear that the equating of the lover with 'l'âme' is an argumentative convenience rather than the reflection of any spiritual conception of love.

But the use of the image does not thereby seem ill judged or extraneous to the meaning of the poem; rather it gives to the whole plea the appealing air of transparent opportunism which is appropriate in one for whom the passionate ends justify the rhetorical means. When it has served its purpose the image is dropped and the sestet moves on to an equally eloquent but totally direct plea for reunion, accompanied

> ... non de severité
> Non de rigueur: mais de grace amiable,
> Qui doucement me rende ta beauté,
> Jadis cruelle, à present favorable.

VII is primarily a poem of deprivation and supplication, the final timid hope contained in 'favorable' being reached only tentatively through a sentence of (for Louise) halting complexity, delayed by the greater reality of fears and memories and obstacles. But perhaps Louise Labé's finest single poem, and certainly her most dramatic exploitation of the sonnet form, is the dream of a fulfilled love triumphing over death:

> Oh si j'estois en ce beau sein ravie
> De celui là pour lequel vois mourant:
> Si avec lui vivre le demeurant
> De mes cours jours ne m'empeschoit envie:
>
> Si m'acollant me disoit, chere Amie,
> Contentons nous l'un l'autre, s'asseurant
> Que ja tempeste, Euripe, ne Courant
> Ne nous pourra desjoindre en notre vie:
>
> Si de mes bras le tenant acollé,
> Comme du Lierre est l'arbre encercelé,
> La mort venoit, de mon aise envieuse:
>
> Lors que souef plus il me baiseroit,
> Et mon esprit sur ses levres fuiroit,
> Bien je mourrois, plus que vivante, heureuse.
>
>   (XIII)

The movement of the poem is by way of the progressive elimination of obstacles. These—personal and social—are powerfully present to block the flight of the imagination at the end of lines 2 and 4; in the second quatrain we are more securely within the imaginative experience, and the only remaining threat is the violence of the physical universe which, however, is confidently and expansively defied. In the first tercet the imaginative experience is the central reality, the conditional now attaches to the obstacles. But the arrival of death is unable to destroy the impetus and incipient ecstasy which have been built up. It can be incorporated as a challenge; and indeed the syntactical parallel with the previous clauses, in which the conditional introduced the *desirable* imagined situation, means that we already partly sense that death is not merely an interruption to, but also an element of, the yearned-for fulfilment. The fulfilment is acted out in the closing lines. The final moment is prolonged in the rapturous drive of lines 12 and 13, and the sonnet expires with its single, sustained, complex sentence consummated on the word 'heureuse'. One can think of few other short poems of the century in which a set of values or aspirations is so perfectly enacted and worked out. It is a similar sort of structural achievement to Ronsard's 'Comme on voit sur la branche...': here too death is triumphed over, though in a different way—the poet, as it were, embalming physical beauty in beautiful sounds, meeting and assimilating the momentary violence of 'La Parque t'a tuée...' and bringing the poem safely through 'mort... corps...' to its conclusion on the keyword 'roses'.

If Louise Labé has only recently received her due as a major figure in sixteenth-century love poetry, it is probably because of the smallness of her output and, even within that, the relative narrowness of her scope. Her strength is that her single note is one rarely sounded by even her most talented contemporaries. We ought perhaps in this connection to allow that it is the unfamiliarity of the emotional standpoint, as well as more strictly literary considerations, which makes her work so attractive to us. The male poets worked under the disadvantage that their very numbers and output tend to make their attitudes seem more stereotyped and derivative. Thus the rather self-consciously feminine audacity of the final lines of

'Baise m'encor...' ('Permets m'Amour penser quelque folie:
Tousjours suis mal, vivant discrettement...') leads the poem away
from the sententious and reflective ending to which lines 9–10
might well have taken it—and into which Ronsard's comparable
'Sinope, baisez moy...' naturally moves. We are amused and
attracted by the tone, but the appeal is perhaps as much a matter
of personality as of poetry. At any rate this sort of immediacy and
individuality ought not, as is so easy when using other poets for
comparative purposes, to be erected into an absolute literary virtue.
If a poet has thoughts he is entitled to put them down without being
accused of being discursive, and if he has conclusions they may even
be best expressed in a *pointe*. Comparison is better used to help
characterize a poet's work than to establish a hierarchy of values.
To turn from the range of feeling and reflection in, say, Ronsard's
'Ces longues nuicts d'hiver' to Louise Labé's variant on the same
theme (IX) may well be to feel that one is turning to a narrower
emotional as well as intellectual world. It will make us want to do
justice to Ronsard, sardonic final *pointe* and all; but we shall also be
made more aware, as we are led with absolute directness to the
heart of the poetess's experience ('Tout aussi tot que je commence
à prendre / Dans le mol lit le repos desiré...'), as we hear the simple
notation of misery ('Que de sanglots ay souvent cuidé fendre') and
supplication ('Faites au moins qu'elle en ait en mensonge'), of the
total distinctiveness of Louise Labé's 'amoureuses noises'.

In the opening sonnets of the *Regrets* Du Bellay promises a
similarly direct record of his experience—'De(s) papiers journaux
ou bien de(s) commentaires' (I), 'Ce que la passion seulement me
fait dire' (IV). But his choice of the sonnet form in which to record
these day-to-day experiences already prepares us for something
slightly more literary, less private than these statements of intention
might suggest: once again the personal is to be framed in the
formal and conventional. The accomplished Petrarchist of the *Olive*
may have lost his aspirations, but he has not lost his memory; and in
terms of literary history part of the novelty of the *Regrets* consists in
the application of a certain fund of inherited techniques and images

to—for the first time—a subject other than love. Here is an example
of what Du Bellay's 'passion' makes him say:

> La nef qui longuement a voyagé (Dillier)
> Dedans le sein du port à la fin on la serre:
> Et le bœuf, qui long temps a renversé la terre,
> Le bouvier à la fin lui oste le collier:
>
> Le vieil cheval se void à la fin deslier,
> Pour ne perdre l'haleine ou quelque honte acquerre:
> Et pour se reposer du travail de la guerre,
> Se retire à la fin le vieillard chevalier:
>
> Mais moy, qui jusqu'icy n'ay prouvé que la peine,
> La peine et le malheur d'une esperance vaine,
> La douleur, le soucy, les regrets, les ennuis,
>
> Je vieillis peu à peu sur l'onde Ausonienne,
> Et si n'espere point, quelque bien qui m'advienne,
> De sortir jamais hors des travaux ou je suis.
>
> (XXXV)

We only have to turn back to Scève's similarly constructed, similarly
derivative 'Le laboureur de sueur tout rempli' (briefly discussed in
the previous chapter) to see what Du Bellay does not do with his
imagery. Scève starts with the commonplaces of the ploughman
and the pilgrim, but, with the image of the two rivers and the shift
to the second person, he comes nearer a dramatization of his own
position. The Rhône's violence is personified, a moment of tension
is established—the Saône waits 'froidement', which could be cold-
heartedly as well as calmly—and we feel a palpable relief with the
'tant doux' which resolves the doubt in the next line. The conclusion is not argued out: two lines, introduced not by 'mais' but by
'et', convey by their brevity and dismissiveness Scève's pathetic role
in the world of harmony and justice; his indignity too, 'suant à (sa)
fin grandement', compared with the ploughman of the first line,
'rempli', filled, and also fulfilled, with the sweat of his labour.
Both poets use the basic Petrarchan techniques of enumeration

and antithesis. Scève, however, achieves his effects through compression and dramatization, while Du Bellay is unashamedly discursive in his leisurely elaboration. He might seem to risk achieving all too well his aim of writing 'une prose en ryme ou une ryme en prose'—not by being too personal and particular but rather by being over-schematic, over-explicit, over-general, by his reliance on unqualified abstract nouns, by his rather routine distribution of the poem's subject-matter between octet and sestet. But Du Bellay has his music too, as we see when we compare his sonnet with the tripping argumentative movement of his Italian models, piling up their trite examples of virtue rewarded, to conclude with the contrasting fate of 'chi alla femmina serve'. By comparison with these Du Bellay's sonnet seems pure incantation—and the evocativeness it has is a direct result of the symmetrical pattern, the weary systematic enumeration. The change from the decasyllable to the alexandrine (still suspect of prosiness in the theory of the time and not yet in common use among the sonneteers) allows the repeated insertion of the adverbs 'longuement', etc., while such a device as the inversion and withholding of the subject in lines 7–8 perhaps helps to convey the feeling of delayed fulfilment in addition to those of fatigue and yearning already built up. The division between octet and sestet, though schematic, is also the most natural and appropriate one, the more open structure of the sestet translating the poet's unfulfilled desires, as the embracing rhymes of the octet had defined and circumscribed the world of order and justice.

All the same, in spite of its achievements in elegiac orchestration, the sonnet remains something of a rhetorical exercise. Elsewhere the exploitation of the form can be vindicated in a more positive way. Sonnet VI

> Las, ou est maintenant ce mespris de Fortune?
> Ou est ce cœur vainqueur de toute adversité?

begins with a catalogue of youthful aspirations. This time the tone is more complex: the technique of enumeration provides an elegiac strain, but the vocabulary has a certain attack which echoes the confidence that the quatrain describes: the poet does not dissociate himself completely from the idea of the poetic gift 'au peuple non commune', the repetition in 'honneste desir', 'honneste flamme' hovers between rueful self-mockery and nostalgic pride. The second quatrain warms into a more expansive recall of actual achievement:

> Ou sont ces doulx plaisirs qu'au soir, soubs la nuict brune,
> Les Muses me donnoient, alors qu'en liberté
> Dessus le verd tapy d'un rivage esquarté
> Je les menois danser aux rayons de la Lune?

The image condenses all the characteristics of the youthful Pléiade—their feeling for beauty, their sense of emancipation, their exclusiveness; while Du Bellay's vigorous insertion of himself as leader in the traditional dance of the Muses translates the poets' almost playful confidence in their mastery of the divine art. After this high point the sestet registers the present reality in language which, when not calculatedly clumsy ('Et mon cœur, qui souloit estre maistre de soy') does little more than systematically negate what has been evoked earlier: the list of aspirations is as it were checked, each failure bleakly recorded, until with the fine last line

> Et les Muses de moy, comme estranges, s'enfuyent

we feel the stage of the poet's life left completely empty, aspiration relentlessly and efficiently drained by reality.

In this sonnet the rhetorical scheme, though still rigid, seems much less obtrusive—the sonnet gives appropriate general expression to what emerges, in the course of the *Regrets*, as Du Bellay's particular brand of melancholy. To put it in terms as prosaic as the poet himself could have wished: enumeration is the natural mode of a mind and a moment which, as the *Deffence* shows us, formulated their ideals in explicit lists, and broad antithesis that of an individual whose suffering is not so much felt in its individuality as measured against a very literary but none the less real vision of happiness and success. Du Bellay's simplicity is justified and gains its resonance partly from his relation to a particular moment of literary history. His, like Baudelaire's, is 'une douleur très simple et non mystérieuse': those who live by the programme perish by the programme.

Throughout the *Regrets* Du Bellay revolves this central antithesis,

and the related contrasts which present themselves equally obses-
sively to a representative of the Pléiade, whose devotion to antiquity
was matched by their intense nationalism: the nostalgic comparison
between Italy and France and the contrast within Rome itself
between the humanists' dream and the present particularly squalid
political reality. The antithesis expresses itself in many ways and
at many different levels of emotion. The sonnets to Ronsard and
Baïf evoke the world of Pléiade love poetry, now affectionately re-
called, even though, in the imitative vocabulary, there is a note of
the irony and detachment of the maturer man. The joys of singing
'ta Cassandre divine' and

> ... la doulce rudesse
> D'une belle, courtoise et gentille maistresse

are set against Du Bellay's exile

> Sur le bord incogneu d'un estrange rivage
> Ou le malheur nous fait ces tristes vers chanter.

The sonnets have an emphatic rhetorical structure; the contrasts
are articulated on phrases like 'Las, et nous cependant', 'Moy chetif,
ce pendant' which might seem to isolate the poet in a posture of
repetitive self-pity and envy. Yet it is precisely the allusiveness of
the poems that often saves them from these dangers. The resounding
orchestration of Ronsard's successes:

> Tu t'honores toymesme et celuy qui honore
> L'honneur que tu luy fais par ta docte chanson

recalls the language of the *Deffence*; it is the celebration of promise
fulfilled rather than an expression of personal jealousy. Both the
successful and the failed poet are part of the fortune of a larger
enterprise; and in the variants on the antithetical theme we hear the
cumulative music of the splendours and miseries of adherence to
an ideal.

As the comparison with Scève suggested, we do not find in
Du Bellay a novel or dynamic exploitation of the traditional fund of
imagery. Rather we feel that he is laying out the stored analogies of

his mind as they rise to the surface. The image enlarges and prolongs simple statement, it is the natural clothing for a complaint which is both personal and representative. Du Bellay's mind moves easily between the real world and the mythological, with its archetypes of fulfilment and deprivation. The poem to Ronsard discussed above is followed by another (XVII) also apparently addressed to him:

> Après avoir long temps erré sur le rivage
> Ou lon voit lamenter tant de chetifs de Court,
> Tu as attaint le bord ou tout le monde court,
> Fuyant de pauvreté le penible servage.

The scene is not precisely localized—it recalls the 'estrange rivage' of Italy on which Du Bellay himself is languishing. The next quatrain with its explicit Virgilian reminiscence

> Nous autres ce pendant...
> En vain tendons la main vers le Nautonnier sourd

evokes the shores of Lethe; without, however, totally effacing the realistic element—the two are wrily fused in

> ... pour le faire court
> Nous n'avons un quatrin pour payer le naulage.

The shore changes again in the last line, with the image of the sailor who has reached safety and no longer cares about those 'Criant dessus le port ou tirant à la rame'. The effect is not of a hopelessly mixed metaphor but of the poet revolving and maintaining beside one another a complex of elegiac associations, personal and literary, which arise naturally out of his position on the 'onde Ausonienne' and each provide partial images of his condition.

But in general the firmer structure prevails, and Du Bellay's most famous sonnet is based on the antithetical technique. 'Heureux qui, comme Ulysse...' is only the most genial of his combinations of the oratorical and the personal, the rhetorical elaboration and the simple unexpanded contrast. An analysis might point to the expansive rendering of achievement—the stately yet familiar antonomasia, the leisurely syntax, the emphatic position of 'vivre' in the first quatrain; the abrupt shift to the personal plight in the second—no 'cependant' this time but a rueful 'hélas'; the traditional image of the smoking chimney followed by the more urgent elaboration with its yearning anapaestic drive ('Revoyrai-je le clos de ma pauvre maison'); and another conventional comparison—'qui m'est une province'—personalized by the more vibrant colloquialism of 'et beaucoup d'avantage'.

When we come to the sestet we feel, again, a sort of Pléiade shorthand at work. Du Bellay's lost world is a world already cherished and celebrated by his fellow poets. In particular the 'ardoise fine' evokes the *châteaux* of Touraine and Anjou and the whole civilization of François I and Henri II from which, culturally and financially, Du Bellay had expected so much. Du Bellay's nostalgia may be nourished primarily by personal memories; but when we read his regret for the 'champs blondissans' we feel also that he is drawing on a vision of natural beauty already opened up by Ronsard. It is against this that the marble of Rome stands out hard, alien, sterile. Ever since the *Chanson de Roland* hotter and stonier countries had been compared unfavourably to *la douce France*. It took the Pléiade's particular brand of nationalistic aestheticism for Du Bellay to demote the ruins of Rome—ironical sacrilege in a humanist—to the inert status of a 'grand monceau pierreux'.

The satirical sonnets are less frequently constructed on antithetical schemes and often, in the descriptions of carnivals, cardinals, and courtesans, observation completely replaces reflection. Yet the underlying contrast between France and Italy, or between the poet and the courtier, or between expectation and reality, is rarely far from the surface, and still determines the structure of many of the sonnets. They overtly set reality against a known or expected standard:

> Ne pense (Robertet) que ceste Rome cy
> Soit ceste Rome là, qui te souloit tant plaire...
>
> Veulx-tu sçavoir (Duthier) quelle chose c'est, Rome...

The attempt to *define* Rome, to define his own failure, is Du Bellay's constant concern, and again enumeration is given significance by the synthesizing intention, the desire to catalogue and sum up in fourteen lines the shame and smallness of a whole way of life. Sonnets like 'Marcher d'un grave pas...' offer vivid pictorial notations, Du

Bellay mimes his countrymen and himself with bitter lucidity; but the succession of infinitives links the sonnet with those of elegiac regret; a single technique conveys intellectual vigour and spiritual lassitude. Life is a sordid failure, and disjointed observations provide the most faithful description of reality. The claim that this *is* in fact the whole picture is repeatedly made at the end of the poems— 'Voila, mes compagnons, les passetemps de Rome', 'Voila, mon cher Morel (dont je rougis de honte) / Tout le bien qu'en trois ans à Rome j'ay appris'.

Though life at Rome provides constant spectacle, reflection cannot be kept out for long. Sonnets CXX and CXXI describe the carnival in prospect and retrospect:

> Voici le Carneval, menons chascun la sienne,
> Allons baller en masque, allons nous pourmener...

The rhythm is sprightly, mockery is subordinated to the almost enthusiastic evocation of a colourful if slightly absurd scene:

> Voyons courir le pal à la mode ancienne,
> Et voyons par le nez le sot bufle mener;
> Voyons le fier taureau d'armes environner,
> Et voyons au combat l'adresse Italienne:
> Voyons d'œufz parfumez un orage gresler...

But in the next, complementary poem the remorseless, disabused list of infinitives is back: the scene has shrunk, been assimilated, become another illustrative token of the emptiness of life. It is the bull as victim that now holds the poet's attention:

> Se fascher tout le jour d'une fascheuse chasse,
> Voir un brave taureau se faire un large tour...

and so on through the shabbiness and boredom of the feast to the final dismissive conclusion:

> Dresser un grand apprest, faire attendre long temps,
> Puis donner à la fin un maigre passetemps:
> Voila tout le plaisir des festes Romanesques.

Wherever Du Bellay looks he finds nothing but illustrations of his central thesis. Another sonnet (LXXX) shows him in vain quest of a nobler sight. And again the form, with its series of conditional clauses, serves to give the impression of a reality bizarre but essentially repetitive, whose pettiness can be totally encompassed and dismissed in a few words:

> Si je monte au Palais, je n'y trouve qu'orgueil...
> Qu'un bruit de tabourins, qu'une estrange harmonie...
> Si je descens en banque, un amas et recueil
> De nouvelles je trouve, une usure infinie...

Elsewhere there is 'de Venus la grand'bande lascive', a sad substitute for the Muses whom he formerly led to dance. And the retreat into humanistic contemplation too has lost its savour:

> Si je passe plus oultre, et de la Rome neufve
> Entre en la vieille Rome, adoncques je ne treuve
> Que de vieux monuments un grand monceau pierreux.

The ruins are only further reminders of moral disintegration. The effect of the symmetrical, enumerative structure is of a reality totally dominated, briskly surveyed and found wanting. The tour is soon over, the vastness and monumentality of Rome are contracted into a few representative samples of decay.

Antithesis and enumeration as technique and poetic habit of mind have been the chief theme of this discussion. They cannot, of course, provide a full characterization of the *Regrets*: even in the more uniform elegiac section important poems such as 'France, mere des arts...' and 'Si les larmes servoient de remede au malheur' elude this sort of categorization. But the emphasis seemed worth while as a way of examining how a poetic personality expresses itself in conventional literary terms. In so far as it tries to prove anything about *value* the discussion is, of course, open to large criticisms: it is essentially circular—the authenticity of the feeling is partly deduced from the recurrence of the forms, and is then used to confer value on their repetitiveness. Further, the poems are seen as mutually authenticating pieces of self-expression, not as autonomous poetic artefacts. An unfashionable approach: but to be fashionable and to appreciate sixteenth-century poetry in any bulk, as distinct from its anthologized masterpieces, are perhaps irreconcilable undertakings.

The argument that the approach is anachronistic is perhaps less strong: the sixteenth century in general did not think of poetry primarily as self-expression, but Du Bellay came very near to this position in writing the *Regrets*. And certainly the whole century did ask to be read in units greater than the single poem. Boileau's praise of the 'sonnet sans défaut' is a strictly seventeenth-century notion. The sonnet sequence *is* a 'long poème'; and by attending to the cumulative effect of the *Regrets* we may come to see how confidently Du Bellay could follow up his admission of prosiness with the prediction that

> ... tel se pense bien habile,
> Qui trouvant de mes vers la ryme si facile,
> En vain travaillera, me voulant imiter.

NOTE

LOUISE LABÉ, 1524?–66, was a leading figure in the cultural and gallant life of Lyons and, after Scève, the most important member of the so-called *école lyonnaise*. She achieved early local notoriety by appearing in male attire at a tournament, and Calvin refers to her in a letter as a *plebeia meretrix*. But apart from her relations with the poet Olivier de Magny, to whom her sonnets are almost certainly addressed, the details of her life have remained largely a matter of speculation and legend.

JOACHIM DU BELLAY, 1522–60, was an orphaned and impoverished member of a distinguished family. He met Ronsard in 1547 and the pair studied the classics together at the Collège de Coqueret in Paris. They became the centre of the group of poets known as the *Pléiade* and evolved a new poetic, based on the imitation of antiquity, of which Du Bellay became the spokesman. In 1553 he went to Rome as secretary to his cousin the Cardinal Jean Du Bellay, and his experiences there were the source of his most important work, the *Regrets* and the *Antiquités de Rome*, both published in 1558.

Modern editions. Louise Labé's complete works, including the prose dialogue *Le Débat de la folie et de l'amour*, are available in an edition by Bernard Jourdan (1953) and in the critical works by Guillot and Giudici mentioned below.

The standard edition of Du Bellay's poetry is that of H. Chamard in 6 volumes (1908–31). Chamard also edited the *Deffence et Illustration de la Langue Francoyse* (1948). There are several other useful editions of the *Regrets* and *Antiquités de Rome*, the most recent being that of M. A. Screech (1965).

Criticism. Dorothy O'Connor, *Louise Labé, sa vie et son œuvre* (1926), Enzo Giudici, *I Tempi, la vita, l'opera et la fortuna di Louise Labé* (1955), and Gérard Guillot, *Louise Labé* (Écrivains d'hier et d'aujourd'hui, 10, 1962) provide a useful introduction. L. E. Harvey, *The Aesthetics of the Renaissance Love Sonnet* (1962) offers rather complex and technical textual analysis.

V.-L. Saulnier, *Du Bellay* (1951), J. Vianey, *Les 'Regrets' de J. Du Bellay* (2nd ed., 1946), and F. Boyer, *Du Bellay* (Écrivains d'hier et d'aujourd'hui, 3, 1958) all contain useful material. From the critical point of view the detailed treatment of Du Bellay in H. Weber, *La Création poétique au XVIᵉ siècle en France* (vol. i, 1956), is superior to that in Chamard's classic four volume *Histoire de la Pléiade* (1939–40). For historical background see G. Dickinson, *Du Bellay in Rome* (1960). J. Vianey, *Le Pétrarchisme en France* (1909) is still an important general study, though its references to Louise Labé are now inadequate and out of date.

8. Ronsard

NEITHER Ronsard nor his contemporaries were in any doubt as to his extraordinary powers as a poet;[1] kings and courtiers, poets, painters, and scholars were all agreed not only that this Prince of Poets was the 'Grand Démon' of French poetry, as Nicolas Rapin called him, but also that he deserved the royal title 'Phébus des Français'. For the warrior-king Henri II Ronsard's poetry was as necessary as food; for Charles IX, lover of poetry and music, Ronsard was indispensable. Mary Queen of Scots sent him presents, Queen Elizabeth I gave him diamonds, and Margaret, Duchess of Savoy foretold that his work would be read in every country where the French language is held in esteem.

Such, indeed, was Ronsard's reputation that he stands for the sixteenth century as the embodiment of their 'ideal' poet, more than fulfilling all the giant claims made for French poetry by Du Bellay in *La Deffense et Illustration de la Langue Francoyse* (1549)—a manifesto calling upon poets to enrich and renew the French language by an inspired imitation of Greek, Latin, and Italian models. Having abandoned a diplomatic career at the age of twenty, Ronsard had devoted himself to study with a curiosity almost unparalleled even for the Renaissance. With apparent ease, he quickly mastered the intricacies of the Greek and Latin languages, enthusiastically imitated their style, form, and matter, and triumphantly presented the fruit of his knowledge and his art in his first four books of *Odes* (1550).

This publication was well timed. The public waited on such a work, since the virtues and splendours of Greek and Latin poets had

---

[1] A discussion of Ronsard's contribution to the literature of the Court will be found in Chapter 5.

long been sung—some of their works had even been translated—
but never had their myths been explored with profit in French. In
his *Odes* Ronsard immediately satisfied many learned hopes, and in
some ways he sets the pattern for his future career. At once, he
gained the unbounded admiration of the humanists who delighted in
the display of erudition they found. He earned the praises of fellow
poets who appreciated the skill with which the form of the ode was
handled, and recognized the newness not only of Ronsard's intentions, but also of his performance. Some envied his obvious facility
and criticized his ostentatious learning, but it was his very success
that had awakened their opposition. Such immediacy of impact as
that of the *Odes* on the public of 1550 placed Ronsard on a pedestal
high above poets like Baïf, Jodelle, and Belleau—even above Du
Bellay, who shared the same aims but lacked the 'master's' voice and
prolific gifts. With little hesitation they recognized his exalted
position and were willing to become his disciples rather than his
peers or his rivals.

The *Odes* not only assured Ronsard a personal triumph; they
established, once and for all, the noble status of the poet in the world.
Endowed with heavenly gifts, the poet was henceforth to provide
more than songs of love or amusements for princes; he was a
prophet of God, the interpreter of Nature, a doctor whose words
have power to heal and to understand the dictates of the stars. He
was also the worthy guide and recorder of royal deeds. In short,
poetry was 'le langage des Dieux'; it was a kind of magic, a means of
communication with the innermost secrets of nature, with 'la vérité
des choses'. Such grand notions on the power of poetry and the
extraordinary role of the poet in the world had often been expressed
by commentators of Plato such as Ficino in Italy or Louis Le Caron
in France (*Dialogues philosophiques*, 1545). Ronsard was the first
French poet to demonstrate them clearly in his verse. It is in the
longest and most celebrated of his early poems, 'Ode à Michel de
l'Hôpital' (1550), that Ronsard for the first of innumerable times
outlines his own poetic ambitions. Free from all misgivings as to the
lasting power of his 'chansons immortelles', he allows the Muse of
epic poetry—Calliope—to express his hopes and intentions. His
words are seen as a voice from God discovering the beauties of

Nature for people less privileged who cannot otherwise understand.
He imagines their humble lives transformed by his poetic revelations
which have

> ...la puissance
> D'arracher les âmes dehors
> Le sale bourbier de leurs corps,
> Pour les rejoindre à leur naissance.

Not only humble folk, but kings too, will be moved to glorious deeds
by the power of his words. In them they will see reflected, as in a
mirror, the morals of good kingship, accounts of virtuous princely
deeds, counsel for present dangers, and prophecies of future events.
Already he seems to foresee the scope of future enterprises, such as
his two books of *Hymnes* (1555–6) which were to break new ground
in poetry, giving sustained lyrical expression to moral and philosophical themes: thoughts on death, justice, and eternity, for
example. Already in 1550 he prepares us for the detailed political
preoccupations of his *Discours sur les misères de ce temps* (1562),
where, provoked by the disorders of the Wars of Religion, he
ardently and eloquently argues the Catholic cause against the violence
of Protestant attacks. Such emotional involvement in the political
and religious events of his time as he shows in these *Discours* must
naturally have directed his thoughts towards other means of defend-
ing and supporting his monarch. Meditations upon this problem
eventually led him to the composition of an epic poem, *La Franciade*,
conceived in 'une extresme envie d'honorer la maison de France, et
par surtout le Roy Charles neufiesme mon Prince'. The first four
books of this ambitious work were published in 1572, and Ronsard
obviously expected to hear again the compliments of Nicolas Filleul:
'On revoit un Virgile, un Homère, un Horace', or Pasquier: 'en
imitant les anciens il les a ou surmontés ou pour le moins égalés'.
He was disappointed in his expectations. Neither the king nor his
contemporaries were sufficiently forthcoming as far as money and
praise were concerned, and Ronsard reluctantly abandoned all hope of
rivalling and surpassing the epic achievements of Homer and Virgil.

Disillusions of this kind must have been far from his thoughts in
1550, when we find Ronsard easily intoxicated by his new-found

knowledge. Myths proliferate, particularly in his early writing, but these are not mere displays of needless erudition as some envious contemporaries implied. They are frequently his most powerful means of expression. In an early sonnet of his first cycle of love poems, *Les Amours de Cassandre* (1552)—'Je vouldroy bien richement jaunissant...'—Ronsard tells of his passionate desire to make love to his mistress. In order to convey the urgency of his passion, he has recourse to certain well-known stories from antiquity: Jupiter's various transformations to seduce Leda and Europa— a shower of gold, a white bull—and Narcissus' impassioned love of his own image. Ronsard modifies this last story to suit his purpose: Narcissus does not pine away from the contemplation of his own beauty in the waters of a fountain: the fountain becomes the image of his mistress which draws him slowly, but irrevocably, towards her, almost describing the very act of love. Thus Ronsard's choice of myth gives an air of nobility to his desires, it keeps their urgency intact (an urgency not only suggested by the content of the myth but perhaps also evoked by the speed of the decasyllabic line and the repetition of 'Je vouldroy'), and yet hides the whole under a decorous veil:

> Je vouldroy bien richement jaunissant
> En pluye d'or goutte à goutte descendre
> Dans le sein de ma belle Cassandre,
> Lors qu'en ses yeulx le somme va glissant.
>
> Je vouldroy bien en toreau blandissant
> Me transformer pour finement la prendre,
> Quand elle va par l'herbe la plus tendre
> Seule à l'escart mille fleurs ravissant.
>
> Je vouldroy bien afin d'aiser ma peine
> Estre un Narcisse, et elle une fontaine
> Pour m'y plonger une nuit à sejour:
>
> Et vouldroy bien que ceste nuict encore
> Durast tousjours sans que jamais l'Aurore
> D'un front nouveau nous r'allumast le jour.

Myth has other ways of enhancing the value of poetry, since it prefigured Christian truth and was thought to provide the most effective means of bringing together pagan and Christian belief.

Such an attempted fusion was often the express aim of Ronsard and his contemporaries; one has only to look at the title of his poem, 'L'Hercule Chrétien' (1555), for example, or study 'L'Hymne de la Mort' (1555), which mingles stories of Hesiod and Homer, illustrations from Virgil, and Platonic inspiration with the religious sentiments of a convinced Christian aware of the richness of life, of the inevitability of death, and of the need to remind himself and others that 'ton âme n'est pas païenne, mais chrétienne'.

The range of Ronsard's ambitions and his discoveries gave him success in every sphere of poetic endeavour outside dramatic poetry. 'Jamais Poète n'écrivit tant comme lui', exclaimed Pasquier, and Ronsard himself wrote in *Le Bocage Royal* (1554): 'Entre tous les Français, j'ai seul, le plus écrit.' It would be difficult to overplay the variety of his poetic invention, to ignore the diversity of forms used from the playful, ingenious early *Odes* and *Gayetés*, the tightly controlled sonnets and expanded elegies of the love cycles, to the long, sustained discourse of the *Hymnes*, the *Discours*, and *La Franciade*. 'Cette âme universellement née pour la poésie', as the Cardinal du Perron described him in a sincere and eloquent funeral oration, perfected poems to delight the courtier and his mistress, poems which combined the lightness of touch of the old medieval lyrics with the elegance of Petrarch. Great simplicity and spontaneity is the impression created by lines such as:

> Mignonne, allons voir si la rose
> Qui ce matin avoit déclose
> Sa robe de pourpre au Soleil...

where Ronsard's immediate and direct appeal to his mistress holds the tone of the poem on a light, conversational note. Yet this illustrates only one of Ronsard's many poetic styles. They range from such lyrical and often playful naturalness—a tone inherited from Marot—through impassioned denunciation to the studied grandiloquence of *La Franciade*. A typical piece of invective is the following passage:

> Ne vois-tu que le Pape est trop enflé de Biens!
> Comme il presse soubs soy les Princes terriens!
> Et comme son Église est toute depravée
> D'ambition, de gloire, et d'honneur abreuvée!

Ne vois-tu ses suppots paresseux et poussifs,
Découpez, parfumez, delicats et lascifs,
Fauconniers et veneurs, qui occupent et tiennent
Les biens qui justement aux pauvres appartiennent,
Sans prescher, sans prier, sans garder le troupeau,
Dont ils tirent la gresse, et dechirent la peau?
('Rémonstrance au peuple de France', ll. 277–86)

In all these multiple aspects Ronsard is as convinced as his contemporaries that he had renewed the power of poetry by inventing new forms, diversifying his style, and discovering new themes. It was as an innovator that Ronsard made his principal claim to glory:

... tout le premier je suis
Qui de Grèce ai conduit les Muses en la France
Et premier mesuré leurs pas à ma cadence...
Je fis des mots nouveaux, je restaurai les vieux...
('Discours contre Fortune')

He had made such a claim in the very first publication of the *Odes* where, in the preface, he assured his reader that 'quand tu m'appeleras le premier auteur lyrique français... lors tu me rendras ce que tu me dois'. It was also as innovator that he fulfilled the demands made by Du Bellay's manifesto; and this is the side of Ronsard which did, and still does, fascinate the literary historian. Yet a complete artist, so thoroughly embodying all the poetic ideals of his age, inevitably suffers by being discussed as a representative of his time. It is true that he needs to be shown standing out against his background so that one may appreciate the scope of his achievement, that one may see the public image which aroused such admiration and emulation on the part of his contemporaries. And without doubt it was his own powers of innovation and his ability to master all aspects of the art of poetry which persuaded Ronsard that he would live 'à tout jamais, de siècle en siècle'. Nevertheless, for a lover of poetry living in the twentieth century, it is debatable whether this is really the aspect of Ronsard which has most interest. One wants to ask: are there signs in his poetry, constants which mark him out not as a national hero who writes what he is expected to write, who never forgets that 'il a en notre langue représenté Homère, Pindare, Théocrite, Virgile, Catulle, Horace, Pétrarque' (Pasquier), but which show him as a private individual who enjoys certain experiences and wants to write about them?

It is probable, of course, that Ronsard never forgot the Ancient and Italian authors he had read and admired, and here again he reveals himself a true product of the Renaissance, whose writers, artists, and scholars knew they would be judged by how near their work came to being a perfect imitation of earlier Greek or Latin achievements. It seems to me, however, that Ronsard's best poems are precisely those where he gives the impression of having forgotten that he imitates, and leaves us with a feeling that he is conveying his own thoughts and emotions, authentically felt.

As soon as we try to record what these thoughts and feelings are outside their historical context, we are immediately drawn back into the sixteenth century by the discovery that there is nothing spectacularly different in the themes Ronsard chooses to write about in his poetry from those conventional themes of Nature, Love, Death, and Transience of Life which had currency throughout Europe at that period. If one examines the detailed elements of style which Ronsard elects to give to his own version of these themes, inevitably again one finds a use of the same images (the rose, the sun, the stars, jewels, the seasons, classical myths, and so on), gleaned from the same common source by all poets. How then can one define Ronsard's individuality? It can be said that it lies in Ronsard's particular handling of an image or a theme, but I feel we need to go beyond these to find a basic attitude in Ronsard of which he might or might not have been fully aware, which informs the whole of his poetry and makes this work characteristic of Ronsard alone.

Nature in all its aspects was a constant source of inspiration and even consolation for Ronsard. It provided him with a dynamic world which could match his every change of mood, which could set his imagination to work and offer an inexhaustible supply of material upon which to reflect:

> Je n'avois pas quinze ans que les mons et les boys
> Et les eaux me plaisoient, plus que la Court des Roys,
> Et les noires forests en feuillages voutées,
> Et du bec des oiseaux les roches picotées...
>
>   ('Hymne de l'Automne')

Ronsard responds with deep perceptiveness to the vitality of Nature, the life which animates the woods and the flowers reborn every year. The natural world in which he lives is never still or silent. Even on a hot summer's day as he lies in languid ease 'sous l'ombrage auprès d'une fontaine', the scene about him suddenly becomes peopled with Nymphs and Dryads, creatures playing and dancing in the sunlight. The world we watch through Ronsard's verse seems an unreal one, a world of happy make-believe and of romance, where the trees and flowers are taller and more beautiful, and their existence more privileged, than ours, their vigour and their beauty constantly renewed by the advent of spring:

> Ja les forests ont pris leurs robbes neuves,
> Et moins enflés glissent aval les fleuves,
> Hastés de voir Thetys qui les attent...
> ('Avantentrée du Roi', ll. 49–51)

His vision of the calm beauty of the Loire on which he longs to ride with his mistress is filled with the gaiety of water-nymphs who gently and playfully rock his boat along:

> Que les bords soient semez de mille belles fleurs
> Representant sur l'eau mille belles couleurs,
> Et le tropeau gaillard des gentiles Nayades
> Alentour du vaisseau face mille gambades,
> Les unes balloyant des paumes de leurs mains
> Les flots devant la barque, et les autres leurs seins
> Descouvrant a fleur d'eau, et d'une main ouvriere
> Conduisant le bateau du long de la riviere...
> ('Le Voyage de Tours', ll. 207–14)

beings which live in water, presented to us as vividly as those which can still be seen adorning the walls of the Château de Fontainebleau:

> Les autres moins terrains, sont à-part habitans
> Torrens, fleuves, ruisseaux, les lacz et les estangs,
> Les marrais endormis, et les fonteines vives,
> Or'paroissant sur l'eau et ores sur les rives:
> Tant que les aërins ilz n'ont d'affections,
> Aussi leur çorps ne prend tant de mutations,

Ils n'ayment qu'une forme et voluntiers icelle
Est du nombril en haut d'une jeune pucelle
Qui a les cheveux longs, et les yeux vertz et beaux,
Contre-imitans l'azur de leurs propres ruisseaux.
                        ('Hymne des Daimons', ll. 261–70)

Such a view of the world explains the grief which Ronsard felt when
his beloved forest of Gâtine was threatened with destruction:

Ecoute, Bûcheron! arreste un peu le bras!
Ce ne sont pas des bois que tu jettes à bas;
Ne vois-tu pas le sang lequel degoutte à force
Des nymphes qui vivoient dessous la dure écorce?
        ('Élégie, contre les Bûcherons de la Forêt de Gâtine')

In Ronsard's eyes the wood-cutters deserve the most frightful death
for such an act of sacrilege. The forest is a place of refuge for certain
beauties of life and Ronsard particularly regrets their loss:

Forest, haute maison des oiseaux bocagers,
Plus le cerf solitaire et les chevreuils légers
Ne paistront sous ton ombre, et ta verte crinière
Plus du Soleil d'esté ne rompra la lumière.

He chides himself for having placed such confidence in the perman-
ence of Nature's gifts, reminding us 'Que l'homme est malheureux
qui au monde se fie!' Yet such a solemn note of Christian truth
hardly makes up for the loss of the Forêt de Gâtine. True consolation can only be positively found in the final reflection: 'La matière
demeure et la forme se perd', which restates the vital power of renewal which constantly draws Ronsard's affections towards Nature,
and which also, incidentally, ends the poem on a neat maxim—
a stylistic means of distilling truth, particularly appreciated by an
age which firmly believed in the moral worth of literature.

   This destruction of a beautiful, vigorous, shady forest, full of life,
is presented by Ronsard as a personal and physical loss. One might
ask why *such* a display of personal grief? Is this merely a means of
persuasion used by the poet to convince us that an outrageous act
has indeed been committed? Or is it that Ronsard really does feel
human affection for beings which only his imagination can see living

in the forms of nature? Or rather, as I think, is it not a way of showing the living beauty of the forest, of making us appreciate the divine spectacle we are deprived of once the forest is destroyed? The fact that Ronsard seeks to arrest the arm of the wood-cutter in the very act of destruction gives added power to the forest's beauty, which seems never more attractive than at that moment before it disappears. Ronsard's acute appreciation of beauty is at the heart of his emotion and his comments in this poem. This is, I think, that basic attitude which is present in all his best poems. His sense of beauty, his ability to catch at its fragility, its variety, and its vitality, and to record it in the lines of a poem, is his most enduring achievement.

The beauty of the rose is a commonplace of Renaissance literature. Ronsard forces us to look at it anew when he links its sweet flowering, its moment of glory picked out against a clear blue sky, its swift and silent fading, with the same phases in the life of his beautiful Marie. It is important to see that Ronsard is primarily concerned— in the very celebrated sonnet 'Comme on voit sur la branche au mois de mai la rose...'—with Marie's beauty, with the need to create for himself and us a permanent thing of beauty which cannot be touched by the laws of death. Marie's death was the starting-point for the poem, but her earthly beauty is what Ronsard preserves for eternity.

Vision, the power to see and appreciate the beauty of what is perceived, sets Ronsard's imagination alight, arouses and explains the nature of his emotion which, however physically it is expressed, seems somehow to be held afar off. Ronsard seems to be able to detach himself from what he feels, able to examine and explain his emotions almost as though they belonged to somebody else. Also, he chooses to present those uncomplicated feelings which we have all experienced and which demand no deep heart-searching, no profound analysis, only simple and direct evocation. This impression of apparent detachment might well be a result of Ronsard's almost total reliance on vision and expression through imagery. In the sonnet 'Le soir qu'Amour vous fist en la salle descendre', his affections for Hélène have been engaged and he seeks to project his sense of her beauty which acquires divine aspects as he describes the beautiful movement of her winding dance:

> Le ballet fut divin, qui se souloit reprendre,
> Se rompre, se refaire, et tout dessus retour
> Se mesler s'escarter, se tourner à l'entour,
> Contre-imitant le cours du fleuve de Meandre.

A flowing, seductive grace is mirrored in this long sentence which twists its way back and forth. Moreover, Ronsard wishes us to have a precise picture of the nature of the dance, and he describes the pattern meticulously:

> Ores il estoit rond, ores long, or estroit
> Or en pointe, en triangle...

Then, suddenly, Hélène's feet take flight, and the poet's own sense of surprise carries his vision of her beautiful dancing body heavenwards, and Hélène assumes a form of divine beauty:

> Je faux, tu ne dansois, mais ton pied voletoit
> Sur le haut de la terre: aussi ton corps s'estoit
> Transformé pour ce soir en divine nature.

Of course, it was the sight of the beautiful woman which was the starting-point of the neoplatonic view of love which Maurice Scève had explored in his *Délie* and which had inspired many poets, including Ronsard. Nevertheless, even in those poems where Ronsard seems closest to a neoplatonic interpretation of love, such as 'Si seulement l'image de la chose' (*Amours de Cassandre*), he does not push the theory very far. He simply uses the notion that the earthly beauty of a woman is a reflection of an ideal beauty, in order to intensify the impression of the beauty of his mistress here and now. Again and again in his love poems Ronsard dwells on the external delights of a beautiful woman, and is content to leave us with an image of physical perfection, only hinting at the twinges of desire which colour the poem with light sensuality. Cassandre's hair, as she dresses in the morning, tantalizingly hides the beauties of her form, just as Venus modestly covered her perfections as she rose on a shell out of the sea (*Amours*, xlii). Another time Ronsard catches sight of her:

> Dedans des Prez, je vis une Dryade
> Qui comme fleur s'assisoyt par les fleurs...

Cassandre is thus the focal point of a scene. Once more his love has turned into a flower, an embodiment of beauty to be admired and contemplated from afar.

There is always a nobility about Ronsard's vision of beauty and of Nature. There is a warmth and a freshness which preserves them from decay. Rarely do the cold of winter, the fierce aspects of storm, the wild or arid parts of Nature encroach upon his poetry. These are reserved for the picture of the world out of joint which he paints with so much passion in the *Discours*, precisely because he is aware how opposed this view is to the noble, civilized painting he wants to leave with us. Like all representations of beauty in the Renaissance, Ronsard's view of Nature is also very formalized. There is none of the untidiness of a 'jardin anglais' in his vision. He orders the scene, unconsciously beautifies the elements of Nature, and arranges them into a pattern. Even the vast trees of the forest of Gâtine are seen in their mass, as a tall comforting roof to house its teeming life. The flowers of his garden all have their assigned places, given by the hand of the artist. This formal nobility has never been more perfectly rendered than in his poem written on the departure of Mary Queen of Scots from France. It opens with a statement of intention to record the portrait of her beauty in the pages of his book:

> Bien que le trait de vostre belle face
> Peinte en mon cœur par le temps ne s'efface,
> Et que tousjours je le porte imprimé
> Comme un tableau vivement animé:
> J'ay toutesfois pour la chose plus rare
> (Dont mon estude et mes livres je pare)
> Vostre portrait qui fait honneur au lieu,
> Comme un image au temple d'un grand Dieu.

The queen is dressed in all the white simplicity of royal mourning.

As she stands erect on the deck of the ship which sails away with her from France the wind catches at her garments, and blows them gently out like the sails of the ship in which she rides. This moment of sad, quiet beauty reminds Ronsard of the queen in a different setting, in the gardens of the Château of Fontainebleau:

> Lors les rochers, bien qu'ils n'eussent point d'âme,
> Voyant marcher une si belle Dame,
> Et les deserts, les sablons, et l'estang,
> Et maint beau Cygne, habillé tout de blanc,
> Et des hauts Pins la cime de vert peinte
> Vous contemploient comme une chose sainte,
> Et pensoient voir (pour ne voir rien de tel)
> Une Déesse en habit d'un mortel
> Se pourmener, quand l'Aurore estoit née,
> Par ces jardins cueillant la matinée,
> Et vers le soir, quand désjà le Soleil
> A chef baissé s'en alloit au Sommeil.

The presence of Queen Mary walking in the palace gardens at dawn and at the fall of night has imposed respect upon the elements of Nature. Hushed and silent they seem to feel and share in her regret. They know that a personage more than worthy of their formal splendour walks among them.

It was not always possible for Ronsard to sustain a picture for very long in some of his more extended poems. Even in this poem where a single figure is a point of departure and return, there is a long middle section of dialogue with Charles IX of France which seems to limp along after the calm and beauty of the opening evocative passages. His *Hymnes* are often constructed on a series of extended images, each one seeming to unfold out of the previous image, a little regardless of the argument of the poem, as though Ronsard has no control over the bounds of his imagination. His 'Hymne de l'Éternité', for example, after its grand, epic, ambitious beginning:

> Je veux plein de fureur, suivant les pas d'Orphée,
> Rechercher les Secrets de la Nature et des Cieux...

is then built up by a near catalogue of personifications which describe eternity's empire. It is important, however, not to condemn out of hand poetic structures which do not measure up to our own strict rules. We have been brought up to distrust rhetoric, even to erect barriers between ourselves and the power of persuasion of the poets. At one and the same time we question the validity of their art and fear the force of their magic. We have become slaves to the pithy saying, willingly giving our admiration to thoughts well condensed, to density of structures, and we are thus impatient of forms of art which build up their effects slowly. Such twentieth-century prejudice has no doubt prevented us from assessing the beauties of *Les Hymnes des Saisons*, so justly appreciated by Ronsard's contemporaries. He himself said that he would have preferred some of the *Élégies* to be shorter, but that his readers demanded lengthy works. The *Hymnes* are long, expanded descriptions of the beauties of Nature at all stages of growth, stressing her dynamism and ever-renewed vitality. 'L'Hymne de l'Automne' brings the whole sequence together in so far as it opens with a long elaboration on the purpose of poetry, on the nature of the poet, and on the need to be worthy of divine inspiration, which reveals the secret workings of Nature—workings that only the prophet Ronsard can interpret. After many such deep reflections, Ronsard finally announces:

> Je te donne
> Pour present immortel l'Hymne de cet Automne.

Thus the poem is offered as a conscious act of revelation, an imparting of truths about the workings of the universe, and it is not surprising therefore that Autumn is presented as a beautiful young woman who only gradually discovers what she is and who her parents are. To gain this knowledge she sets off on a journey of exploration, glimpses her father—the Sun—who recoils from his daughter and disappears in haste. She visits her brother, the Spring, in his balmy palace. Not finding him she calls in on the Summer palace and sees an abundance of crops enjoyed by the goddess Ceres. From there she wanders to the most magnificent seat of all, 'Le Palais superbe où Nature habitait'. Only here does she find out about herself. Appalled at the ravages she must commit upon

Nature, Autumn turns away to see the triumphant Chariot of Bacchus approaching. They fall in love and Autumn's destiny is fulfilled. In spite of Ronsard's assertions at the beginning of the poem, the charm of this anecdotal work does not, of course, lie in the revealing of truths. It is to be found in the sense of the beautiful and of the richness of Nature which Ronsard communicates through his descriptions of the various palaces; such descriptions provide the main structural fabric of, and perhaps the excuse for, his poem. In an atmosphere of 'Volupté, gentillesse, amour et gaillardise', Ronsard sets out the noisy garden of Spring:

> Les pins et les cypres y voisinent les Cieux,
> Et le Cedre embasmé d'un flair délicieux:
> Les Rossignols logés dans les boys y jargonnent,
> Par les jardins carrés les fontaines resonnent,
> Qui arrosent le pied des pommeux orangers,
> Et des myrthes sacrés qui nous sont estrangers.

The deliberately constructed formal garden is thus described in a very general way; and it is precisely the absence of any concentration on particular detail which allows Ronsard to create over all a mysterious atmosphere. We sense an existence beyond our ken, finally confirmed by the presence of the strange myrtle trees which belong to the realm of the gods. In this *Hymne*, whatever Ronsard says he is doing, he has created a framework in which he can indulge the feelings of joy he experiences whenever he contemplates the grand spectacle of the beauties of Nature grown to maturity.

Even in the last years of his life his constant preoccupation with beauty as it is manifested in Nature and in Woman remains firm. His desire to feel the delights of beauty are, in fact, more strongly expressed at this time when his own physical frame is obviously weakened. The elegy on the Forêt de Gâtine comes from this period, and the sonnet addressed to Hélène: 'Vous triomphez de moi', which recalls the fervour and strength of the early Cassandre poem: 'Je vouldroy bien richement jaunissant'. On this occasion Ronsard has chosen a conventional theme from Nature—the climbing ivy— to describe the urgency of his desires, which are mingled here with a confidence in his own immortality. Hence in a lordly way he can continue his poem:

> Vous triomphez de moy et pource je vous donne
> Ce lierre, qui coule et se glisse à l'entour
> Des arbres et des murs, lesquels tour dessus tour,
> Plis dessus plis il serre, embrasse et environne.

The insinuating, clinging nature of the ivy is deliberately stressed to parallel the vain stretching of the poet's wants. Yet all the time the ivy grasps not a warm, yielding body, but the cold beauty of a marble form:

> Je voudrois, comme il fait, de nuit et de jour
> Me plier contre vous, et languissant d'amour,
> D'un nœud ferme enlacer vostre belle colonne.

The sensuality of the poem has thus been checked by the poet's knowledge of the cold beauty of his mistress, and immediately the picture he is creating recedes from us and we see only the curling of the plant relieved of its emotional overtones. Ronsard remembers this picture in one of his last poems: 'Élégie à Candé', where memories of natural beauty give him his greatest consolation as he waits for a Christian death:

> Regarde ce bocage, et vois d'une autre part
> Les bras longs et tortus du lierre grimpart
> En serpent se virer à l'entour de l'écorce
> De ce chêne aux longs bras, et le baiser de force.

Desire has now disappeared altogether; the ivy is presented to us as something pleasurable to look at, and yet a lingering thought of love remains in the choice of the verb 'baiser'.

The starkness of many of Ronsard's final exclamations acquire an extra grim dimension when we remember that they are uttered after a lifetime of worship of beauty. It is no gentle comfort or compliment for Hélène to be abruptly told: 'Vous serez au foyer une vieille accroupie'. 'Vous êtes déjà vieille, et je le suis aussi', he asserts in another place, with all the terrible recognition of old age creeping over him, blurring his desires and his vision. He can yet remember beauty, seen in all its variety, treasured both for its abundance and its transience, presented as a product and a source of love and aesthetic joy—a vision which commands our continuing admiration and regard. Perhaps the Cardinal du Perron was thinking of this particular achievement as well as of Ronsard's many-sided genius when he concluded his friend's funeral oration with these wise and prophetic words: 'Il vivra, il sera lu, il fleurira, il se conservera dans la pensée, et dans la souvenance des hommes, tant que la langue française aura quelque cours et quelque son parmi les nations étrangères, tant que les lettres seront en estime, et en reverence, et bref, tant qu'il y aura des hommes qui voudront jetter les yeux sur les actes de leurs dévanciers.'

NOTE

PIERRE DE RONSARD, 1524–85, first studied at the Collège de Navarre in Paris. In 1536 he became page in the household of François II, and until 1540 played a minor role in various diplomatic missions (Scotland 1537, England 1538, Germany 1540). Suddenly stricken with deafness he abandoned politics for poetry and learning, studying Greek under Jean Dorat, first at the Baïf's house in Paris, later (1547) at the Collège de Coqueret. His fellow pupils included Baïf, Jodelle, and Belleau. Hailed by most of his contemporaries as 'arch-poet of France', he devoted the rest of his life to his own glorification and that of France, being favourite poet of Henri II and Charles IX. His style was not so pleasing to Henri III, but Ronsard still spent some time at Court after his official retirement in 1575. The major part of his last days was passed in the quiet beauty of his native Touraine editing collected editions of his works.

Works. A prolific writer, Ronsard published at least one work every year from 1547 ('Ode à Jacques Peletier') until his death. We note here his most significant works. The first book of *Odes* came out in 1550, and was added to in 1551 and 1552, when he published the first of the cycles of love poems *Les Amours*. 1553 saw the publication of a *Livre de Folastries*, 1554 *Le Bocage* and *Les Meslanges*. The following year, 1555, produced his first set of *Hymnes*, longer and more complex poetry than he had before attempted. The next years were spent adding to these various collections which culminated in 1560 in the first of six collected editions published in Ronsard's lifetime. 1562 produced *Discours sur les misères de ce temps*, 1565 *Élegies, Mascarades et Bergeries*, dedicated to Queen Elizabeth I, and 1572 *La Franciade*, which constitutes Ronsard's last extended work, although he continued to write and revise poems until the very day he died.

Editions. The definitive *Œuvres complètes* published from 1914 to 1959, edited by P. Laumonnier, comprises 17 volumes. These are squeezed into two large

Pléiade volumes, edited by Gustave Cohen (1950). Garnier has a useful *Poèmes choisis*, and a very good complete edition of *Les Amours* by H. and C. Weber (1963). The *Odes* were published in 1952 by Charles Guérin. The complete 'Ode à Michel de L'Hôpital' can be found in A. M. Boase, *Poetry of France 1400–1600* (1964).

Criticism. General studies on Ronsard include P. Champion, *Ronsard et son temps* (1925), an old-fashioned but sound biography. G. Gadoffre, *Ronsard par lui-même* (1960), provides an excellent introduction. H. Chamard, *Histoire de la Pléiade* (1939–40: 4 vols.), deals efficiently with Ronsard's relationship with other poets; P. de Nolhac, *Ronsard et l'humanisme* (1921), remains the best work on the poet's erudition. M. Raymond, author of *L'Influence de Ronsard* (1937: 2 vols.), also writes a penetrating essay on his poetry in *Baroque et renaissance poétique* (1955). H. Weber, *La Création poétique au XVIe siècle* (1956: 2 vols.), sets Ronsard's love poems in the context of other sixteenth-century poetry.

9. Aspects of the Theatre

MENTION the neoclassical theatre of France and subsequent discussion will turn upon Corneille, Racine, and Molière. Such is their stature that other dramatists of the time tend to be ignored. And yet, as Viollet Le Duc asked over a century ago: 'Est-il raisonnable de croire que ceux-ci [i.e. Corneille, Racine, and Molière] ont atteint tout à coup au degré de perfection qui les distingue, sans que les essais des anciens, plus ou moins habiles, leur aient tracé le chemin ?' The path to which he refers was not a long one, and those who trod it numbered some of the most talented poets of the two centuries, the sixteenth and seventeenth. Perhaps it is precisely here, in what they would have considered their strength, that we today find their weakness: that they were above all else poets, men who delighted in words, and who sought to move their hearers by the grace and sublimity of their voice.

This will be borne out particularly in the field of tragedy. The majestic movement and measured cadences of much sixteenth-century tragedy are not always to our modern taste; but we are expecting too much. The fruit requires time to ripen, and tragedy had been cultivated in France for only eighty years before its first undoubted masterpieces, Tristan L'Hermite's *La Mariane* (1636) and Corneille's *Le Cid* (1636), were produced. Nor were these eighty years of steady progress towards what we now call classical tragedy: they were years of trial and error, of rivalry between the regular and the anti-regular, years during which the authority of the critic increased so that ultimately, by the following century, he was able to dictate to the artist.

Such conflicts and rivalries are no doubt indicative of a healthy state of affairs: such speculation is the dialogue of literature with society. But old traditions die hard, especially a tradition reaching back as far as that which divided drama into mystery, morality, and farce: and such, indeed, was very much the way of looking at the theatre at the beginning of the sixteenth century. Little appeared to happen to disturb this view until the mid-point of the century. I say 'appeared to happen' because it is difficult to plot the stages in the development of an idea or outlook until it has shed its hesitancies and will stand in the light. A new approach takes place gradually, whereas we become aware of it suddenly. It was within a traditional form, religious drama, that the first outlines of neoclassical tragedy were to be seen.

In 1549, some three years before Jodelle's *Cléopâtre captive*, Théodore de Bèze (1519-1605) produced a tragedy on a Biblical subject, *Abraham sacrifiant*. Written in the vernacular, it was first staged in Lausanne and published in Geneva (1550). As so often in the sixteenth century, college precincts provided the theatre, and the audience was drawn from amongst the more educated citizens of the region—perhaps not an unmixed blessing for the playwright.

Théodore de Bèze himself was a convert to the Protestant Church, and this becomes apparent as the tragedy pursues its course. For the author, the stage forms part of a higher purpose: it provides a pulpit from which to instruct and exhort, and to ensure that the faithful keep to the straight and narrow path. Its role is therefore complementary to that of the Church, but the Church is, of the two, clearly the more important; it would be deplorable if congregations dwindled, which seems perpetually to be a danger in this world:

> Que pleust à Dieu que toutes les sepmaines
> Nous peussions voir les églises si pleines.

Few have so strong a faith that it stands in no need of support; it is subject to the strains which life necessarily generates, as even Abraham finds:

> En cest endroit vous le verrez tenté,
> Et jusqu'au vif attaint & tourmenté.
> Vous le verrez par foy iustifié:
> Son fils Isaac quasi sacrifié.

> Bref, vous verrez estranges passions,
> La chair, le monde, & ses affections
> Non seulement au vif representées,
> Mais qui plus est, par la foy surmontées.

Abraham comes through his doubts; Satan is vanquished; and salvation seems there to be plucked like a ripe fruit for all whose belief and trust in God are equal to the burdens which the times may bring. For these *were* troublous times. All could see

> Les grans abus esquels nous voyons estre
> Le povre monde, hélas, tant perverty.

Montaigne later painted the same sombre picture of the society in which he was living, when discontent, doubt, and hatred expressed themselves in the violence of civil war as well as in the stealth and fear of nocturnal murder. And the deep rift within the Christian Church itself adds fuel to the flames. Naturally enough, Théodore de Bèze cannot refrain from making propaganda out of his play: he paints Satan 'en habit de moyne', and from time to time he alludes to the struggle between Protestant and Catholic.

It is only too easy for us to overlook the fact that sixteenth-century tragedy does reflect some of the most important aspects of contemporary life; the frequently slow, measured tread of the poetry may well disguise the urgency of the problems to be found there. But any work of art maps the contours of its creator's mind, a mind subject to the strains and pressures of its environment; and to survey the panorama of these tragedies is to become aware that their themes are in the main of two kinds, religious and political. Both themes, clearly, bear upon society. The tragedy distilled from such ingredients looked to the clash of personalities and the conflict of creeds for its strength: Mark Antony, Julius Caesar, Pompey. It left aside the Phèdres of this world, for it was extrovert rather than introvert. The torment of a soul divided within itself—perhaps the deepest and most disturbing tragedy—was not for such writers.

The trilogy of Louis Des Masures (1515–c. 1574), *David combattant*, *David triomphant*, and *David fugitif*, gives the same impression: the theatre at the disposal of religion; not surprisingly, since, like de Bèze, Des Masures was a proselyte. He was not a dramatist born, but he *was* a writer; he was not the equal of de Bèze, who may not have been outstanding as a dramatist, but certainly had an ear for dialogue and a shrewd, penetrating eye for human behaviour and weakness.

We know, of course, how all these plays will end: the Devil will be vanquished, and Abraham and David will have their reward, especially Abraham. All's well that ends well; but it is not really tragedy. Indeed it is the reverse of tragic, if we are to accept what Aristotle said; and the contemporaries of Des Masures and Théodore de Bèze certainly would accept Aristotelian pronouncements. Aristotle, Horace, and Donatus, these are the trinity in matters of drama and theory. As the century rolls on, the stream of criticism swells. Italian commentators such as Castelvetro did, in fact, embroider pages of explanation, elaborate, sometimes perceptive, frequently highly speculative. French theorists, Scaliger, for example, added their voice. And each page tended to distort the ancient wisdom a little more. Contemporary social promptings begin to assert themselves, and theorist as well as dramatist sees tragedy in terms of the violence, the cruelty, and the despair of the times: 'res tragicae grandes, atroces, iussa regum, caedes, desperationes, suspendia, exilia, orbitates, parricidia, incestus, incendia, pugnae, occaecationes, fletus, ululatus, conquaestiones, funera, epitaphia, epicedia.'[1] The words are those of Scaliger (1484–1558) in his *Poetices libri septem.* The whole attitude is most concisely summed up in the formula of Pierre de Laudun (1575–1629): 'Plus les tragédies sont cruelles, plus elles sont excellentes.' In this, as in many ways, Pierre de Laudun is echoing Scaliger; and a world of difference lies between such an approach to tragedy and the reflections of Aristotle. It would, however, be expecting the impossible if we looked for little change over some two thousand years. Even Jean de la Taille (*c.* 1540–1608), who is nearer to the classical ideals in his outlook on tragedy than were many of his contemporaries, is none the less a child of his own times.

---

[1] 'The matter of tragedy is lofty and violent—commands of kings, murder, acts of despair, hangings, exile, bereavement, parricide, incest, arson, fighting, blinding, weeping, wailing, lamentation, death, elegies, and dirges.'

If the theorists as a whole show a tendency to depart from the intentions of Aristotle, they seem to be confirmed in their position by Seneca, author of the only Latin tragedies to be handed down to posterity. It was inevitable, therefore, that these plays should exercise some influence upon the tragic poets of the Renaissance, and in many respects this influence is regrettable. If only more translations of the Greek tragic poets had existed they might have succeeded in counteracting the Senecan hold. As it was, however, Seneca was the model whom they more or less had to follow; and Seneca chose from amongst the Greek myths and legends some of the most appalling stories to be found there. He seems to have delighted in violence and suffering and cruelty: the banquet of Thyestes, the murder of Agamemnon, the madness of Hercules, the rage of Phaedra, the fury of Medea. Horror takes the place of terror in the Senecan aesthetic, as La Mesnardière was to recall with sorrow in the seventeenth century. The stage reeks of blood, and the characters paint their suffering in full, lurid colours. This, of course, calls forth the art of the poet in conveying their distress and the depth of their emotion, and this gives Seneca scope to indulge his undoubted gifts for high poetry as well as for rhetorical effusion. But it holds up the action; indeed, these practices lead to the stagnation of drama.

And here we touch sixteenth-century tragedy on a tender spot; for many of the plays which were written then do seem to us slow-moving. In fact some of them appear to be almost devoid of movement. *Cléopâtre captive* (1552) is such a tragedy. Jodelle (1532–73) in writing it—and it was the first regular classical tragedy—reduced the story to the few hours immediately around the moment of her death, and in doing so, he restricted the action to that one event. The rest is discussion and decision. Such a conception of tragedy may lead naturally into the Unities and so on of the following century, but it does bring the action to a desperate state, to the point of vanishing before it really begins.

It would be difficult to imagine anything less dramatic than this sort of treatment. Indeed, what Jodelle has done is to reduce tragedy to a form of elegy; lamentation and regrets are the staple of this play rather than psychological analysis and consequential action. The poetry is what matters, and Jodelle was certainly gifted with a poetic pen. Love may not have found in him a profound analyst, but it has found a sympathetic interpreter, as in Cléopâtre's final speech:

> Antoine, ô cher Antoine, Antoine ma moitié,
> Si Antoine n'eust eu des cieux l'inimitié,
> Antoine, Antoine, hélas! dont le malheur me prive,
> Entens la foible voix d'une foible captive,
> Qui de ses propres mains avoit la cendre mise
> Au clos de ce tombeau n'estant encore prise:
> Mais qui prise et captive à son malheur guidée,
> Suiette et prisonniere en sa ville gardee,
> Ore te sacrifie, et non sans quelque crainte
> De faire trop durer en ce lieu ma complainte...

The queen will live no longer: and the final act is devoted to describing her death.

In contrast to Jodelle's tragedy, the *Jules César* (1560) of Grévin (1538–70) *has* some action in it. The story is that of the conspiracy of Brutus and Cassius, which Shakespeare has made so familiar to generations of English audiences. Calpurnia tries to prevent her husband from going to the Senate, and he almost yields to her pleas and fears, for which Decimus Brutus reproaches him:

> ... vous qui avez tenu
> Les guerres par dix ans contre l'audace fière
> D'un barbare étranger, et or' par la prière
> Qu'une femme vous fait, je vous vois surmonté.
> Chose étrange! de voir César qui a dompté
> Les plus braves du monde être serf d'une femme!

And so César goes to the Senate, with the results which we know.

That events take place, then, is evident. Once more, however, as with Jodelle, characters express themselves at length, and this blunts the edge of the drama. The entire first act is devoted to an examination of forms of government, and the whole movement of the play is held up accordingly. But despite this there is some gain for tragedy. Grévin has developed a story; he has tried to explain events rather than simply state them. To this end the dialogue is harnessed: everything works towards a climax in which the event is no shock and the mind is freer to dwell upon the suffering.

It is in very much the same vein that Garnier (*c.* 1545–90) treats his material. He draws at first upon Roman history, as Jodelle and Grévin had done; and he seeks out naturally those events which portray human suffering. *Porcie* (1568) is the story of a woman's anxious wait, in her own home, for news of her family which war keeps on distant shores. The news as it continues to arrive adds blow upon blow to her hopes for the safety of those whom she loves. Much the same is true of Cornélie, eponymous heroine of the tragedy written in 1574: she remains in Rome whilst those whom she depends upon, Pompée and Scipion, are being slowly crushed. Another play, *Marc-Antoine* (1578), treats a familiar tragic pair, Antony and Cleopatra. It recounts the last few hours as they ebb away—bitterly for Antony himself—and culminate in the suicide of the two lovers.

To these plays taken from history, Garnier adds three inspired by Greek mythology: *Hippolyte* (1573), *La Troade* (1579), and *Antigone* (1580). All three are concerned with suffering and the horror which so often accompanies it. Indeed, *La Troade* is a story so full of woe and heartbreak that we may well wonder how the human frame could bear the strain without breaking. Garnier tells here of the women of defeated Troy, who stand, defenceless, awaiting news of the fate in store for them. And the final blow comes to Polyxène who learns that she is to be sacrificed to appease the shade of Achilles.

It is all very harrowing and depressing because so much of the suffering is completely undeserved. Those who suffer in these tragedies—usually the main characters—are victims, hapless, helpless, frequently women. They are caught up in the hatreds that ambition and lust for power so often breed: politics is no arena for the sensitive and the scrupulous. In such a world right and wrong become blurred, but through it all we have the feeling that Garnier's heart is in the right place. He was living through troubles too great to let that lesson go unheeded.

Of course, from the dramatic point of view, the theme of vengeance has its attractions, as the Spanish *comedia* and the English theatre's Revenge Tragedy illustrate. And often vengeance can take courage behind the shield of legality: private hatred can be identified with public welfare, and the despot, construing criticism of any degree as *lèse-majesté*, needs no further excuse to pursue his vengeful designs. Garnier, exercising authority as he did, was interested in this type of question: the way in which authority is indeed used. Tyranny he disliked, but equally he was horrified by rebellion. His concern over such matters is clear in *Les Juives* (1583), a work which calls for some comparison with *Athalie*. And obviously he was thinking of France itself as reflected to some extent in the plight of the Jews: this he makes apparent in the dedication of the play.

The drama moves on two planes, the human and the supernatural, the vengeance of Nabuchodonosor on the one hand and the vengeance of God on the other; and both seem to exact a harsh retribution. Le Prophète (Jérémie), however, is able to reveal the shape of things to come, and God's justice will then be apparent. Garnier's ardent Catholic faith inspires him to write here some of his most moving poetry; it carries conviction, and nowhere more so than in the final act:

> *Le Prophète* — Le soleil septante ans dessus nos chefs luira
> Tandis qu'en Babylon Israël servira.
> Mais le cours achevé de ces dures années,
> Ses infélicitez se verront terminées.
> Un roy persan viendra, plein de bénignité,
> Qui fera rebastir nostre antique cité.
> Ses tours s'élèveront et ses murailles fortes;
> Les portaux redressez se fermeront de portes;
> Et au temple dévôt par nous rédifié,
> Dieu mieux qu'auparavant sera glorifié.

Les Juives is one of the most imposing monuments of sixteenth-century tragedy; but if we are looking for a work which reaches down into the depths of tragic experience, *Saül le furieux* (1572), by Jean de la Taille, is arguably superior. Here is a man, Saül, pursued by his fate as unremittingly as any hero of old. He sees the net drawing ever more tightly round him, but there is nothing he can do. Escape is impossible; the path he has trodden knows no return. He struggles, he curses his God, he refuses to submit, even though he realizes the hopelessness of it all: the witch of Endor, or rather the shade of Samuel, has shown to him the irrevocable pattern of the future. Saül's suicide is followed by further suicides, and the play ends in agony and wretchedness.

What is memorable about this tragedy is the study of Saül himself. He completely dominates the action; and the dramatist has managed to convey all the anguish, fury, despair, and resignation of this doomed king, with whom it is impossible not to sympathize and whom we cannot help admiring. There is good in all men, but all have their weaknesses. So with Saül: his misfortune was that the better sometimes failed to assert itself. But fate was against him: what could he do? Here lurks the helplessness of man; and the story is as old as humanity.

The sixteenth century has little more to offer in the field of tragedy, now, until Montchrétien (1575–1621) appears. Strictly speaking, his plays open the seventeenth century—the first edition is dated 1601—but they wear a familiar look. His technique harks back to his precursors: speeches are lengthy and the action often wilts. The Chorus is there to add to the moralizing and to deepen the feeling of impotent sadness which clings like a robe.

Again it is religious and political themes which attract the author. The result is at least one remarkable commentary upon history so recent that passions still had not had time to cool. *La Reine d'Écosse* (or *L'Escossoise*, 1605) is the story of Mary Queen of Scots, executed by Elizabeth, an event which shocked France and to which Montaigne also alludes. Montchrétien, however, refrains from adding fuel to the fire of political hatred: he prefers to seek out the tragic essence in the unfolding drama. In so doing he distils from the events an elegiac sadness. Mary, a noble figure, dignified and admirable, meets her fate with fortitude, showing an unshakeable faith in the justice of Heaven. Her farewell to life and what it has meant to her breathes a nostalgia which the poetry felicitously enhances:

> Il ne me reste plus au partir de ce lieu
> Que faire a tout le monde un éternel adieu.
> Adieu donc, mon Ecosse, adieu terre natale
> Mais plutôt terre ingrate à ses Princes fatale...
> Adieu France, jadis séjour de mon plaisir,
> Où mille et mille fois m'emporta le désir,

Depuis que je quittai ta demeure agréable;
Par toi je fus heureuse et par toi misérable:
Si toutefois chez toi pouvaient loger mes os,
La mort me tiendrait lieu de grâce et de repos...
Adieu finablement chastes et belles Dames,
Le beau désir des cœurs, l'ardeur des belles âmes,
Qui dedans l'air françois brillez plus vivement
Que ne font par la nuit les feux du Firmament.

Montchrétien does not in all this neglect the figure of Mary's opponent, Elizabeth. He tries to show the depths of her doubts, and he endeavours to bring out some of the pressures which played upon the wretched queen as she came to the fatal decision. It is only too easy for private vengeance to convince itself that public welfare is at stake—especially if that private vengeance happens to be in a position of authority, as Elizabeth's was.

Montchrétien's religious tragedy, *Aman* (1601), has roots in similar soil. The tragedy tells of the downfall of Aman, an event in which Esther has a vital part to play; and obviously the dramatist felt attracted to this young queen, so warmly does he paint her. To save her people from what she refers to as 'l'orgueil étranger' she will risk death, however greatly the prospect may daunt her. The measure of her success is the disgrace of Aman; but little sympathy may be felt for this man whose pride places him in so vulnerable a position. He draws from it all a moral which is not entirely unexpected in sixteenth-century tragedy:

Fol l'homme qui se fie en la faveur d'un Roi
Sa plus grand'certitude est n'avoir point de foi;
Car tirant la fortune à son intelligence
Celui qui s'avançait elle le desavance.

To which the Chorus adds its agreement:

La Fortune de cour est semblable à la roue,
Dont le plus haut endroit vient d'un tour en la boue.
Qui s'enfle trop du vent de cet honneur mondain
A la parfin en crève ou se voit en dedain.

Such reflections are, as we have seen, typical. In fact, the Chorus is there mainly to distribute these grains of comfort, to comment

upon the moral implications of events as they take place. With
Seneca this would be largely from a Stoic angle, and this way of
looking at things certainly came down into the sixteenth century.
Many of the great commonplaces of the time are of this nature, an
amalgam of classical reminiscence and valid contemporary reaction
to the human situation as it appeared. This life is hard: rewards are
not guaranteed to those who deserve them; it is useless to struggle
against Fate, Destiny, *Fortuna*—call it what you will—for this
goddess continued to exist well into the Christian era. The wise man
is he who has learnt to despise worldly success, whose prizes seem
so irresistible to ambition. *Naturam sequere*: learn to accept whatever life may hold. And such reflections can readily be assimilated
into a Christian outlook, so that it becomes impossible to separate
each strand, to affix to each an identity label. A timeless wisdom
emerges.

The Chorus, therefore, stultifying though it might be dramatically,
had the virtue of retaining some sort of ethical grasp upon events as
they were happening upon the stage. It could exhort and instruct
and influence. Dispense with the Chorus in the interests of realism,
and difficulties can (and did) arise in this field of ethics. Tragedy, as
Aristotle noted, is based upon injustice, and this can easily come to
mean that we are all part of a 'sorry scheme of things'. Such a view
accords ill with the Christian position, and thus with the normal
way in which the people looked at life at the time. An obvious
escape from this dilemma is to make the hero deserve his fate. But
a gain for morality may well be a loss for sympathetic appeal; the
hero might appear a monster.

Hardy (*c.* 1570–1632) seems to have found himself in a dilemma
of this nature. His dramatic technique was superior to that of his
precursors; he often managed to convey the impression of greater
movement though he still sometimes clogged his action with the
traditional devices of tragedy: ghosts, messengers, lamentation,
rhetoric. But he did reduce the role of the Chorus, suppressing it
entirely in *Mariamne* (published 1625),[1] *Lucrèce* (published 1628),
and *Alcméon* (published 1628). In so doing, he deprived himself of
the most obvious means of moralizing upon the events taking place.

[1] Not to be confused with Tristan L'Hermite's *La Mariane* of 1636.

He therefore had to use the plot to show approval or disapproval, to reward virtue and to punish vice, as La Mesnardière suggests. However, it is by no means the rule that with Hardy the wicked suffer most, or even at all, for example in *Scédase* (published 1624). On the other hand, many good characters do suffer: Achille, Mariamne, Daire. All this doubtless has to do with a type of thinking that emerged from the framework of theoretical opinion produced in the previous, the sixteenth, century: 'Plus les tragédies sont cruelles, plus elles sont excellentes.' Blood is what dyes a tragedy in its appropriate hues. Probably the very titles of some of the plays, for example *Tragédie Mahommetiste* (1612) and *More cruel* (1614?), suggest that cruelty will be an essential part of their composition; and so it is. Violence there will be in tragedy, but this is the violence of the wicked towards the good. Sometimes, though rarely, we do however gain a glimpse of what tragedy can well convey: the anguish of a mind divided against itself. The torment of Hérode, torn between his desire to hurt Mariamne and his desire to possess her, is of this nature. But this is a different type of tragedy and Hardy was not of a generation refined in its powers of analysis or one which had come to know a gentler philosophy such as was cultivated on the banks of the Lignon. There they might have learnt, if nowhere else, that despite its weaknesses human nature still has its worth, that there is still something to admire in it. Pity for the weaker qualities should be matched by admiration for the stronger. Greek tragedy could have shown the same lesson. The humanists had seen this, but the vision somehow had faded when it came to writing tragedy or, at best, was glimpsed only occasionally. Corneille was later to restore it to its eminence. 'L'école du devoir, de la vertu, de l'héroïsme' is the way in which Rotrou referred to the theatre of his, and therefore of Corneille's, time, doing so in a letter to Corneille himself.

Tragedy, then, at the beginning of the century seems to have enjoyed little popularity; but there was one exception gleaming like a fresh spring in the arid stretches. *Pyrame et Thisbé* (1617) by Théophile de Viau (1590–1626), although dismissed as virtually worthless by Boileau some years later, did captivate Parisian audiences, a fact mentioned by Georges de Scudéry and Mahelot.

It is very much the story of Romeo and Juliet once again, but it is far less tightly knit as a tragedy. Indeed, it stands in this category simply by virtue of its ending, which tells of the death of the two lovers. But this death is a purely fortuitous event, clearly not the sort of denouement to appeal to a later generation of dramatists. The play does, however, have one refreshing feature: the character of the hero, and the heroine too, is such as to ensure the sympathy and admiration of an audience. Pyrame will stand comparison from this point of view with Corneille's Rodrigue. He may lack Rodrigue's filial piety, but he has the other virtues of courage, honour, and loyalty to Thisbé. And all this Théophile built up himself out of the slenderest of character sketches contained in his source, the fourth Book of Ovid's *Metamorphoses*.

1634 saw a change: Mairet's *Sophonisbe* was staged only a short while after Rotrou's *Hercule mourant*. From this moment, tragedy never faltered, and within three more years had two masterpieces to its credit: *Le Cid* and Tristan L'Hermite's *La Mariane*.

But is *Le Cid* really a tragedy? Or is it a tragi-comedy? Corneille hesitated. It is very like *Bradamante* (1582), Garnier's tragi-comedy, the first *notable* example of this genre. The tone is for the most part noble, as it was later to be in *Le Cid*; the events which Garnier recalls have importance, and the rank of some of the participants is regal—that of Charlemagne, for instance. But there is in *Bradamante* the breath of comedy. Much of the dialogue between Aymon and his wife, Béatrix, has the ring of natural domestic conversation, which will inevitably lower the tone from that which a tragic poet would hope to sustain. An obvious example is Act II, Scene 1. Then again there is the happy ending; the lovers, Roger and Bradamante, overcome the obstacles which keep them apart, to be united in the end. The pattern is that of almost any tragi-comedy, and could be repeated in almost any novel of the late sixteenth and early seventeenth centuries, as well as in the Greek romances which so delighted readers in the time of Garnier and Hardy. And tradition, the inheritance from past literary experience, can be seen working, too, through the same pair of lovers, Roger and Bradamante. In a number of ways they recall the heroes of the *chanson de geste* and the *roman d'aventure*, as does Renaud, Aymon's son. Roger, courageous in battle and constant in love, has a sense of honour so strong that it leads him to repay his debt towards Léon, even at the expense of his love. This type of hero was to appeal greatly to the seventeenth century: is it too much to see in him a descendant of Aristotle's magnanimous man? On such a hero some of the aspirations of a society can be focused and concentrated; he will be the more readily accepted for that.

Nobility, in rank and in sentiment, may be essential in tragedy, but it is out of place in comedy. Such, at least, was the idea current in these early centuries of the French theatre. Jacques Peletier du Mans (1517–87) speaks of 'les personnes comiques, qui sont de basse condition', whereas, he points out, 'en la Tragedie s'introduisent rois, princes et grans seigneurs'. He is, of course, repeating a distinction drawn centuries before by Donatus, who referred to comedy as dealing with 'mediocres fortunae hominum'. In this sense, therefore, if in no other, comedy will be nearer to daily life. But beyond this, when properly, if cautiously, interpreted, comedy can and does provide a commentary upon the society which inspires it. It is, to quote Jacques Peletier again, 'le miroir de la vie, par ce qu'en elle s'introduisent personnes populaires'.

There are two comedies of the sixteenth century which probably more than any others give the impression of having their roots in the society of the time. Perhaps this is because they are better written than most, though such a judgement may be unfair to Jodelle or Jean de la Taille or Pierre de Larivey (c. 1540–c. 1619), the most prolific comic writer of the time, and one whom Molière drew on occasionally.

The two comedies I have in mind are Grévin's Les Esbahis (1561) and Les Contens (printed 1584) of Turnèbe (1553–81). Both of them take love as their subject. In Les Esbahis an elderly widower, Josse, plans to marry the young daughter, Madalène, of his friend, Gerard. Madalène, however, is in love with a young advocate, who returns her affection. Finally the young lovers triumph, Josse is discomfited, not least in the discovery that the wife he thought to have escaped from is back again, alive and well, and all ends happily. The amusement derives largely from the situations; the salt of verbal wit is there, but only in pinches. Rather it is the quickwittedness and *savoir-faire* of some of the characters, especially servants, which entertains. If some characters, then, are glib and can talk their way out of trouble, others are there to be duped. Amongst these is one Pantheleone, an Italian, who was to become well known in France subsequently, like Arlequin, imported by Italian actors schooled in the *commedia dell'arte*.

Again, in *Les Contens*, the wit of servants carries the action along, and once more disguise and discovery play an important role in shaping events. This may suggest that it is all far-fetched, yet the reverse is true. The realism of the play is striking. Turnèbe has an ear for the natural conversation of people and his use of prose, unusual at the time, gave him an added advantage. Through the perceptive way in which he has moulded his characters, he has given a delightful picture of the *mœurs* of the period. Naturally, echoes will sound from previous authors through a number of the stock situations. One reared as Turnèbe had been must have had a tremendous fund of characters and situations on which to draw. But if we see in Rodomont something of the *miles gloriosus* and in Françoise something of the bawd of that remarkable Spanish play of the beginning of the century, *La Celestina*, this should not blind us to the freshness, the spontaneity and the verve of Turnèbe's own portraits. If, too, the moral of the story, as with so many of these comedies, seems disquietingly dubious—Basyle's way of winning a bride would be alarming if generally adopted—we should remember that we are looking at a century not quite as delicate as our own in its daily practice.

Doubtless many more comedies were written than are now extant, but comedy will always find an audience. Tabarin knew this as he sold Mondor's drugs on the Pont-Neuf. On the whole, however, comedy developed less than one might have expected from this time until Molière. But we should be wrong to look for a Molière in every generation; here, in comedy as in tragedy, the sixteenth and early seventeenth centuries have most to offer the present-day reader who can approach them on their own terms.

NOTE

Biographical. No less than three of the principal dramatists discussed in this chapter were educated at the Collège de Boncourt in Paris: Étienne Jodelle (1532–73), Jacques Grévin (1538–70), and Jean de la Taille (*c*. 1540–1608). Here they presumably came into contact with Muret, who appears to have had a great interest in the theatre.

The most important dramatist discussed is Robert Garnier (*c*. 1545–90). As a young man he went to Toulouse to study law, and whilst there devoted some of his time at least to writing poetry. In 1564 he took second prize in the *jeux floraux* in Toulouse, and two years later won the first prize. In 1567 he became *avocat au Parlement de Paris. Porcie* was published in the following year, and then in 1569 he moved to Le Mans, as *conseiller au présidial*. His tragedies continued to be published at regular intervals: *Hippolyte* (1573), *Marc Antoine* (1578), *La Troade* (1579). The first collected edition of his tragedies (1580) also included *Antigone*. A second edition followed in 1582, with the addition of *Bradamante*, and in 1583 came *Les Juives*. Two further editions of the complete tragedies were published in 1583 and 1588.

Modern editions. These are often difficult to find. A most useful general conspectus is offered by D. Stone, *Four Renaissance Tragedies*, published 1966 from Harvard and containing the texts of George Buchanan, *Jephté ou le vœu*, Théodore de Bèze, *Abraham sacrifiant*, Étienne Jodelle, *Didon se sacrifiant*, and Jean de la Taille, *Saül le furieux*. Jodelle's *Cléopâtre captive*, *Eugène*, and *Didon* can be read in vol. iv of the *Ancien Théâtre français* series which is being reprinted. In the same collection can be found Grévin's *Les Esbahis* (vol. iv), Larivey's comedies (vols. v and vi), and Turnèbe's *Les Contens* (vol. vii). Jodelle's *Cléopâtre captive* has been edited recently by L. B. Ellis (1946), and L. Pinvert published his *Théâtre complet et poésies choisies* (1922). Jean de la Taille's *Art de la Tragédie* was edited by F. West (1939): his tragedy was reprinted in 1908 and a photographic reissue has come out: *J. de la Taille und sein 'Saül le furieux'*, ed. A. Werner (1908). For Garnier see *Œuvres complètes*, ed. L. Pinvert (1923), and for Hardy *Le Théâtre d'Alexandre Hardy*, ed. E. Stengel (1884).

Criticism. Useful articles include those of G. Lanson in the *Revue d'histoire littéraire de la France* of 1903 and 1904: 'Études sur les origines de la tragédie classique en France' and 'L'idée de la tragédie en France avant Jodelle', and R. Lebègue, 'La tragédie française au XVIe siècle', *Revue des Cours et Conférences*, 1930–2. See also his *La Tragédie religieuse en France* (1929), and 'Tableau de la comédie française de 1573 à 1610' in *Bibliothèque d'humanisme et renaissance*. A more recent study is E. Forsyth, *La Tragédie française de Jodelle à Corneille* (1962). H. W. Lawton, *Handbook of French Renaissance Dramatic Theory* (1949), and B. Weinberg, *Critical Prefaces of the French Renaissance* (1950), should also be consulted.

10. The Poetry of Violence: D'Aubigné and the Wars of Religion

THE Wars of Religion involved France in violent, though spasmodic, internal conflict for over thirty years—years in which both Catholics and Protestants relied on destructive and bitterly resented foreign intervention. The savagery of the fighting, the intractable social and ideological issues which lay behind it, and the conditions of near-anarchy which it led to, inspired a rich production of pamphlets, memoirs, tracts, and histories, some of which are discussed in Chapter 11.

Here we are concerned with the contribution of the Protestant Agrippa d'Aubigné. His long and powerful poem, *Les Tragiques*, both chronicles and interprets these events with a partisan hatred and vehemence which give it a unique status in literature grounded in war and violence. It is, we shall see, as much the history of a tormented soul as of a tormented country. D'Aubigné also described the religious wars in his *Histoire universelle* which, unlike the *Tragiques*, does not aim to interpret the religious wars, but simply to chronicle and commemorate the acts of the Huguenots. The *Tragiques*, on the other hand, are explicitly both an indictment of the acts of the Catholics, and a vindication and celebration of the Huguenot cause.

The universality aimed at by the *Histoire universelle* is European: like previous histories it sets events in France against contemporary developments in the other main European countries. The *Tragiques* claim a much wider universality, embracing as they do the entire universe and the entire course of human history from the Creation to the Last Judgement, and beyond. But both works take up the story of the religious struggles where modern histories of the wars also begin: with the peace treaty signed between Spain and France at Cateau-Cambrésis in 1559. This treaty ended over half a century of active involvement in European affairs, and France now turned inwards to tackle the problem of heresy, which by this time was an organized and disciplined power within her borders. This is how d'Aubigné sums up this fateful moment, with his usual trenchancy:

Voilà les conventions d'une paix, en effect, pour les royaumes de France et d'Espagne... désadvantageuse aux François, redoutable aux reformés, car... après la paix establie, les princes, qui par elle avoyent la paix du dehors, travaillèrent par émulation à qui traicteroit plus rudement ceux qu'on appelloit hérétiques. Et de là nasquit l'ample subject de 60 ans de guerre monstrueuse. (*Histoire universelle*, ch. xviii.)

He is here putting the blame for the wars squarely on to the Catholic monarchs of Europe. Moreover, by seeing the French civil wars in a European context, he can think of them as still raging in 1619: in Germany the Thirty Years War is being fought out, and in France d'Aubigné, at least, has not laid down his arms. All the same, the *Histoire universelle* does describe the French civil wars with a genuine and partly successful effort at impartiality, as Plattard has demonstrated in his introduction to its *Supplément*.

Not so the *Tragiques*. The difference in tone between the two works, conceived at about the same time, describing the same events, and published close together, is quite remarkable. D'Aubigné remarks of his history: 'c'est chose merveilleuse qu'un esprit igné et violent de son naturel ne soit monstré en aucun point partisan, ait escrit sans löuanges et blasmes, fidelle tesmoin et jamais juge, se contentant de satisfaire à la question du faict sans toucher à celle du droict' (*Tragiques*, Aux Lecteurs). The slightly self-flattering confusion between what he wanted to do and what he did is repeated in his judgement that the *Histoire universelle* is the more important of the two works. For the modern reader finds incomparably more substance in the *Tragiques*. He is one of those deplorable readers referred to by d'Aubigné in the preface to the *Histoire universelle*, who, in this instance at least, 'aiment mieux un historien pathétique et faux, qu'un astorge (impartial) et véritable'. In the final analysis, he feels that the violent emotionalism and distorting passion of the *Tragiques* is more truthful, more convincing, more adequate to the events described, than an attitude of impartiality. The poem is quite openly grounded in hatred, and is always true to its obsessions. However, the reader ought not to forget that this emotional integrity might not have been achieved, had d'Aubigné not been able to concentrate his emotions and pursue them to their bitter end, thanks to his equally single-minded struggle to be impartial in his historical work.

Because the way things are said is as important as what is said; because the poem sets out to irritate, disorientate, and overwhelm; because the narrative continuity is deliberately torn and twisted around—for these and similar reasons it is barely possible to summarize the grandiose sequence of events in the seven books of the *Tragiques*. The first book (*Misères*) laments the horrors of civil strife, and deplores the impious connivance of the French monarchy, manipulated by Catherine de Médicis and the Cardinal of Lorraine, in treachery and murder. It ends with a plea to God to avenge the wrongs suffered by the Huguenot Church, seen as the humble victim of tyrannical oppression. The second book (*Princes*) is given over to a ferocious attack on the Court, and ends with a warning to the moderates at Court to flee the wrath to come. The courts of justice, brilliantly satirized in *Chambre dorée*, act out their bloody charades in a frenzied oblivion of the ultimate victory of true justice. After two books about the persecutors, two about the persecuted: *Feux* is d'Aubigné's *Book of Martyrs*, a sickening survey of Protestant martyrdom; *Fers* treats the civil wars as the great period of trial, when the constancy of the Huguenots is tested to the limit by the blandishments of political compromise, the temptations of military success, and the ordeal of massacre. In the concluding books the tables are turned. The sixth book (*Vengeances*) embraces the history of God's revenge on the persecutors of Israel, the early Christian Church, and the Huguenots. *Jugement*, the last book, castigates Huguenot renegades and draws a savage picture of the coming overthrow of them and their allies in oppression. Leisurely arguments for the resurrection of the body then precede and justify the depiction of the terrifying splendour of the Last Judgement. With the unspeakable terrors of eternal torment, and the ineffable joys of eternal bliss which d'Aubigné, in the last lines of the poem, ecstatically describes, this strident poem—and history itself—issue into the silence of the apocalypse.

Such a summary perhaps brings out the rigorously dichotomized and oversimplified view of history and humanity in the *Tragiques*. There are and always have been only two classes of men according to this picture: the meek and the arrogant, the persecuted and the persecutors. Each book of the poem, whilst focusing on different aspects of this opposition, contributes to the poem's general movement which follows the simple rhythm of the great reversal of fortunes promised at the beginning of the Sermon on the Mount to those who are persecuted for the sake of righteousness. History lies under the shadow of the last days, and is moving inexorably towards the second coming of the avenging Christ. Most of the readers of the poem, like those for whom the Sermon on the Mount was written down, can be addressed as having witnessed the beginning of history's final phase (*Misères*, ll. 715–26): some will live to experience its cataclysmic end; all, like d'Aubigné, are caught up in the firm purposes of history whose urgency is matched by the strong purposiveness of the poem, insistently, persistently soliciting this ultimate consummation.

The *Tragiques* were first published in 1616, some twenty years after the cessation of armed hostilities in France, and their crude though grandiose evocation of the wars revived memories which most Frenchmen wanted to forget. Now, as then, an appreciation of their subject-matter requires the reader to immerse himself in violence of a hypnotic intensity, and to live through scenes of such distressing cruelty that his sensibility is soon battered into something like the poet's own mesmerized acceptance of a world gone wrong. What had gone wrong in d'Aubigné's eyes?

Two events, in particular, seem to have dictated the furious vindictiveness of the *Tragiques* and to have sustained the poet's obsessive sense of a great betrayal of the Huguenot cause, just as they echoed in the minds of all politically conscious Frenchmen at the time. The first event, the Saint Bartholomew Massacre, was the most dramatic of the disasters suffered by the Huguenots, the greatest political crime of the century. The second, the conversion of Henri IV to Catholicism in 1593, was, for those who identified the success of the Huguenots with the establishment of a Protestant monarchy, its most fundamental, because irretrievable, reverse. That the one event led fairly directly to the poem's conception, and that the other occurred when the poem was in large part written, does much to explain its tone of frustrated anger and its structure, based on the idea of divine retribution (urgently called for in the first five books, before being accomplished in the last two).

In 1572 there seemed a real chance that France would return to the policy of hostility to Spain which it had pursued until the treaty of Cateau-Cambrésis, a chance to reunite warring factions behind the French monarchy, against a common foe. This policy was being canvassed energetically by the moderate party of the 'Politiques', and due to the powerful personal influence of Coligny, the Huguenot leader, was enthusiastically backed by the neurotic king, Charles IX. It was excitedly discussed throughout July and August in Paris, where the nobility of France had assembled for the wedding of Henri de Navarre (later Henri IV). Catherine de Médicis, the powerful Queen Mother, and the influential, staunchly Catholic Guise family (which included the Cardinal of Lorraine), resorted to an extraordinary expedient to prevent these discussions coming to anything: on 24 August, Saint Bartholomew's Day, the order was given for a general massacre of Huguenots, women and children included. Only two Huguenot names were excluded from the executioners' lists, those of Navarre and Condé, who were princes of the blood. Among the few who escaped this brutal and deliberate act of mass murder was d'Aubigné, who shortly afterwards was attacked, seriously wounded, and left for dead.

The episode of the *Tragiques* in which he relates a mystic vision which he then experienced forms the hinge on which the pattern of Providence and the pattern of the *Tragiques* both turn:

> Parmi ces aspres temps l'esprit, ayant laissé
> Aux assassins mon corps en divers lieux percé,
> Par l'Ange consolant mes ameres blessures,
> Bien qu'impur, fut mené dans les regions pures.
>
> (*Fers*, ll. 1195-8)

In his vision d'Aubigné sees the past and future vicissitudes of the Huguenots, and their final triumph when (in 1666) the Antichrist will be struck down. As we have seen, the whole poem is written in the perspective of that restoration of the persecuted with which the following two books are concerned. And it is this vision, we now realize, which compelled the eloquent denunciations of the preceding books, starting from the mysterious, but now more understandable, imperative of the opening lines, with their impulsive obscurity and rhythmical irregularity:

> Puisqu'il faut s'attaquer aux legions de Rome,
> Aux monstres d'Italie, il faudra faire comme
> Hannibal...   (*Misères*, ll. 1–3)

Such, however, were the necessities of war that the task of vengeance laid upon d'Aubigné by the angel had to be pursued in intervals of fighting, perhaps even on horseback or in the trenches. At any rate, the poem was actually begun in 1577, when d'Aubigné was again seriously wounded. A great deal was completed by the 1590s, but by then it must already have begun to seem outdated and unnecessary, for in 1589 the Protestant Henri de Navarre had succeeded to the throne as Henri IV. Heaven seemed to smile. Pen and sword might soon be laid aside. The Huguenots appeared to be on the brink of a political triumph so complete that it would wipe away all memory of martyrdom and trial. But God had not done with d'Aubigné yet. In July 1593 Henri announced his conversion to Catholicism. This turn of events brought the light of peace and reconciliation to France. To d'Aubigné it brought only despair, and it darkens the whole of the *Tragiques* in their final form.

The blow was all the more bitter to d'Aubigné for his personal involvement in the career of Henri. Referring to his part in the escape of Henri from the Court, where he was virtually imprisoned after the Saint Bartholomew Massacre, d'Aubigné writes of himself 'comme ayant esté choisi de Dieu pour instrument de la liberté de mon prince' (*Histoire universelle*, Preface). The *Tragiques*, as first conceived, almost certainly saw in Henri the providential saviour of the oppressed, as opposed to the sons of Catherine: Charles IX, Henri III, and the Duc d'Alençon. Significantly enough it is the

last of these three, the tragic, sickly d'Alençon, who excites most
wrath, as he had excited the greatest hopes. He it is who is most
terrifyingly attacked in the preface, and in *Princes*, both of which
look beyond him to the resolute figure of Henri, 'prince choisi de
Dieu' (*Misères*, l. 1021). July 1593 revealed the folly of such hopes.

There is in the vision of Henri something of the haunting
tragedy, the sense of large historical irony, which we feel in the
Divine Comedy over Henry VII of Luxembourg. But there is in
Dante's poem a much greater degree of acceptance and under-
standing. D'Aubigné keeps some of his harshest prophetic words for
Henri IV's apostasy:

> Princes, qui vomissans la salutaire grace
> Tournez au ciel le dos et à l'enfer la face,
> Qui, pour regner ici, esclaves vous rendez
> Sans mesurer le gain à ce que vous perdez,
> Vous faittes esclatter aux temples vos musiques:
> Vostre cheute fera hurler vos domestiques.
> Au jour de vostre change on vous pare de blanc:
> Au jour de son courroux Dieu vous couvre de sang.
> (*Jugement*, ll. 175–82)

This apostasy—this betrayal, as it seemed to many Huguenots—
was a political necessity, since France was still overwhelmingly
Catholic in sentiment. Such was the distrust of Henri's intentions
that it was another year before he was able to enter his capital. He
proved to be a strong, fair-minded king, determined to implement
the Edict of Nantes (1598). This edict restored many of the political
concessions and guarantees which the Huguenots had several times
previously secured from the Crown. All the same, it did not restore
all previous concessions; it was not fully implemented; and, above
all, it only tolerated Protestantism and did not grant it full recognition. No wonder many Huguenots saw it as the defeat which in
some degree it was.

Soon after the assassination of Henri IV in 1610, confessional
antagonism was openly renewed. The Huguenots, only too well
aware of their own weakness, were led into acts of rebellion which
made their position even more vulnerable, a fact bitterly underlined

for d'Aubigné by the demoralizing failure of a revolt in which he took part in 1616. The publication of the *Tragiques* in this year is a symbolic event, a celebration of defeat, an acknowledgement of the harsh inevitabilities of history. It is as though d'Aubigné finally admits that the heroic age of French Protestantism is past, and that it can never be revived. Though he still lived in France, he writes as if exiled. Some seventy years later the Edict of Nantes was revoked, and all Huguenots were in fact exiled from France.

It has frequently been suggested that the *Tragiques* were originally conceived in answer to a patriotic urge to write a great epic poem which should crown the literature of the vernacular in the way that the epic poems of Homer and Virgil were thought to crown classical literature. The national consciousness of the Pléiade poets had in fact demanded this proof that the moderns really did equal the ancient world in genius and achievement. D'Aubigné, however, was not inspired by any archaizing vein. It never occurred to him to fill his poem with the classical machinery of the Olympian gods, with the funeral games, and with the legends about national origins which we find in Virgil. Nor was he much taken up with the love intrigues, magic spells, and voyages of adventure so common in the epics deriving through Ariosto from Apollonius of Rhodes. On the other hand, like his Protestant contemporaries, Du Bartas and Spenser, he is little touched by that humanist rejection of the medieval past which characterizes most Pléiade poetry. The *Tragiques* embody something like the medieval view of epic as an exemplary portrait. In them the Protestant martyrs present the 'loftie image of such worthies (which) most inflameth the mind with desire to be worthy', which Spenser saw as being the task of epic to create. There is a medieval flavour about the divine predilection for worms as instruments of retribution in *Vengeances*, and about the naïve, jingling didacticism of Montalcino's profession of Protestant faith in *Fers*. The beast-fable satire of the court in *Princes*, and perhaps, above all, the powerful and creative use of allegory throughout, have a medieval vigour and crudity. The frenzied figures of Belonna, Libitina, and Melpomene which the poem conjures up, are more like figures from a 'danse macabre' than from a classical frieze.

Perhaps the nearest epic analogue to the *Tragiques* is Lucan's *Pharsalia*, which is closely imitated in the first book (and practically only there), especially at moments of melodramatic sensationalism. Like the *Tragiques*, the *Pharsalia* is hyperbolic, scornful of poetic tradition, and thoroughly uncivilized. Both poems are lacking in the sense of the warmth and stability of human society which epics usually have. They respond only to the brotherhood of shared suffering. Thus the swords, the palaces, and the drinking-bowls of the *Tragiques* are not described as beautiful examples of human ingenuity as they are in Homer or *Beowulf*. Instead, the drinking-bowls are human skulls; the palaces are built of bones; and the swords are seen only as instruments of death (cf. *Chambre dorée*, ll. 175-216). Gone are magnanimity and optimism and national confidence. For Lucan as for d'Aubigné, the enemy is completely bad; compromise and mutual endeavour are rejected; all belief in national institutions is lost.

D'Aubigné's subject is a large, immediate tragedy in which he had participated emotionally and physically. It hardly needed imaginative re-creation. The vocabulary and the mood of the *Tragiques* are part of contemporary experience, and form the very basis of his aesthetic:

> Si quelq'un me reprend que mes vers eschauffez
> Ne sont rien que de meurtre et de sang estoffez,
> Qu'on n'y lit que fureur, que massacre, que rage,
> Qu'horreur, mal-heur, poison, trahison et carnage,
> Je luy respons: amis, ces mots que tu reprens
> Sont les vocables d'art de ce que j'entreprends.
>
> (*Princes*, ll. 59-64)

The actions that he portrays irrupt into his mind. He is haunted by scenes of perversion, massacre, and lust: 'comme par force l'œil se destourne à ces choses' (*Misères*, l. 681), 'l'esprit lassé, par force advisa le monceau / Des chrestiens condamnés' (*Fers*, ll. 1215-6), 'ces exemples m'ennuient (torturent) / Ils poursuyvent mes vers et mes yeux qui les fuyent' (*Vengeances*, ll. 925-6). For the nightmarish intensity of the poem is made of the violent world around him. It was a world in which humanism was on the retreat, as the conditions of the late Middle Ages returned to France.

D'Aubigné is, of course, far from being the only witness to the way men's sensibilities were coarsened and exacerbated at this time. Montaigne comments in his gently sardonic manner: 'A voir nos guerres civiles, qui ne crie que cette machine se bouleverse et que le jour du jugement nous prent au collet?' (*Essais*, i. 26). The *Journal* of L'Estoile gives a reliable account of the hair-raising excesses common in besieged Paris. Monluc's *Commentaires* have the brutal directness of his own actions as a military leader. Written from a blindly Catholic viewpoint, they are a frighteningly innocent panegyric of violence. Perhaps we come even closer to the fears and obsessions of the *Tragiques* in the many treatises on witchcraft which were written throughout this period.

Even in the *Printemps* collection,[1] most of the poems we remember, poems of frustrated love, are expressed in a tone of characteristic original vehemence. There are also poems describing happier moments spent with Diane, such as the pretty song of delight at relaxing with her

> Soubs la tremblante courtine,
> De ses [?ces] bessons arbrisseaux,
> Au murmure qui chemine
> Dans ces gasouillans ruisseaux,
> Sur un chevet touffu esmaillé des coulleurs
> D'un million de fleurs
> (*Ode* VIII)

The shrubs, the flowing murmur of the brooks, the flower-sprinkled grass are noted with unforced simplicity through the gentle underlining of the unobstructed rhythm. The atmosphere of relaxed sensuousness is gracefully expanded in the next stanza:

> O doux repos de mes pennes,
> Bras d'yvoire pottelez,
> O beaux yeux, claires fontaines
> Qui de plaisir ruisselez,
> O giron, doux support, beau chevet esmaillé
> A mon chef travaillé!

[1] See Note at end of this chapter.

The jarring note set up by the unprepared mention of the tormented head is far from being effectively resolved by the rather contrived closing stanza. The poem as a whole makes us feel that the mood d'Aubigné wishes to convey is not adequately communicated through the conventions of pastoral.

The more unified and yet more decorative sonnet on the same subject (*Hécatombe* XIX) makes even more apparent this tension between form and content. D'Aubigné rarely seems at ease in the sonnet, which forces him into a compression and regularity of form in which his emotion seems trapped. His effects are too large to submit to the contained antithesis of, for example, the sonnets of his contemporary, Sponde. Several of d'Aubigné's sonnets are not in fact self-contained but form part of a larger unit of two or more. In *Hécatombe* VIII, which runs on from the preceding poem, the allegorical struggle between love and fortune comes memorably to life in:

> Je suis le champ sanglant où la fureur hostile
> Vomit le meurtre rouge, et la scytique horreur
> Qui saccage le sang, richesse de mon cœur,
> Et en se debattant font leur terre sterile.

But its vigour is weakened by the precious conceit which continues these lines:

> Amour, fortune! helas! appaisez tant de traicts,
> Et touchez dans la main d'une amiable paix.

The most successful poems in the *Printemps* are the *Stances*, whose length and loose organization allow the waves of emotion to pour over from one stanza to the next, as they do in the *Tragiques*.

It is the decorative, pagan poetry of the *Printemps* which d'Aubigné brutally rejects near the beginning of the *Tragiques*:

> Ces ruisselets d'argent, que les Grecs nous feignoyent,
> Ou leurs poëtes vains beuvoyent et se baignoyent,
> Ne courent plus ici: mais les ondes si claires
> Qui eurent les sapphirs et les perles contraires
> Sont rouges de nos morts; le doux bruit de leurs flots,
> Leur murmure plaisant heurte contre des os.
>
> (*Misères*, ll. 59–64)

Just as the brooks are now choked with bleeding bodies, so the dis-located alexandrine is held up by phonetic and syntactical obstacles. The imagery, the rhythm, and the mood have gained strikingly in vigour and expressiveness, to convey the full power of d'Aubigné's furious indignation.

No one has ever thought of the *Tragiques* as a masterpiece of pleasing reticence, or insinuating charm. D'Aubigné rarely draws from his alexandrines the suave and easy fullness of a Ronsard, nor yet the grave melodic firmness of Chassignet, an important poet whose poems communicate a stronger control of emotional tensions than his own. Sometimes d'Aubigné does bring his verse-paragraphs to a successful rhythmic climax, and in the description of Ann Askew's martyrdom in *Feux*, for example, he succeeds in building up a variety of rhythmical patterns into a satisfying whole. Characteristi-cally, however, success comes in the single line: 'Desirs, parfaits amours, haut desirs sans absence' (*Jugement*, l. 207), 'Pures dans les cieux purs, le beau pays des ames', 'Les orbes tournoyans sonnent harmonieux' (*Chambre dorée*, ll. 114, 116). The last line of each verse-paragraph frequently lacks force, as if d'Aubigné is already thinking of the striking image to be created in the next.

D'Aubigné's alexandrine can be grave, noble, elegiac; but it is above all impassioned, energetic, varied. Thus Caesar, seeing Rome:

> Il vid Rome tremblante, affreuze, eschevelee,
> Qui en pleurs, en sanglots, mi-morte, desolee,
> Tordant ses doigts, fermoit, defendoit de ses mains
> A Cezar le chemin au sang de ses germains.
>
> (*Misères*, ll. 9–12)

This is a good example of d'Aubigné's power of communicating states of distress, a distress which is mirrored here by the broken movement of the lines and the fiercely hammered syntactical point-ing. The diffuse concluding line is typically weak—perhaps because a full communication of Caesar's humanitarian hesitations would check the impulsive onward movement of the opening pages of the poem.

The constantly changing rhythms in the *Tragiques* help to excite
and recharge the reader's attention as he responds to the way narrative gives place to spectacle, to direct speech, to vigorous apostrophe:
'Vous ne m'escoutez plus, stupides endormis!' (*Chambre dorée*, l. 1006).
The poem's concern is with excitement, to the virtual exclusion of
inquiry or ease. To this end sensationalism to some extent replaces
imaginativeness. Good taste about atrocities would anyway be an
impertinence. It is, then, in keeping with the subject of the poem
that d'Aubigné's use of language should be unhampered by the
restrictions of decorum laid down by the humanist poets of the
Pléiade. He strives for physical immediacy, dramatic intensity, and
visionary sublimity, as in the following passage (the first two lines of
which are part of an extended illustrative image but, by a fine disregard of logic, become part of the narrative sequence):

> Le bon Roy quitte lors le sceptre et la seance,
> Met l'espee au costé et marche à la vengeance.
> Dieu se leve en courroux et au travers des cieux
> Perça, passa son chef; à l'esclair de ses yeux
> Les cieux se sont fendus; tremblans, suans de crainte,
> Les hauts monts ont croullé: cette Majesté saincte
> Paroissant fit trembler les simples elements,
>
> Tout s'enfuit, tout s'estonne, et gemit à sa veuë;
> Les Rois espouvantez laissent choir, paslissans,
> De leurs sanglantes mains les sceptres rougissans;
>
> Le meschant le sentit, plein d'espouventement,
> Mais le bon le connut, plein de contentement.
>
> (*Chambre dorée*, ll. 137–60)

With each change of tense, the action clicks into a new focus. The
repetitions, the heavy alliterations, the disordered syntax convey the
chaotic and universal up-turning in images derived from the *Book of
the Apocalypse* and the Old Testament. Again, in these images,
d'Aubigné pursues the isolated brilliant effect to the neglect of strict
logic, for the whole point of *Chambre dorée* is the total oblivion of
earthly rulers to God's presence, yet in these lines they are not only
aware of this presence, but it thoroughly frightens them.

God is, of course, present throughout the poem. The poem revolves, as we have seen, around d'Aubigné's awareness of God and of His plans for mankind: retribution for the many, and the supreme reward for those who, like d'Aubigné, achieve election. It is the sure basis of the poet's utter sense of certainty which sets off the *Tragiques* so sharply from the explored, unresolved tensions of Sponde's verse. D'Aubigné met his own tensions, not by contemplating them, and thereby refining his self-knowledge like Sponde, but by identifying his tensions with the conflicts of the Huguenots, defeated in this world, victorious in the next.

Some well-known lines of *Misères* (372–4) describe the devastation caused by civil war:

> J'ai veu le reistre noir foudroyer au travers
> Les masures de France, et comme une tempeste,
> Emporter ce qu'il peut, ravager tout le reste.

These lines are echoed in *Jugement* (260–4) by magnificent lines of imprecation ('les propres mots des organes de Dieu') against the Catholics, which prophesy the coming miseries of besieged Paris, and the victorious arrival of foreign armies:

> Bien-heureux l'estranger qui te sçaura bien rendre
> La rouge cruauté que tu as sçeu cercher;
> Juste le reistre noir, volant pour arracher
> Tes enfans acharnés à ta mamelle impure,
> Pour les froisser brisés contre la pierre dure.

It is clear that the ever-present God of the *Tragiques*, whilst He may lack pity, does not lack eloquence or wrath. The God of this poem, unforgettably majestic, and quite without mystery or compassion for His enemies, is indubitably made in the image of d'Aubigné.

NOTE

AGRIPPA D'AUBIGNÉ, 1552–1630, born near Pons (Charente-Maritime), was the son of an ardent Huguenot soldier and scholar. At nine he was pledged to avenge the Huguenots executed after the Amboise conspiracy, which preceded the civil wars. Refugee at ten, orphan at eleven, he was schooled for a time in Geneva, and at eighteen was already a resourceful officer. His love for Diane de Talcy, whose family sheltered him after the Saint Bartholomew Massacre of 1572—from which he was lucky to escape with his life—inspired the poetry of *Le Printemps*. His suit was rejected in 1573. For the next twenty years d'Aubigné was a turbulent comrade of Henri de Navarre, until the latter's conversion to Catholicism in 1593, when already King of France. As a spokesman of Huguenot intransigeance, d'Aubigné was now in the political wilderness. In 1616 he published anonymously his historico-religious epic, *Les Tragiques*, begun as he recovered from battle wounds in 1577. His last ten years were spent in exile in Geneva, partly due to his complicity in revolts, partly to his blunt *Histoire universelle* (1619–20).

Editions. The *Œuvres complètes* (6 vols.) edited by Réaume and Caussade do not include the *Histoire universelle* (10 vols.), edited by A. de Ruble (1886–1909). The important *Supplément à l'Histoire universelle* was edited by J. Plattard in 1925. The three parts of *Le Printemps* can be read in the following editions: ed. B. Gagnebin, *L'Hécatombe à Diane* (1948); ed. F. Desonay, *Stances et Odes* (1952); ed. H. Weber, *L'Hécatombe à Diane et les Stances* (1960). *Les Tragiques* (4 vols.) edited by A. Garnier and J. Plattard (1932–3) were re-issued in 1962–5.

Criticism. There is a useful general study by J. Plattard, *Agrippa d'Aubigné* (1931). The chapters on *Les Tragiques* in H. Weber, *La Création poétique au XVIᵉ siècle en France* (1956) and in T. Greene, *The Descent from Heaven* (1963) are most helpful. The emphasis of two full-length studies is indicated in their titles: I. Buffum, *Agrippa d'Aubigné's 'Les Tragiques', a Study of the Baroque Style in Poetry* (1951), and H. Sauerwein, *Agrippa d'Aubigné's 'Les Tragiques', a Study in Structure and Poetic Method* (1953). Suggestive remarks are made by A. Boase in *The Poetry of France*, vol. 1 (1964), by M. Raymond in *Génies de France* (1942), and by R. Lebègue in *La Poésie française de 1560 à 1630* (1951). A. Garnier's *Agrippa d'Aubigné et le parti protestant* (1928: 3 vols.) is useful on historical points.

11. Problems of the Religious Wars

IN about 1552 a young law student at Orleans, Étienne de la Boétie, composed a minor literary masterpiece, the *Servitude volontaire*. Like the edition of Seneca's *De Clementia*, which Calvin had produced at Orleans twenty years before, to emulate the heroic scholarly achievements of his recent teachers at the newly founded Collège de France, Budé, Vatable, and Danès, it is essentially a work of humanist enthusiasm and idealism. It gives magnificent expression to those humanist preoccupations at the heart of much humanist writing, which Calvin, for his part, was soon to modify. But although the *Servitude volontaire* contains a rigorous analysis of the psychological mechanisms of despotic government, and develops a clear theory of passive resistance, it is no less of an academic exercise, and has no more immediate political relevance, than Calvin's Seneca edition. It describes an ideal, abstract world, constructed out of La Boétie's classical reading.

La Boétie's grounds for rejecting tyranny are ethical and aesthetic rather than practical and political, being based on an optimistic sense of the nobility of the individual. 'Si nous vivions avec les droits que la nature nous a donnés et avec les enseignemens qu'elle nous apprend, nous serions naturellement obeissans aux parens, subiets à la raison, et serfs de personne', La Boétie firmly declares. The exercise of despotic power by the tyrant and its acceptance by the tyrannized, therefore, involve the destruction of personality and of worthwhile human relationships.

How then, we may ask, can men re-create their sense of spiritual independence? The answer is found in literary culture, seen as the source of moral regeneration and the means to the spiritual collapse of tyranny: 'les livres et la doctrine donnent plus que toute autre chose aux hommes le sens et l'entendement de se reconnaître et d'hair la tyrannie.' The message is clear: 'soies résolus de ne servir plus et vous voilà libres.' Sentiments like these inspired the passionate friendship of Montaigne, whose later exploration and assertion of his own personality in the *Essais* is conducted inside a largely classical culture, in the manner and memory of La Boétie.

However classical the mould of La Boétie's mind, his *Servitude volontaire* is something of a sport in Renaissance political thinking, as Montaigne implies. Machiavelli's *Prince* (written in 1513) is perhaps closest to it in mood. For, although it is written in praise of tyranny, and has the contemporary situation more in mind, it is equally a declamation. This type of passionately theoretical writing was to be common enough in the Enlightenment: Rousseau's *Discours sur l'origine de l'inégalité* is a good example and may well be directly inspired by La Boétie's discourse.

The wars of religion, which broke out in 1562 and lasted for most of the century, were soon to pose questions which could not be solved by rhetoric. France, like Europe as a whole, was to be split into two armed factions, glowering resentfully or scornfully across ideological barriers which each side was increasingly unwilling to cross. The capacity even to conceive the possibility of confessional reconciliation and compromise grew faint. At the same time the authority of the monarchy, which had grown steadily in the first half of the century, was severely weakened, and the very strength of the forces arrayed against it led men to construct new and fruitful theories of political obligation and social order. But after thirty or so years of fierce conflict, the political reunion eventually achieved under Henri IV was far more the product of physical exhaustion than the creation of political idealism.

The aims of Court policy in the 1560s are clearly set out in a speech made at Fontainebleau by Monluc, Bishop of Valence, in 1560. His first point is that the whole nation should turn to God in penitence and prayer, the king to set the example by encouraging the singing of psalms; secondly, a General Council or, maybe, a national one, should be called to settle the main points of difference between Catholics and Protestants; thirdly, persuasion and not force should be used against heretics. The last two points were soon put to the test at the colloquy of Poissy (1561), an assembly of Catholic and

Protestant theologians arranged by the Court. The colloquy foundered in complete and predictable disagreement over the doctrine of the Real Presence.[1] The Court persevered, however, in its policies of compromise, and by a royal edict of January 1562, gave legal toleration to French Protestants, the Huguenots, allowing them to worship outside towns.

This was an event of momentous importance, the first official recognition ever granted in Christendom to a second religion. But the government was far too weak to ensure the success of so revolutionary a step on its own, and there was no strong body of moderate opinion to which it could appeal. Polarization had gone too far, as La Boétie's last work, a clear-sighted, tough-minded memoir on the edict, shows. Referring to civil disturbances, he says that 'tout le mal est la diversité de religion, qui a passé si avant, qu'un même peuple, vivant sous même prince, s'est clairement divisé en deux parts'. La Boétie is acutely conscious of the potentially disruptive power of the situation, and urges quick action. First, the king must vigorously assert his authority over the nation: 'on ne saurait croire de combien, après cette terreur, il [le peuple] sera plus traitable.' Only then should he contemplate, and himself initiate, measures to reform the traditional religion, and thus preserve national unity. Like all the really constructive political writing of this period, La Boétie here champions the monarchy as the arbiter of conflict, and as the leader in the search for formulae to secure unity and peace. For, like Ronsard in his poetry of the early 1560s, La Boétie is now grappling with urgent problems of social disorder and religious turmoil, which make earlier humanist preoccupations seem irrelevant and self-indulgent. It is a change of emphasis, brought about by the onset of civil strife, which can be seen nowhere more clearly than in the works of Jean Bodin, whose reflections on these problems are the most valuable and consistently original of the age.

In 1559, four years after his translation into Latin verse of Oppian's Greek poem on hunting, Bodin published a long address, an *Oratio*, to the notables of the town, urging the creation of a

---

[1] A Catholic doctrine which asserts the actual presence of Christ's body and blood in the eucharist.

'collège' which should provide a thorough humanist training for in-
tending law students. It is a proposal in line with his historical and
philological approach to Roman Law. Like the most progressive
jurists of the time, he did not consider Roman Law a static and
eternally valid codification, but thought that it should be approached
like any other historical document. Whereas the earlier humanists
possessed little or no sense of history, Bodin remained interested
throughout his life in the particular historical and social circumstances in which any legal, political, or indeed religious enactment
had been made. The *Oratio* shows how he was already developing a
strong and inquiring historical imagination.

In many ways the *Oratio* is Bodin's most attractive and most
generous work. He eulogizes the encouragement by François I of
scholars and poets with a buoyant optimism which includes even
theology among the disciplines forwarded by his creation of the
Collège de France, and he praises contemporary improvements in
mechanical crafts, agriculture, architecture, and the arts of war. His
description of the fervent devotion inspired in noble minds by the
pursuit of knowledge is, of course, a Renaissance commonplace,
though none the less deeply felt for that. But he is also original when
advocating the use of French as the medium for teaching and for
scientific discourse. He speaks feelingly of religious and social unity,
and of common spiritual endeavour by all Frenchmen, ideals which
remain leitmotives of his thought, and which he hopes to see realized
by a system of publicly organized and supervised education of the
young in an (unspecified) 'pure' religion. This is a programme he admits having derived from the theocratic states of German-speaking
countries. The Gallican, monarchical attitudes of this speech do,
however, clearly favour the interests of the Crown against religious
extremism on both sides.

Those who supported these interests were soon to be known as the
party of the 'politiques', or 'tiers parti'. The word 'parti' is unfortunately misleading, for the tragedy of the wars of religion was that
men of the 'politique' outlook were not an effective or stable group-
ing until the very last years of the conflicts for which France was
already preparing in 1559. At Toulouse, the moderate party was
declining in influence at the Court, and the *Oratio* fell on deaf ears.

In 1561 Bodin became a member of the Paris Parlement where, after civil war had actually broken out early in 1562, he signed an oath of Catholic allegiance along with the majority of his colleagues (including Montaigne, a member of the Bordeaux Parlement and in Paris at the time). But his real loyalty was still to learning. His first important work, the *Methodus ad facilem historiarum cognitionem* (1566), is in part what its title implies, an art of reading historians critically. In the prefatory epistle Bodin explains that he has decided to dedicate all the time he has free from judicial affairs (the Paris Parlement was the highest court of justice) to the pursuit of scholarship. He hopes in particular to develop a methodology for the study of comparative law. But the *Methodus* itself so defines history that his programme of study sounds more like the plan of an encyclopedia of the human and natural sciences, together with metaphysics. And that is precisely what it is: a comprehensive programme of universal knowledge. This grandiose and original concept was very nearly carried out over the next thirty years, though not without many interruptions and complications due to the wars.

In the introduction to the *Methodus*, Bodin gets down to the task of mapping out a comparative approach to law which Baudouin had merely indicated in his important book on the conjunction of history and jurisprudence (*De institutione historiae universae, et de eius cum iurisprudentia conjunctione*, 1561), and takes the decisive step of rejecting Roman Law as the framework of investigation, a step Baudouin had not taken. Baudouin, however, had insisted that the legal profession should provide public servants to help society in its present difficulties, 'not inexperienced, foolish, adolescent orators, who bring the state to rapid ruin' but 'senatores', competent, public-minded men. The times urgently demand action, not rhetoric. For, as he says in his conclusion, 'man is placed on earth not merely to be a spectator and commentator, but to take a hand ('ut sit actor')'.

Similarly pragmatic and practical tendencies are already apparent in the *Methodus*, especially in those sections which analyse different types of constitution, and deal with questions of political stability. But obviously Bodin is not, as yet, especially worried by these questions, and although many additions to book six in the second edition (1572) are concerned with political instability, he observes confidently that the wise tolerance of the Valois kings is maintaining a reasonable degree of order. And book seven paints an even more optimistic picture of the onward march of Renaissance civilization than the *Oratio*.

The first open abandonment of Bodin's programme of encyclopaedic scholarship in favour of works more immediately relevant to incipient social collapse comes in his *Réponse au Paradoxe de M. de Malestroit* (1568). Unlike, for example, Budé's work on the *As and its Parts* (see ch. 3, p. 38), an elegant work of pure scholarship and unlike Bodin's previous works, the *Réponse* makes no claims to stylistic elegance. It is about a matter of mundanely practical concern. In this largely pioneering study of economic mechanisms, Bodin analyses some of the causes of the serious inflation of the period of which, he says, 'la cause principale et presque seule (que personne jusques icy n'a touchée) est l'abondance d'or et d'argent'. His analysis is no doubt incomplete, since the depreciation of coinage antedated the influx of Spanish bullion, and was probably in part due to a population explosion. Nevertheless, Bodin has clearly given the first clear expression of the quantity theory of money, and isolated a specific cause of social instability. In the *Réponse* Bodin begins to introduce the element of justice into his notion of legitimate political authority, and consequently attacks Machiavelli, whose grasp of political realities he had praised in the *Methodus*. He also urges the social necessity of charity, pointing out for instance that the abolition of smaller coinage by Elizabeth of England, due to inflation, had made the giving of charity to the poor more difficult.

This concern with justice and charity is carried much further in Bodin's *magnum opus*, the *République* (1576), which was written in the vernacular and is commonly accepted as the most important work of political theory between Machiavelli and Hobbes. Its significance was immediately acknowledged: as well as being translated into English, German, Italian, Spanish, and, by himself, into Latin, the *République* went through nineteen French editions before the turn of the century, nine of them by 1580. Its appeal is understandable, as France was now in a state of near-anarchy. The Saint Bartholomew Massacre of 1572 had hopelessly compromised the Crown in the eyes of Protestants, who had replied with angry, uncompromising, and rather muddled theories of resistance to tyranny. Hotman's *Franco-Gallia* (1573), the anonymous *Réveille-Matin* (1573/4), and Simon Goulart's oddly entitled *Mémoires de l'Estat de France* (1576) were, in fact, incitements to tyrannicide and defences of popular sovereignty. Goulart's *Mémoires* is a collection of works including La Boétie's *Servitude volontaire*, now published for the first time, apart from a section already included in the *Réveille-Matin*.

La Boétie's real, monarchical position of 1562 is vigorously upheld by the *République*, far more absolutist in tone than the *Methodus*. In the seventeenth century it inspired fully fledged theories of divine right—Bossuet used it a great deal. But Bodin's own theory of sovereignty is not a theory of the divine right of kings. True, he goes further than any previous theorist in claiming that all authority in a monarchy stems from the king, who only consults the representatives of the people (the States General, in France) because he can thereby govern more effectively. But the sovereign need not be a king. Some states are more effectively governed as democracies, and others as aristocracies, depending partly on the psychological characteristics of the people. Bodin's largely original reflections in the *République* and *Methodus* on the geographical and climatic factors which condition these characteristics, and on the need to adapt the constitution of any State to the psychologically and culturally conditioned requirements of its citizens, are pursued with a speculative flexibility which even Montesquieu does not match.

As we have seen, Bodin gives a role to the States General in the procedures of monarchical government. In the same year as the *République* appeared, Bodin was deputy of the Third Estate, representing Laon, at the States General held at Blois. The king, Henri III, was coming increasingly under the influence of extremist Catholics, and hoped to get financial support from the States for military action designed to eradicate the Huguenots once and for all. That he failed was apparently due entirely to the courageous oratory of Bodin who obstinately stood by his 'politique' support of a strong but tolerant monarchy, able to stand above religious faction. From this moment onwards, not only was Bodin's political career ruined, but the Crown was forced inevitably into the hands of Catholic intransigeance. Very few people could now hope, as Bodin still did in his speeches at the States (cf. his own *Commentaire*), that the king would be able to 'maintenir ses suiets en bonne paix, et dedans deux ans tenir un Concile general ou national pour regler le fait de la Religion'.

Two of the books Bodin wrote after the *République* have gained notoriety rather than fame, the *Démonomanie* and the *Heptaplomeres*, the one for its illiberalism towards witches, the other for its liberties towards Christianity.

The preface of the *Démonomanie* (1580) begins with Bodin's now habitual directness. He recounts how he was called on 30 April 1578 to the trial of a witch who faced a serious charge—carnal knowledge of the devil—to which she had pleaded guilty. One judge thought it sufficient to hang her, the others thought she should be burnt alive, a sentence which was carried out on the same day. Bodin concurs in the majority view, and the *Démonomanie*, addressed mainly to magistrates, is devoted to the proposition that 'il n'y a crimes qui soient à beaucoup près si execrables que cestuy-cy [la sorcellerie], ou qui meritent peines plus griefves'. A witch is guilty of sacrilege, for she deliberately adores God's creatures, instead of worshipping God their creator. The last of the four books of this disturbingly rigorous work gives detailed advice on the extraction of confessions through intimidation and torture.

The *Heptaplomeres*, which Bodin wrote towards the end of his life, remained in manuscript until the middle of the nineteenth century. Anyone who had a copy of it guarded it carefully. For it eradicates Christ from the true religion, and the ethics of Christ from the true morality. As its author is clearly anti-Christian, and equally clearly Catholic, the interpretation of the *Heptaplomeres*, which is still not easily accessible, has not always been very pertinent.

These two extraordinary works give us many clues to the under-lying tensions of the period. Just how are they related to Bodin's analysis of the problems raised by the civil wars?

Bodin's book on witchcraft had at least half a dozen editions in his lifetime. He discusses a topic of contemporary concern with vigour and conviction. Since the book is lucid and well arranged, it is not surprising that it became a standard European textbook. Nowadays, because of its distressing contents, it is usually neglected or regarded as a sign of mental deterioration. Such views are commonly linked with a reference to Montaigne as a writer whose serene scepticism dismisses this type of book for good in a couple of lines. The lines most frequently chosen come from 'Des Boyteux' (*Essais*, iii. 11): 'A tuer les gens, il faut une clarté lumineuse et nette', or again: 'Apres tout, c'est mettre ses conjectures à bien haut pris que d'en faire cuire un homme tout vif', together with his prescription of a purge rather than a poison for some women accused of witchcraft whom he had visited in prison.

In 'Des Boyteux' the examples used suggest that Montaigne is thinking of the *Démonomanie*: like any opponent of witch-trials at the period, and there were not many, he cannot, however, refute its arguments intellectually, and merely condemns the violent way witches are treated, and the violent way the case against them is put. He argues his case on grounds of humanity rather than logic.

Bodin bases his case in the first place on the strong Biblical authority for persecution, such as Leviticus 20: 4, which the extremely liberal Johann Wier had already translated as referring to poisoners rather than witches. But for most and perhaps all people at this time, like Bodin, or like Louis le Caron (in his *Questions Diverses*), the witches' own trial confessions gave overwhelming evidence of objective guilt even if, like le Caron, they accepted it reluctantly. The few who could not condone witch-trials and executions, tended to refrain from mentioning them in their diaries, just as Montaigne refrained from mentioning by name any of the writers against witchcraft.

It was inevitable that anyone with an interest in the way society functions in general, and a concern with the mal-functioning of France in particular, should think about the nature of witchcraft. The rise of witch-terror in continental Europe had been startlingly rapid, coinciding suggestively with the cultural and social disturbances associated with the break-up of the unity of Christendom. At Geneva the witch-terror had been particularly intense since the 1530s. The susceptibility of the Genevan government to popular pressures, the tendency to make the Old Testament the basis of legislation, and the Calvinist belief in man's complete corruption were all perhaps elements behind the recurrent witch-trials in Geneva, which set a pattern for Europe.

It may well be that there was a real increase in superstitious practices amongst the uneducated. In France, quite apart from the miseries of guerilla warfare, rapidly changing economic, social, and political conditions may well have induced a sense of helplessness which increased the need for religious reassurances at a time when these were frequently lacking. In many areas the Reformation had taken away the traditional props of the faithful who could no longer, for instance, expect prayers to be automatically answered, and thereby gain a sense of reparation when things were going badly. In areas immediately affected by fighting or rioting, established ways of living were easily broken up, and where churches were destroyed and priests were absent, the difficulties of picking up old patterns were aggravated. Witches, moreover, came almost entirely from the most vulnerable section of the peasant community. They were usually old, impoverished, unsupported females, perhaps dependent on charity. When crops were burnt, or plundered, or went unharvested, charity must have been hard to come by. It might not help much to go to the towns, where conditions could be as bad, and where a capitalist, individualist mentality was growing up, unsoftened by older ideas of mutual help. In any case, both town and country were plagued with rising food prices. No wonder such people were led to curse their fate and, by cursing those who refused them help, to initiate an accusation of blasphemy or witchcraft against themselves.

We may hopefully think that a witch is totally deluded, or define her as a person prosecuted for badly defined or impossible actions. Montaigne may have thought these things too (though even he never clearly stated them), and in the Middle Ages the practices of witchcraft had in fact been regarded by the educated with something like Montaigne's detached open-mindedness. But witchcraft had been assimilated with heresy towards the end of the fifteenth century, and later still became a matter for the civil courts rather than the potentially understanding priest. Unfortunately, the lawyers of the sixteenth and seventeenth centuries proved as much victims of contemporary fears and insecurities as the uneducated. Now in almost all his writings, Bodin shows profound concern for the distress caused by poverty and, as we have seen, he was acutely conscious of the need for charity. Yet, although he was intelligent enough to glimpse a link between witchcraft and poverty in the *Démonomanie*, he could not comprehend its significance. He was trapped by the universal association of witchcraft with heresy and blasphemy.

As early as 1566, in his *Apologie pour Hérodote*, Henri Estienne wrote a partly tongue-in-cheek exposure of the blasphemous habits of his age. As a Protestant he makes unoriginal and not very funny jibes about Catholic idolatry. However, although he may be wrong about the author of the *Cymbalum Mundi*: 'Qui ne sçait quel contempteur et mocqueur de Dieu a esté Bonaventure des Periers', and is certainly wrong about Rabelais, described as the author of 'rescrits brocardants toute sorte de religion', these words are seriously meant. They indicate a new development of sensibility, a real awareness of the possibility of considered unbelief, and a fear of its consequences for society.

As the political pressures to conform to the various national religions increased, so dogmatic divisions had sharpened. At the same time confessional disputes increasingly revealed the problematical nature of religious choice. Large numbers of men were faced with totally new issues of personal commitment when forced to choose between competing catechisms. Accusations of blasphemy and atheism begin to be common, and they are liable, in these circumstances, to have a defensive ring about them, and may reveal more about the deeper insecurities of the accuser than about those of the accused. They are nearly always made by people against whom the accusation could be returned in kind.

Moreover, it was usual to believe that whole communities suffered retribution for the sins of the few, a belief which added considerable urgency to the widespread and passionately felt fear of blasphemy. The search for religious reunification was therefore very frequently impelled on both sides by the sense that disunity itself was the retribution for impiety, which could be, and was, conceived in a supraconfessional and unpartisan manner. As late as 1575, at a meeting of 'politique' Catholics and Protestants at Nîmes, the causes of discord were said to arise from 'le courroux de Dieu par le manquement de piété et justice... l'examen de ceste piété fut bien et legitimement commencé au concile de Poissy, où la vérité obtint quelque liberté' (quoted by d'Aubigné, *Histoire universelle*, vii. 17). Such opinions were quite common even through the early 1580s in intellectual Court circles, where Bodin's 'politique' desire that the Court should set an example of piety and lead the religious reform of the country was seriously pursued.

So we might expect the *Démonomanie* to view the Court of Henri III with a less jaundiced eye than it does. Nowadays, Bodin claims, the Court is advised by its sorcerers to commit murder and pardon crimes—indeed the rulers themselves use magic. But if the ruler is a sorcerer, 'les mignons et courtisans, puis le peuple y est attiré, et par conséquent à toutes impiétés'. This attitude towards the Court was by no means uncommon, nor was it completely unjustified. In its best-known versions (such as d'Aubigné's scathing attack in the *Tragiques*), it is obviously excessive. Yet the Court, as we have seen, was isolated and weak. Under the uncertain guidance of Catherine de Médici, its policies oscillated between brutal acts of force, like the Saint Bartholomew Massacre, which was lauded by many of the Court poets, and the semi-magical use of music and poetry and dancing in Court festivities designed to effect reunion as by a spell. These expensive festivities and the increasingly histrionic religiosity of Henri III and his inner circle of devoted courtiers repelled many outside observers. At the Court there was a fashionable interest in conjuring tricks and fortune-telling at which d'Aubigné, for one, proved a great success with the ladies. There was probably also widespread and serious use of magic for political ends.

Bodin's attack on impiety embraces the Court as well as the uneducated. Above all, Bodin is incensed and disappointed by the Court's failure to proscribe blasphemy successfully since, 'd'autant que cette impiété là regnait du temps de Charles IX plus que jamais, le Roy Henri troisiesme à sa venue fit un édit tressaint contre les blasphemeurs'. This particularly unpleasant 'holy edict', as Bodin calls it, offers a reward to informers, and ordains graduated penalties culminating after various other brutalities in the excision of the tongue with a hot iron. Bodin, who does not quote it, does describe

approvingly the infliction of these penalties under a similar edict of
1569. We should remember that the graduated punishment of witchcraft and blasphemy which Bodin himself advocated was explicitly,
in part, curative and deterrent. He did not, therefore, advocate the
torture of a hardened witch or blasphemer. One of the main grounds
for the criticism of Christianity in the *Heptaplomeres* will be its in-
consistent and arbitrary use of the deterrent of Hell, and its socially
dangerous encouragement of forgiveness.

Bodin's quest for the 'pure' religion which he posits in the *Oratio*
led him ultimately to compose, in about 1593, his most original and
imaginative work. The *Heptaplomeres* is in the form of a discussion
between a Catholic, a Lutheran, a Zwinglian, a deist, a Moslem, a
Jew, and a pagan. The atmosphere of its six books is curiously
blended of passion and piety and scholarship. All the speakers join
in the singing of psalms, often to the accompaniment of music performed by young boys, which may remind us of the reunionist psalm-
singing which Monluc, Bishop of Valence, had praised in his speech
of 1560 and which did, in fact, take place at the Court to settings
composed by Catholic and Protestant Court musicians. At various
times individual speakers are impelled to sing or recite religious
poems, and their more fervent speeches may be preceded by a
dramatic pause, or followed by an exhausted silence.

The extremely circumstantial nature of many details suggests that
the *Heptaplomeres* may well be based on the proceedings of an actual
academy in Venice which, as Naudé told Patin, were kept by
Guillaume Postel, and came into Bodin's possession. However that
may be, the work has a distinctly 'real' flavour, which becomes of
interest when we consider the difficulty of reconstructing the actual
mood of the proceedings at the many Renaissance academies from
the speeches which have been recorded. It may be that the *Heptaplomeres* allows us to get nearer to their encyclopaedic enthusiasms
and pious reunionist aspirations than any other document.

Some of the characters stay in the mind. Apart from the courteous
Catholic host, and the dignified Jew, we remember, for example, the
impulsive, easily deceived Lutheran, Frederick. At the beginning of
book five, which is concerned with the criteria to be used in religious

disputes, he falls into a nice trap. The trap is set by the mischievously obliging Catholic. The apples he offers his guests contain artificial ones, made of wax. Frederick takes an injudicious mouthful: like all Lutherans, it is implied, he has bitten off more than he can chew. It is a position all the Christian speakers get themselves into. We remember, too, the curious pagan, Senamy, critic of all positive religions, and no respecter of persons, who is resolutely convinced with the others of the necessary function of all religion, however superstitious, as a socially cohesive force, and consequently worships in all churches. He reminds us of the universally eclectic piety of Bodin's contemporary Bruno, sincerely taking part in Lutheran worship in Germany, and Calvinist worship in Switzerland. In fact, all seven characters are convincingly individualized; and their exchanges often have an honest vehemence reminiscent of Montaigne's ideal conversationalist (see *Essais*, iii. 8).

The realities of much ideological discussion are well caught in the *Heptaplomeres*. The participants often talk at cross-purposes, and none is persuaded to change his beliefs. There is, consequently, no explicit conclusion in favour of one speaker. At the same time, the presentation of the arguments is not deliberately enigmatic, nor are the issues, on the whole, ill defined or confused. Although sometimes concealed by the richness of exemplification, the structure is clear: in the first three books all the speakers agree on rigidly monotheist and strictly voluntarist ethical principles, which in the last three books are met only by a simplified form of Judaism, approved by the deist and the Moslem. Throughout the book, so scornful of arguments from authority, the credentials of the Old Testament are never questioned, not even by the pagan. (Platonic truths, according to a common sixteenth-century view, derived from Moses.) Solomon, the Jew, has a peculiarly strong advantage in a discussion conducted on this presupposition, due to his acknowledged pre-eminence in Biblical exegesis. He can and does therefore lay down the law throughout the *Heptaplomeres*, either to support, or to be supported by, the deist and the Moslem, and usually one or more of the Christians, depending on the point in dispute. He is the oldest speaker, and accepted as wisest and best by the others, who plead with him, at the beginning of book four, to join in the discussion of their varying religious views. Coroni solemnly promises him: 'Je vous promets et me rends guarend pour tous que quoy que vous demeuriez victorieux ou que vous soyez vaincu, nous n'en serons pas moins amis pour cella.' It is a uniquely solemn procedural moment in the dialogue, looking forward to its serene but disillusioned ending, with its acceptance of mutual religious disagreement and renunciation of religious debate. Confessional reunion has proved impossible, but the pursuit of knowledge goes on, to the accompaniment of pious singing of the psalms, which express a basic, monotheist piety acceptable to all.

The *Heptaplomeres* is a nobler and larger re-enactment of the colloquy of Poissy, seeking to establish a basis of tolerance, and a return to a shared spirituality. Like the Protestant Acontius and the Catholic Cassander, whose views were influential at Poissy, the speakers in the dialogue attempt to reach agreement on a limited number of basic articles of belief. Indeed, tolerance spreads even further to include Senamy, the pagan, who has no known religious allegiance, and sees in all religions, monotheist or not, some part of a truth which no positive religion adequately defines. Even in the *République*, Bodin's advocacy of religious toleration includes any religion whatsoever. It will be remembered, however, that the colloquy of Poissy finally came to grief over mutual instransigeance on the question of the Real Presence. As at Poissy, so in the Venice of the *Heptaplomeres*. At last Coroni stands his ground, as he must, and states harshly that those who reject the Real Presence burn in the eternal fires.

The unequivocal rejection of eternal torment which follows this assertion, and which virtually concludes the dialogue, is a striking example of Bodin's compassion and intellectual ruthlessness. Such explicitness on the subject was extremely rare before the eighteenth century and had been almost unknown since Origen's attack in the early third century. The rejection of orthodoxy is rationally unanswerable, given the earlier agreement that all sin is finite and that the soul, being corporeal, is not eternal. For, if this is agreed, no sin can merit infinite punishment, nor can any punishment last eternally. The deist argues, furthermore, that an infinitely great threat, supposing it be conceivable, leads to the lethargy of despair and, if it is not conceivable, is pointless. At the back of these arguments lies Bodin's unusually clear conviction that actions performed out of fear or insanity or ignorance are ethically neutral.

The 1580s were an especially dismal and hopeless period of the religious wars. After Bodin had, in 1584, put the finishing touches to his Latin version of the *République* (published 1586) he abandoned his analysis of the problems of political division, and his attempt to construct a comprehensive theory of political obligation. Events were making it plain that force, not reason, would decide the future shape of France. In 1584 the death of the Duc d'Alençon, who had been for some time the pale white hope of the 'politiques', made the Huguenot Henri de Navarre direct heir to the throne. In the following year a despairing Henri III was forced to ally himself finally with the extremist Catholics of the League. There was no longer a centre for 'politique' loyalism. Frenchmen had to decide whether they were Catholic and royalist, or Protestant and rebellious.

In the same year, 1585, Henri III's Palace Academy, the intellectual background of the Court festivities designed to bring about a harmonious return to peace and unity, was disbanded, and one of its leading members, Ronsard, died. In his funeral oration Du Perron declares that Ronsard is lucky to die and escape from so chaotic a world. This note of melancholy world-weariness is apparent in the epitaph Bodin composed for his closest friend, Nicholas Trouillard, who died in 1587, 'luckily taken up ['opportune ereptus'] from the flames of civil wars'. It was this mood which induced Louis le Caron to seek in philosophy some consolation for the agonies of never-ending conflict, as he explains in the dedication of his *De la tranquilité d'esprit*. He published this treatise in 1588, together with a *Discours sur le proces criminel faict à une sorciere*. Both works, the title-page points out, are 'traictez grandement necessaires pour le temps present'. Both of them preach the unity of religion. The work on witchcraft expresses the primitive, retributionist fears we have noted before, being written to incite judges to 'rechercher et punir tels crimes, et admonester les François à prier et invoquer plus devotement Dieu, pour appaiser son Ire, qui permet pour noz pechez telles impietez et meschancetez durer entre nous, qui sont cause de troubler le vray repos de la Chrestienté'. Social, and therefore spiritual, calm can only be restored by a return to the reassurance and stability given by the traditional religion, he explains in the *Tranquilité d'esprit*. Unity of religion was the cry of the League.

Those who had sought to construct the ideal and the reality of national unity on a basis of mutual toleration were now silent, whilst the pamphleteers of the League wrote furiously. Dissatisfied with the lingering irresolution of the king they now composed heady apologies of popular sovereignty and regicide as the Protestants themselves had done in the 1570s. Indeed, in 1588 the League chased Henri III ignominiously from his capital. In desperation he ordered the assassination at Blois of the ambitious and insolent leaders of the League, the Duc de Guise and his brother the Cardinal. The League made sure that its own theories of divine retribution worked: on 2 August 1589 Henri III was killed by the knife of Jacques Clément.

For over four years Paris, terrorized by the League, held out with fanatical courage against their new king, the Protestant Henri de Navarre. Only after he had been converted to Catholicism in July 1593 could he undertake the conquest of Paris with sufficient national support to ensure success. And even then the bitterness and divisions of thirty-five years were to survive for many years, especially amongst the Huguenots (see Chapter 10).

Whilst Paris was under siege in 1590, Guillaume du Vair wrote an eloquent *Traicté de la constance et de la consolation ès calamités publiques*. This dialogue, the most interesting of the discourses on consolation written as a result of the civil wars, is also the most closely related to classical models, such as Seneca's epistolary *Consolatio ad Helviam*. But though the work recaptures the classical eloquence of La Boétie, it has ceased to theorize about politics. Du Vair can merely wait on events. His hopes for the speedy victory of Henri IV and hatred for the excesses of the League are tempered by fear of the violence both may perform. In its urbanity, clarity, and moderation his work is reminiscent of Montaigne, though it is more moving on a public issue than Montaigne knew how to be.

Fundamentally, as we have seen, the *Servitude volontaire* of La Boétie had proposed that ideal of self-awareness and spiritual detachment which had guided Montaigne. Du Vair's work shows a more than verbal echo of the same ideal: 'Or, si nous pouvons persuader de supporter la pauvreté, combien plus aisément la perte de nos dignités et honneurs, qui ne sont qu'une servitude volontaire par laquelle nous nous privons de nous-mêmes pour nous donner au public!' This renunciation of political theorizing in favour of a concentration on the moral and religious exploration of the self will mark the most characteristic writing of the coming century, when peace has been restored.

When Du Vair wrote, the country was still bitterly divided. The reluctance of Catholics to accept a heretic as legitimate king, and their struggles of conscience over the prolongation of the disastrous chaos which this reluctance involved, are honestly and tragically expressed in the *Dialogue du maheustre et du manant*, written in Paris towards the end of 1593. The Catholic 'manant' is only too well aware of the divisions and cynical intrigues within the League, which had become an openly unpatriotic and mercenary cover for conflicting personal ambitions. But his conscience forces him to prefer a foreign but Catholic monarch to a French but heretical one.

By 1594 it was obvious, even in Paris, that Henri IV's conversion had been accepted by the country at large, and that (barring assassination) he would soon enter his capital at the head of a re-united army of loyal Protestant and Catholic believers. The anti-League pamphlet, the *Satyre Ménippée*, is a pungent, vigorous, exuberant attack on an enemy already certain of defeat, and a celebration of the inevitable return of peace. This corporate work catches the mood of the nation in the speech attributed to d'Aubray:

Le Roi que nous demandons est déjà fait par la nature, né au vrai parterre des fleurs de lys de France, jeton droit et verdoyant du tige de Saint Louis. Ceux qui parlent d'en faire un autre se trompent, et ne sauraient en venir à bout. On peut faire des sceptres et des couronnes, mais non pas des Rois pour les porter: on peut faire une maison, mais non pas un arbre ou un rameau vert: il faut que la nature le produise, par espace de temps, du suc et de la moelle de la terre, qui entretient le tige en sa sève et vigueur...

Henri IV may have some defects, d'Aubray concedes, even if the worst is only his excessive clemency in a situation calling for rigour. In any case, peace is the pressing need: 'il n'y a paix si inique qui ne vaille mieux qu'une tres-juste guerre.'

It was a lesson that France had taken long to learn, and tried desperately hard to remember, as the country returned gradually to peace. But the ability to ask original or fundamental questions about the nature of society was seriously weakened in the process, and was hardly to be revived before the eighteenth century.

NOTE

Studies. Introductory discussions of the historical background include G. Livet, *Les Guerres de religion* (1966); R. Mandrou, *Introduction à la France moderne* (1961), an interesting socio-psychological approach; R. Mousnier, *Les XVIᵉ et XVIIᵉ siècles* (1956); J. E. Neale, *The Age of Catherine de Medici* (1943). Political theorists are studied by J. W. Allen, *A History of Political Thought in the Sixteenth Century* (1928); V. de Caprariis, *Propaganda e pensiero politico in Francia* (1959), for the first years of the wars; J. Lecler, *Histoire de la tolérance au siècle de la Réforme* (1955), Eng. tr. *Toleration and the Reformation* (1960); P. Mesnard, *L'Essor de la philosophie politique au 16ᵉ siècle* (1951). There are interesting discussions of Bodin in R. Chauviré, *Jean Bodin, auteur de la 'République'* (1914), the best single book on Bodin; J. H. Franklin, *Jean Bodin and the Sixteenth Century Revolution in the Methodology of Law and History* (1963); J. Plamenatz, *Man and Society* (1963). The philosophical background is treated by H. Busson, *Le Rationalisme dans la littérature française de la Renaissance* (1957); R. H. Popkin, *History of Scepticism from Erasmus to Descartes* (1960); D. P. Walker, *Spiritual and Demonic Magic from Ficino to Campanella* (1958); Frances A. Yates, *The French Academies of the Sixteenth Century* (1946); these last four works are original and important.

Editions. Jean Bodin: *Réponse au paradoxe de M. de Malestroit*, excellent edition by H. Hauser (1932), Eng. tr. by C. A. Moore (1946); *Œuvres philosophiques*, tr. P. Mesnard (1951), contains *Oratio* and *Methodus*; *Method for the easy Comprehension of History*, tr. Beatrice Reynolds (1945); *The Six Books of a Commonwealth*, ed. K. D. Macrae (1962), reproduces Knolles's translation of 1611, has valuable editorial matter; *Six Books of the Commonwealth*, tr. M. J. Tooley (n.d., 1955), is heavily abridged; *Colloquium Heptaplomeres*, ed. L. Noack (1857); *Colloque de Jean Bodin*, ed. R. Chauviré (1914), an excellent partial edition of a good seventeenth-century translation.

Other writers. Étienne de la Boétie, *Œuvres philosophiques*, ed. F. Hincker (1963), also *Discours de la servitude volontaire*, ed. M. Rat (1963); Guillaume du Vair, *Traité de la constance*, ed. J. Flack and F. Funck Brentano (1915); *Satyre Ménippée*, ed. Ch. Read (1876). On other little-edited works and writers, the *Dictionnaire des lettres françaises, XVIᵉ siècle*, ed. Mgr Grente, is usually reliable.

12. Montaigne

THE preface to the first edition of Montaigne's *Essais* gives a provocatively straightforward warning to the reader that they are merely a self-portrait, written for a private and personal purpose; a warning that there is no sense in the reader's leisure being spent on a matter so trifling and useless, 'un subject si frivole et si vain'. Similarly self-disparaging remarks recur just as insistently in the subsequent, enlarged, editions. Thus, if one of the earliest essays (i. 13) begins: 'Il n'est subject si vain, qui ne merite un rang en cette rapsodie', the last of all describes the *Essais* still more mundanely as 'toute cette fricassée que je barbouille icy'. Humble pie, indeed, or even less: for rather as Rabelais's creative persona is that of the drunkard, so Montaigne explains that his work is the excremental product of his dotage (iii. 9).[1] Is this self-disparagement no more than self-defensive irony? How is it bound up with Montaigne's view of man in general? Is it perhaps merely trivial self-advertisement or is it part of a serious artistic purpose? These are some of the questions provoked by Montaigne's preface. We shall examine them in this order, and hope to keep to something like the underlying order of one of Montaigne's own essays. But within each topic we shall progress, like the *Essais*, by digression.

Montaigne's self-critical stance corresponds in part to the adoption of extreme theoretical positions by so many innovating French writers, uncertain of their audience and of their place in literary tradition. It corresponds, for example, to the exaggerations in the manifestos of Romantic and Naturalist writers. For the *Essais* were in fact a surprisingly innovating work. They draw a self-portrait which attempts to re-create, as fully as possible, the

---

[1] Of course there is a psychological difference; drinking is an extroverted, excretion an introverted, activity—a difference characteristic of the two authors.

whole range of Montaigne's memories and experiences—aesthetic, emotional, and intellectual—as they occurred, over the twenty years or so (approximately 1572–92) during which the book was written. They do not have the chronological form of a diary. They are not an attempt to draw a whole life into a single focus, but tend rather to a multiplication of viewpoints and interpretations. They are a continuing, unsystematic, but thorough record of Montaigne's reflections on his life, on his reading, on friends and acquaintances, on contemporary events, on general moral problems. They are, above all, a record of his deepening conviction that as his exploration of his own attitudes became more detailed, more personal, more 'useless', so it increased in value. In many of these points the *Essais* were of course not only novel, but have remained unique, with the possible exception of Gide's *Journal*.

The sixteenth-century reader would have been unprepared for a person with no acknowledged claim to statesmanship, sagacity, or saintliness, a man of no notoriety, to reveal himself so openly in print. European literary tradition forbade the unqualified to indulge in autobiography. Unlike autobiographical writers of antiquity, Montaigne cannot claim to tell us the reasons for military or political success, as Caesar does in his *Commentaries*, or to instruct us how to live, as does Cicero in his *Letters*; least of all to show us the operation of grace in his life, like St. Augustine in his *Confessions*. Again, unlike works such as Dante's *Vita Nuova*, and Petrarch's *Secretum Meum*, the *Essais* do not set out to dignify and stylize a literary vocation in terms of a quasi-religious conversion. Montaigne's first readers might indeed have read the autobiographies of Cellini or Cardano. Whilst neither man impresses us with an essential truthfulness—Cellini is too gossipy, Cardano too self-pitying—their quirky, irrepressible books do give some foretaste of the equally personal *Essais*. But they cannot be said to have much in common with this saner, more objective, and much more ambitious work. Like Cellini and Cardano—only more so—Montaigne wishes to offer us his unqualified, unprofessional views on life in general, and on himself in particular. Unlike them, he seems to have decided to make the best of his impertinence, and to proclaim the insignificance of his enterprise.

But the theme of vanity, or insignificance, is at the heart of Montaigne's view of man in general, as well as of himself and of his book. The theme 'that man hath no pre-eminence above a beast: for all is vanity' (Ecclesiastes 3: 9) is a leitmotif of the *Essais*; nowhere more eloquently espoused than in the essay on vainglory (ii. 17): 'De toutes les opinions que l'ancienneté a euës de l'homme en gros, celles que j'embrasse plus volontiers et ausquelles je m'attache le plus, ce sont celles qui nous mesprisent, avilissent et aneantissent le plus.'

And this theme is nowhere more lovingly pursued than in the essay which took up a quarter of the first edition: the *Apologie de Raimond Sebond*. This is a defence of the Spanish theologian whose *Natural Theology* Montaigne had translated, a translation which he published in 1569. It defends him in two ways. Firstly, a fairly short section approves of a demonstration of the truth of religion by rational argument, such as Sebundus attempts, though only after a prior grounding of the truth in faith, which is very much the position of Pascal. Then follows an extremely lengthy section which 'defends' and excuses the weakness of Sebundus's arguments by demonstrating that all rational argument is weak anyway.

The view that this long essay is evidence of a personal crisis in Montaigne is hardly compatible with the tone or even the contents of the essay. The second section, whilst it develops an increasingly radical attack on human reason, merely restates and reinforces positions which Montaigne had come to well before this date. Even his first essay had concluded: 'C'est un subject merveilleusement vain, divers, et ondoyant, que l'homme.' It is the demonstration of the vanity of man which is indeed the unifying element of the whole apology, rather than the attack on reason. Thus, on the same page, Montaigne may be seen arguing that animals are dignified by the possession of reason, and also that they are dignified by having only instinct—the function of both of these apparently contradictory arguments being to lower the status of man. The eclecticism of the arguments and the multiplicity of examples; the over-mobile, over-curious mind self-indulgently at play; the affectionate, undespairing contemplation of human insignificance: all show us a mind untouched by religious doubt, and undisturbed by philosophical uncertainty. Even the so-called Pyrrhonism of the *Apologie*—the view that no philosophical conclusion whatsoever is immune from doubt—seems negated by the consistency with which Montaigne presses home the theme of vanity.

The *Apologie* reveals reason as a self-contradictory force, a two-edged sword on which religious systems can only be lacerated. Faith, being grounded in divine revelation, escapes destruction. For Montaigne personally, faith seems to be mediated through the Church, and through society, and to have no grounding in the *personal* revelation which the almost liturgical ending of the *Apologie* seems to indicate as the proper religious basis for the sceptical position he has adopted. Montaigne does not experience faith as part of the uniqueness of himself, that uniqueness which the *Essais* are, essentially, devoted to exploring, expanding, and strengthening.

All the same, however problematical Montaigne's Catholicism has seemed to his commentators, it is almost certain that it did not seem so to him. True, he may on occasion put forward a view which, theologically speaking, has Protestant implications: 'Il faut avoir l'ame nette, au moins en ce moment auquel nous le prions [Dieu], et deschargée de passions vitieuses' (i. 56), just as he may, on occasion, write an incidental phrase with an exclusively Catholic implication: 'Les Chrestiens... sçavent... que Dieu regarde agir tout l'homme, et veut qu'entier il reçoive le chastiement, ou le loyer, selon ses merites' (ii. 17). In each case he is not writing from a confessional viewpoint, however, but as an innocent layman. Whenever he does write on subjects of obvious theological relevance, such as suicide or repentance or prayer, he handles theology as if it were moral philosophy. And whilst he does so in a spirit of piety, the fact is, as Dréano well puts it: 'il préfère un acte de vertu à un acte de piété.'

As a convinced deist and a devout Catholic, Montaigne seems to be in the tradition of liberal theologians like Erasmus, preparing the way for a Lord much more loving than the God of Calvin or of d'Aubigné. And on one theological issue Montaigne does speak out boldly, twice commenting forcibly on the injustice, as he sees it, of the notions of eternal torment and eternal bliss (ii. 12), though careful to put the remarks into discussions of the Platonic, and not the Christian, afterworld. Even here, Montaigne's passion is contained within the mould of coolly direct query or comment.

The note of religious enthusiasm is rare in Montaigne, especially where religion itself is concerned. The passionate voice is heard, typically, in vehement denunciation of man's inhumanity to man (see the essay on cruelty, ii. 11), or in celebration of literature or of friendship. Thus the ending of the *Apologie* conveys no feeling of personal involvement: '[l'homme] s'eslevera si Dieu lui preste extraordinairement la main: il s'eslevera, abandonnant et renonçant à ses propres moyens, et se laissant hausser et soubslever par les moyens purement celestes. C'est à nostre foy Chrestienne, non à sa vertu Stoïque, de pretendre à cette divine et miraculeuse metamorphose.' Here the repetitions seem merely repetitious and flat, and fail to concentrate and particularize, as Montaigne's repetitions normally do. Compare them with the emphatically serious praise of Amyot's translation of Plutarch at the beginning of *A demain les affaires* (ii. 4), and the sprightly, humorous and yet deeply personal reaction which sums up Montaigne's gratitude to Amyot: 'Nous autres ignorans estions perdus, si ce livre ne nous eust relevez du bourbier: sa mercy, nous osons à cett'heure et parler et escrire; les dames en regentent les maistres d'escole; c'est nostre breviaire.' Again, whenever Montaigne refers to his lifelong Catholicism he confines himself to bald statement of his submission to the 'Église catholique, apostolique et Romaine en laquelle je suis nay' (i. 56), or to bald statement of his fundamental conservatism: 'en matiere d'opinions universelles, dés l'enfance je me logeay au poinct où j'avois à me tenir' (iii. 2).

The plain impersonality of these remarks stands in contrast to the precise, yet fervent, statement of his lifelong love of poetry: 'dés ma premiere enfance, la poësie a eu cela, de me transpercer et transporter', a statement which is then expanded into a sensitive account of the effect on him of Ovid: 'une fluidité gaye et ingenieuse', of Lucan: 'une subtilité aiguë et relevée', and of Virgil: 'une force meure et constante' (ii. 37).

Finally, with Montaigne's passionately moving description of his love for his dead friend, La Boétie, we can compare nothing in his own work: 'Si je compare tout le reste de ma vie , ... si je la compare, dis-je, toute aux quatre années qu'il m'a esté donné de jouyr de la douce compagnie et societé de ce personnage, ce n'est que fumée, ce n'est qu'une nuit obscure et ennuyeuse. Depuis le jour que je le perdy, je ne fay que trainer languissant...' (i. 29). It is perhaps, among sixteenth-century writers, only in the love poetry of Louise Labé that we find anything to equal the tender, intensely felt sense of loss which these lines, and the entire essay, convey so completely.

No doubt we seem to have moved a long way from the theme of vanity. Yet not so far, after all. With Montaigne's reaction to the death of La Boétie, we may well have returned to the emotional reality underlying his philosophical statement of the world's empty vanity. The actual writing of the *Essais* may be seen, fundamentally, as an attempt to re-create that noble conviction of the essential meaningfulness of human aspiration which his friend inspired. Had La Boétie lived, Montaigne's thoughts might well have been expressed in a correspondence with him, rather than as essays: 'Et (j') eusse prins plus volontiers ceste forme à publier mes verves, si j'eusse eu à qui parler. Il me falloit, comme je l'ay eu autrefois, un certain commerce qui m'attirast, qui me soustinst et souslevast' (i. 40).

We have looked at some of the self-defensive and philosophical implications of the theme of vanity, or insignificance. But how far is the purpose of Montaigne's self-portrait bound up with the vanity which is vainglory, the pretence of the *poseur*? It is at least possible that some element of self-advertisement lies behind the self-disparagement of the preface. Does Montaigne frequently pretend to be less—or more—than he knows he is? There is in fact a hint of vanity, certainly a touch of untruthfulness, in what Montaigne says about his acceptance of the collar of the order of Saint Michael, and of the citizenship of Rome. Both were honours which Montaigne sought, and which meant much more to him than the *Essais* suggest. Similarly, whilst he criticizes the French nobility as 'gens qui ont peu de soing de la culture de l'ame' (ii. 17), he sometimes fosters the impression that he was of the old military aristocracy. He was not. Montaigne's family had prospered in trade, and his father had entered the judicial nobility only in 1519, some fourteen years before

Montaigne's birth. Why is the generally transparent truthfulness of the *Essais* darkened by something like vanity in this way?

Like some of Montaigne's contemporaries, we may legitimately smile at the aristocratic and military pretensions in the *Essais*. But we can try to understand why the aristocratic, military persona is natural to him as a man and essential to him as a writer. Surely, we may think, there is nothing of the natural soldier in a man who only mentions his friend Monluc to draw a touching picture of Monluc's regret at having brought up a son in a manner so strict and military that it excluded intimacy and affection (ii. 8). Yet Montaigne does wish a nobleman's son to be brought up with a love of the military life (i. 26) and he soberly insists on a physical toughness to fit him for a world at war which contrasts strongly with the gay, fantastic exercises in military skill required by the exuberant educational syllabus of Rabelais's Gargantua. Surely a man who cannot even excuse most of the military actions of his own side in the civil wars (iii. 10), in which soldiers act like miserable butchers (ii. 6) and men stir up war, because it *is* war (ii. 1), can have no feeling for military values? Yet Montaigne sees in military valour the one excellence which his contemporaries do achieve, and writes some of his most sustained lines of praise in eulogy of the soldier's life:

Il n'est occupation plaisante comme la militaire... La compaignie de tant d'hommes vous plaist, nobles, jeunes, actifs, la veue ordinaire de tant de spectacles tragiques, la liberté de cette conversation sans art, et une façon de vie masle et sans ceremonie, la varieté de mille actions diverses, cette courageuse harmonie de la musique guerrière qui vous entretient et eschauffe et les oreilles et l'ame, l'honneur de cet exercice, son aspreté mesme et sa difficulté... Vous vous conviez aux rolles et hazards particuliers selon que vous jugez de leur esclat et de leur importance. (iii. 13)

In this description of the soldier's life there is a literariness which resembles the second-hand nature of his description of religious revelation at the end of the *Apologie*. Montaigne is not referring to any specific military engagement in which he personally has taken part. But there is also a literariness which resembles his reflections on the classical moralists; these are not merely second-hand textbook commentaries, but vital reactions to the modes of experience which their philosophies offer. They embody imaginative, and often vivid, re-creations of the possibilities of the moral life, if not of the actualities of his own life. Similarly, whilst Montaigne did have limited military experience, in the passage quoted above he expands his awareness of it into a description which goes beyond the limitations of the merely biographical and factual. The *Essais* are often imaginatively self-transcendent in this way.

The title itself gives a key to this central feature of the book. The 'essai' is the trial, the try-out, the exploration, the flexing of one's muscles and of one's mind. Montaigne twice describes the book as 'l'essay de mes facultés naturelles', twice as 'les essais de mon jugement', before reaching the comprehensive formulation of it as 'le registre des essais de ma vie'. Verbs such as 'essayer', 'exploicter', 'employer', 'exercer', 's'escrimer', 'branler', 'agir', 'agiter', 'savourer', 'goûter', 'tâter', recur and re-echo as he conveys his sensuous, very active apprehension of his own life, and imaginative investigation of the experience of others. Such expressions stand in striking juxtaposition with Montaigne's frequent confessions of an innate lethargy and inertia. Together they can give the impression of a man frightened of inactivity and uselessness; and this fear would almost certainly be heightened, if not entirely produced, by Montaigne's 'retreat', his retirement from the public life into a life of meditation and creation. Montaigne may perhaps be seen as the first man in modern literature to express the weight of ennui, the artist's frustration at the inertness and inadequacy of his life.

However this may be, Montaigne sees movement in all things, and seeks action at all costs. Action, no matter how trivial or vain: 'Nous sommes nés pour agir. Je veux qu'on agisse... et que la mort me treuve plantant mes chous, mais nonchallant d'elle, et encore plus de mon jardin imparfait' (i. 20). Cabbage planting is seen by Monluc as being the negation of the military life (*Commentaires*, Pléiade edition, p. 350). But to Montaigne the defence of king and country, and the planting of cabbages, can both be worthwhile activities and worthwhile topics to discuss, as they are for Lewis Carroll's walrus and carpenter.

Montaigne's praise of the rough vigour of life in the military camp is some evidence of the naturalness with which he assumes the soldierly persona. His vehement, demanding nature finds in war the action which his body and mind both need. 'Mon esprit ne va, si les jambes ne l'agitent' (iii. 3). And he finds too the reaction of others which is equally important to him, especially the reaction of others in conversation, in friendship, or in love: 'Nul plaisir n'a goust pour moy sans communication' (iii. 9). Jousting, fencing, and fighting metaphors give to the chapter on conversation (iii. 8) its unity and dense suggestiveness. Any kind of social intercourse is seen ideally as a military engagement: 'Elle n'est pas assez vigoureuse et genereuse, si elle n'est querelleuse, si elle est civilisée et artiste, si elle craint le hurt et a ses allures contreintes.'

The love affair too is seen as a Stendhalian challenge, an adventure, which thrives on strife and difficulty: 'J'ayme une societé et familiarité forte et virile, une amitié qui se flatte en l'aspreté et vigueur de son commerce, comme l'amour, és morsures et esgratigneures sanglantes' (iii. 8). Montaigne celebrates the pursuit of love as a paradigm of the universal desire for movement and experience, in a manner far removed from any lofty, platonizing metaphysics: 'Tout le mouvement du monde se resoult et rend à cet accouplage: c'est une matiere infuse par tout, c'est un centre où toutes choses regardent' (iii. 5).[1]

Montaigne, then, easily and naturally acted the soldier. It was in his character. And he also wrote as the soldier. It was, at first, not easy and not natural for him to write at all. But for various reasons it was necessary, and inevitable, that he write as the military man, the soldier-aristocrat. When Montaigne began writing the *Essais*, the time to practise the love of women was past. He was too old at forty. And the time of conversation and friendship with the two men for whom he had felt love—his father and La Boétie—had gone. They were dead. They live on, however, in the *Essais*, especially, perhaps, in the apparently less personal earlier essays of the first two books. The Stoic attitudes to life and the questions of military tactics which are so frequently discussed in these essays, were subjects on which Montaigne talked to La Boétie, and to his father, as authorities: La Boétie due to the manner of his life and death (consciously

---

[1] There is a revealing similarity here with Pascal's phrase: 'Jesus-Christ est le centre où tout tend.' Christ is hardly mentioned in the *Essais*.

modelled on Stoic deaths), and his father due to his participation in military campaigns under François Ier. But underneath even the lawyer's robes of La Boétie was a soldier's heart: 'Je lisois sous sa robe longue une vigueur soldatesque' (ii. 17), and the Stoic philosophy itself was suited to a period of strife and violent death in which it had, as a matter of fact, originally developed.

Montaigne could escape neither the memory of the death of La Boétie, which he had described in a classically polished and well-constructed letter to his father (published before the *Essais* were begun), nor the facts of the violent warfare going on around him. The first *Essais* tend to be meditations on unexpected or violent death, written in an apparently detached, purely intellectual manner. This may well be only an appearance of non-involvement. For, if the Stoic philosopher maintained an aristocratic, disdainful equanimity towards pain and death, yet he needed difficulty and danger as a challenge to his fortitude, and he found in death the extreme test, the final 'essay' of his personality. It is probable that in his reflections on death, Montaigne was already 'testing out' his personality. At any rate the verb 'essayer' is frequently used to describe the experience of death (there are several examples in the beginning of ii. 6). In death and in violence Montaigne found an essential imaginative and creative stimulus, before he found a full mastery of the form in which to express himself.

It is normally suggested that Montaigne's original purpose in writing was to produce a compilation of anecdotes, a compendium of golden sentences, thus following a tradition of Renaissance literature. And this purpose is given as proof that Montaigne's original conception was not of a new, personal work. Now as a matter of fact the mere compilation is not what we read anyway in Montaigne. For example, the first essay not only gives *contradictory* examples of the usefulness of kindness in the military commander, but concludes with a judgement which already bears the stamp of Montaigne's individual view of man: 'c'est un subject merveilleusement vain, divers, et ondoyant que l'homme.' The compilation seems in fact to derive from the judgement, at least as much as the judgement is imposed by the compiled evidence. The compilation is then the secondary factor, the means rather than the end. It gave

Montaigne a very simple, fluid form of composition, well suited to express what he felt about the variety and contradictoriness of the moral world. Its typical use in the early essays is to express the extremely diverse ways in which a man's death may be said to fulfil or negate his life; and to demonstrate the extreme uncertainty and complex determination of military success. The defect of anything like the compilation in Montaigne's eyes was almost certainly that it was a traditional form of *literary* activity. In a C addition[1] to an early essay, Montaigne tells us that if he were a *writer*, he would still produce this early type of essay, the compilation with commentary, and still write about death: 'Si j'estoy faiseur de livres, je feroy un registre commenté de morts diverses' (i. 20). But Montaigne never admits to being a professional writer: 'J'ay mis tous mes efforts à former ma vie. Voylà mon mestier et mon ouvrage. Je suis moins faiseur de livres que de nulle autre besoigne' (ii. 37). He even tries to make out that though he translated Sebundus's *Natural Theology*, this was only to please his father, and took no time at all. In fact it is a careful piece of work and probably took him all of four years.

Montaigne writes in the vernacular for the educated laity, not in Latin for the learned. Writing as a non-professional, he writes for the class which was to evolve the ideal of the gentlemanly *honnête homme*, interested in all things but professionally competent in none. It is not surprising that he does all he can to make his own image fit the aristocratic military class which he is addressing. Perhaps the stress on military affairs in the earlier essays is partly due to the nature of his audience. Certainly the stress which Montaigne lays on his amateur status, the fact that he is not writing for gain, as do lawyers, scholars, and even theologians, would be partly a social stress. The man of learning in the aristocratic household was usually a badly paid hireling, whose job kept him exclusively with the children and servants.

The persona of the soldier-aristocrat had further uses for Montaigne. The *Essais* are not only written in French, but entirely conceived in French, the first serious philosophical work of any importance by a Frenchman which could not equally well have been

[1] See Note at end of this chapter.

written in Latin. Even Calvin's *Institutes* were first written in Latin, and though Bodin's *République* and *Démonomanie* were first published in French, their aim was not to appeal exclusively to the unlearned layman, but to him as well as to the scholar. Moreover, unlike the fictional writing of, say, Rabelais, or the poetry of the Pléiade, there was no literary model for Montaigne to follow. The exceptional stylistic awareness of Montaigne derives from this lack of a model, but even more from his extremely original wish for a style completely his own. In so far as Montaigne is conscious of a stylistic model for this 'personal' style, it is the speech of the soldier which provides it: 'Le parler que j'ayme, c'est un parler simple et naïf, tel sur le papier qu'à la bouche; un parler succulent et nerveux, court et serré, non tant delicat et peigné comme vehement et brusque... non pedantesque, non fratesque, non pleideresque, mais plustost soldatesque' (i. 27). Not then the language of the pedant, ecclesiastic, or lawyer, but that of the soldier, speaking as man to man. As a matter of fact the brusque, laconic manner described here is not so typical of Montaigne as an apparently more spontaneous, tentative, unbalanced style. Montaigne sees this looser, and also 'spoken' style, too, as being modelled on the speech of the soldier which he is: 'Mon dessein est de representer en parlant une profonde nonchalance et des mouvements fortuites et impremeditez, comme naissans des occasions presentes: aymant aussi cher ne rien dire qui vaille que de monstrer estre venu preparé pour bien dire, chose messeante, sur tout à gens de ma profession' (iii. 9).

But not only does the soldier provide the model for the 'personal' style, he also provides an example and encouragement in the enterprise of personal revelation and self-communication. For, far from being an exhibitionist, Montaigne is rather shy about physical self-exposure; shyer than he thinks fitting in a soldier like himself: 'J'y souffre plus de contrainte, que je n'estime bien seant à un homme de ma profession' (i. 3). Since Montaigne's literary persona is that of the soldier, it is not surprising that his ideal man has a lot of the soldier in him, a man who is vigorous, direct, and versatile. There is little of the elegant and self-effacing courtier about the *honnête homme* as he is described by Montaigne: 'Il se rejettera souvent aux excez mesme, s'il m'en croit: autrement la moindre desbauche le ruyne… La plus contraire qualité à un honneste homme, c'est la delicatesse et obligation à certaine façon particuliere' (iii. 13). Montaigne has no time for the lily-livered spoil-sport whose hesitations he fiercely castigates, especially in 'un homme de guerre… lequel, comme disoit Philopoemen, se doit accoustumer à toute diversité et inégalité de vie' (ibid.).

The context shows no particular reason why Montaigne should refer to the soldier here. And in fact there is none. Montaigne is simply taking it for granted that his readers are of the aristocracy, and that they are interested in his views on proper aristocratic conduct. We cannot reasonably deny the element of vainglory in this assumption. Can we deny its existence in the preface? Here Montaigne claims to be writing only for the 'commodité particuliere de mes parens et amis'. Yet a manuscript would have done the job as well.

The stress on his insignificance, and on the limited interest of his book, is probably meant to provoke interest in what he has to say: to act, in short, as self-advertisement. Whether we consider this to be merely trivial depends on our reaction to what it is he says.

Montaigne obviously shares the vanity of any writer who has something new to say, and wants to say it as an individual, rather than as the instrument of a higher power or of a larger purpose. We have already seen something of the novelty of the *Essais*, and the quotations will have revealed something of the individuality of Montaigne's language. If we re-read the first of the quotations in this chapter: 'il n'est subject si vain, qui ne merite un rang en cette rapsodie', we may now see that he is making quite a positive statement about the range and variety of subjects which he wants to discuss. His confession of triviality is a claim to an independent inquiry into phenomena that are so innocuous and insignificant that none of the censorships of tradition need infringe its scope. Seen in this way, the theme of vanity is a defensive weapon. For example, by giving harmless titles such as *Coutume de l'isle de Cea*, or *Sur des vers de Virgile*, to his essays, Montaigne can analyse the acts of suicide and of love more intimately and more boldly than a more ambitious title, and a more formal, traditional, and scholarly approach would either have allowed or suggested. And he seems to be aware of this. Thus the sentence: 'Il n'est action si privee et secrette qui se desrobe de leur cognoisance et jurisdiction', which occurs in *Sur des vers de Virgile* (iii. 5), is an excellent description of the scope of the *Essais*. Yet it does not refer to the *Essais* at all, but to the universally prescriptive ambitions of theology and (moral) philosophy of which Montaigne is conscious but which he chooses by and large to ignore since his aims, though different, are equally universal.

It is in Montaigne that the twin Renaissance tendencies to cultivate literary and aesthetic values and to explore this world rather than the next find their fullest expression. Montaigne is both poet and descriptive, un-moralizing 'moraliste'. He is both of these most typically and most originally in his extremely new awareness of his power to fashion and shape himself, to feel his personality at work. He seems to have felt the soul as a sequence of events, rather than an eternal, indivisible essence, as something fluid and discontinuous and malleable, rather than fixed and given for all time. The origins of this very novel outlook are extremely complex. We may suspect that it was stimulated by what seems to have been a prolonged and intelligent effort on his father's part to educate Montaigne in as individual and personal a way as possible. Montaigne likewise would dearly have loved to bring up a son, and his essay on education (i. 26) shows him half-consciously identifying himself with the tutor who tries to shape the pupil in order best to bring out his individuality, his uniqueness. In the absence of a son, the *Essais* seem to have acted as a substitute in which all the potentialities of Montaigne's own individuality are drawn out.

It is usual to write of Montaigne as if he evolved through various philosophical positions—Stoic, Sceptic, and Epicurean—before hitting upon a personal philosophy. This simple scheme has served many useful purposes. But it does obscure the fact that Montaigne does not erase or materially alter what he has published, from one edition to the next. On the contrary, in B and C passages, he expands and enlarges positions which, according to the evolutionary theory of the growth of the *Essais*, he should have abandoned for good. This need not to obliterate the person he once was may well be the real explanation for Montaigne's inclusion in the *Essais* of the document granting him the citizenship of Rome. Montaigne seems to need concrete evidence that he is a real person, and is the person that he was previously. He needs the evidence because the case needs to be proved, and in so far as memory is for most of us the most obvious witness to the existence of a reasonably stable personality, Montaigne is badly equipped as he can remember little. At least this is what he frequently says, though what he means may be that he cannot possess and manipulate his previous self as accurately and sensitively as he would wish.

The Stoic, Sceptic, and Epicurean attitudes in the *Essais* all express genuine aspects of his personality: none of them are inaccurate accounts. But all are merely partial, fragmentary evidence of the whole man, evidence which Montaigne needs to re-read to capture his richly contradictory unity. By standing outside himself he can better feel his solid, three-dimensional existence. The inscriptions that he had carved on the beams of his library to indicate the mood of his 'retreat', the striking of a medal to express his interest in Pyrrhonism, the portraits he had painted of himself, the purely personal travel diary, and the actual publication of the self-portrait which the *Essais* are: all these are expressions of his need to objectivize himself, to see himself acting. Acting, perhaps, in two senses. For a basic metaphor in Montaigne is that of playing a part—that is, of consciously behaving in a ceremonial manner. Ceremonial, but not hypocritical: 'quelque personnaige que l'homme entrepraigne, il joue tousjours le sien parmy' (i. 20).

Montaigne is equally conscious that other people are busily acting too, though more self-deceivingly than himself, particularly in public roles. Thus, if 'le Maire et Montaigne ont tousjours esté deux, d'une separation bien claire' (iii. 10), it is no less true that others 'se transforment et se transsubstantient en autant de nouvelles figures et de nouveaux estres qu'ils entreprennent de charges, et... se prelatent jusques au foye et aux intestins' (ibid.). The gently mocking tone of the verbs here is the closest Montaigne ever comes to satire of the Church, or to satire at all. His sense of human vanity is usually tinged with good-humoured resignation and hardly ever with righteous indignation. It would be wrong to read any bitterness into the ending of the essay on vanity (iii. 9) which addresses man as 'le scrutateur sans connoissance, le magistrat sans jurisdiction et après tout le badin de la farce'. We may wonder how Montaigne views the violence of the civil wars which caused so much distress to less detached minds than his own. Even here he is able to use a theatrical comparison which, by invoking tragedy, effectively denies it: 'Je m'aggrée aucunement de veoir de mes yeux ce notable spectacle de nostre mort publique, ses symptomes et sa forme... Si cherchons nous avidement de recognoistre en ombre mesme et en la fable des Theatres la montre des jeux tragiques de l'humaine fortune' (iii. 12).

If satire and indignation are absent here, they are also absent from another comment on his contemporaries, who may well be extremely brave but in whom may be seen 'tant d'imparfaites et faibles qualitez autres... et, au bout, la nihilité de l'humaine condition' (ii. 6). If *all* is vanity, however, Montaigne's exploration of the 'humaine condition', found in himself and in others, is seen to have a very wide scope indeed. He is able, quite unsatirically, to relate phenomena which European literature had not been able to put together seriously before. This may in fact be the most fruitful result of the theme of vanity in the *Essais*, and is probably responsible for the apparently haphazard suggestiveness of so many essays. Take the short essay *Que nostre desir s'accroit par la malaisance* (ii. 15). Montaigne reflects on the Pyrrhonist maxim that any argument has a counter-argument, and immediately transforms this into the psychological insight that we are stimulated by opposition: 'la difficulté donne pris aux choses.' Opposition is particularly welcome in sexual encounters, and this is true of Cato as well as of horses. But it is also true of the Church which is in much better shape after the stimulating challenge of the Reformers: 'c'est un effect de la Providence divine de permettre sa saincte Eglise estre agitée, comme nous la voyons, de tant de trouble et d'orages.' The Reformers, more like a provocative mistress than an unstimulating prostitute, have not given the Church an easy ride. A little later there is a brilliant switch to the unprovocative nature of his château, which being undefended, has not been attacked. Both silver spoons and deeds have remained untouched. This analysis inevitably makes the essay read like a satire, or like something either impossibly solemn, or stupidly frivolous. In fact the tone is well mannered and fundamentally serious.

At the same time the essay has something of the *boutade* in it, like so much of what Montaigne writes. Whilst recognizing this we should not be worried by it, any more than Montaigne himself who merely notes the fact: 'Ce que j'auray pris à dire en battellant, et en me moquant, je le diray lendemain serieusement' (iii. 5). And we should certainly recognize that the *boutade* is central to the way Montaigne thinks, and to the way he writes.

The *boutade* helps Montaigne to explore the range of human activity and sensibility without analysing, categorizing or systematizing it out of recognition. He is not concerned to arrive at a systematic corpus of knowledge about man, since for him philosophy is a form of activity rather than a description of ultimate truth. His purpose is more personal than theoretical, more poetic than philosophical. In so far as he *is* a philosopher he is a 'nouvelle figure: un philosophe impremedité et fortuite!' (ii. 12). Here we should remember Cotgrave's helpful definition of the *boutade* or *boutée* in his dictionary as 'a violent attempt, a vehement essay'.

In so far as he is a poet, Montaigne learnt to view the world in an increasingly literary and sensuous and individual way. Of the physical world he writes: 'Ay je pas veu en Platon ce divin mot, que nature n'est rien qu'une poësie œnigmatique? comme peut estre qui diroit une peinture voilée et tenebreuse, entreluisant d'une infinie varieté de faux jours à exercer nos conjectures' (ii. 12). In spite of the critical distance implied in these words, which concentrate as much on the intellectual activity of the observer ('exercer nos conjectures') as on the mysterious resonances within nature, the attitude communicated here reaches forward in time to the feeling of Baudelaire's sonnet *Correspondances*. And not only is the physical world perceived in this lofty, poetic manner, but so is the philosophy which attempts to describe it: 'Et certes la philosophie n'est qu'une poësie sophistiquée. D'où tirent ces auteurs anciens toutes leurs authoritez, que des poëtes... Platon n'est qu'un poëte descousu' (ibid.). An earlier version of this passage included the admonition: 'Voyez ces authorités de toute la philosophie antienne, tous leurs ouvrages sont estoilez et emperlez de poësie.' This sensitivity to poetry is equally obvious in Montaigne's own writings which are crammed full of quotations from poets. He might have written verse himself, but found that he could be more original and could better express his very literary mind by combining his prose with other people's verse.

Poetry is very close to his own nature. Thus he writes of women that 'la poësie est un art follastre et subtil, desguisé, parlier, tout en plaisir, tout en montre, comme elles' (iii. 3). If we are tempted to think that this is at least as much a self-portrait as an accurate description of women, or indeed of poetry, we are justified only a few lines later when Montaigne reminds us that 'ma forme essentielle est propre à la communication et à la production; je suis tout au dehors et en evidence'. He is extremely taken up with beauty, adornment, and appearance. In his usual outspoken way he suggests that a bad-looking child actually *deserves* less affection than a beautiful child (iii. 9), and he gives vent to his annoyance that his two greatest heroes, Socrates and La Boétie, are far from being models of human beauty!

Such idiosyncrasies are a small price to pay for Montaigne's love of life, for his exploration of its surprise and variety and joy, for his resolute espousal of a world of sensuousness and ceremony and vigour. Above all, by characterizing himself and his world as useless and trivial he can cause us to reflect, and to wonder. Not least to ask how far we agree with him that 'il n'y a rien d'inutile en nature; non pas l'inutilité mesmes' (iii. 1).

NOTE

MICHEL DE MONTAIGNE, 1533–92, was born at the château of Montaigne, acquired by his father, a soldier and lawyer who came of a prosperous merchant family. He was brought up speaking only Latin, before attending the humanist Collège de Guyenne (1539–46). At twenty-one he began a legal career. The death in 1563 of his friend and colleague, La Boétie, was a profound emotional experience. He became Michel, sieur de Montaigne after his father's death in 1568. He published a translation of the *Natural Theology* of Sebundus in 1569, and some of La Boétie's works in 1571. In the same year he retired to his estates, to write and to meditate. After a long trip to Italy in 1580–1, he was mayor of Bordeaux for almost four years, in which post he pursued the public-minded, moderate, Catholic policies which he consistently held to during the civil wars (1562–98).

Works. The first edition of the *Essais* (1580), in two 'books', was republished with slight alterations in 1582 and 1587. In the next edition, 1588, Montaigne substantially enlarged the first two 'books' and added a third. A posthumous edition of 1595 included many additions based on material written by Montaigne in a copy of the 1588 edition. Modern editions of the *Essais* distinguish between passages which first appeared in 1580, 1588, and 1595 by the signs A, B, and C. The most convenient text is the edition by A. Thibaudet and M. Rat of the *Œuvres complètes* (1965), which includes Montaigne's journal of his voyage to Italy, a private document first published in 1774.

Criticism. Pierre Villey, *Les Sources et l'évolution des essais de Montaigne* (1937) is still fundamental. The most stimulating and thorough general study is H. Friedrich, *Montaigne* (1949, in German). D. Frame, *Montaigne, a Biography* (1965), is readable and reliable. A. Thibaudet, *Montaigne* (1963), although disorganized is suggestive. M. Dréano, *La Pensée religieuse de Montaigne*, is the most sensible book on the subject. Apart from Thibaudet and Friedrich, there are excellent remarks on style in E. Auerbach's brilliant essay in *Mimesis* (1946), and F. Gray, *Le Style de Montaigne* (1958), is helpful.

CHRONOLOGY

History	French literature	English and Italian literature
Voyage of Vasco da Gama to India, 1497–9		
France loses Naples, 1503		Michelangelo writing early poems from 1503 onwards
Treaty of Blois, 1505	Jean Lemaire de Belges, *Épîtres de l'amant vert* (1505)	Sannazaro, *Arcadia* (authorized edn. 1504)
		Bembo, *Asolani* (1505)
		Ariosto, *Cassaria* (1508)
Accession of Henry VIII of England, 1509		Ariosto, *I suppositi* (1509)
		Bibbiena, *La Calandria* (1513)
Fifth Lateran Council, 1512–17		Trissino, *Sofonisba* (1515)
Accession of François I, 1515		
Concordat between François I and Pope Leo X, 1516	Gringore, *Mère Sotte* (c. 1516)	Ariosto, *Orlando furioso* (1516)
Publication of Luther's theses, 1517		Folengo, *Baldus* (1517)
		Machiavelli, *Mandragola* (1518)
Charles V elected Emperor of Holy Roman Empire, 1519		
First circumnavigation of world by Magellan, 1519–22		
Field of the Cloth of Gold (Henry VIII and François I, 1520)		Ariosto, *Il Negromante* (1520)
Excommunication of Luther in Germany, 1521		

Painting and music	Criticism and aesthetic theory	Theology, philosophy, and ideas
Petrucci of Venice prints music from movable type, 1497		Brandt, *Narrenschiff* (1494; 1st French ed., *La Nef des Folz*, 1497)
		Ficino died, 1499
Finck, 1445–1527		Champier, *La Nef des dames* (1503)
Isaac, *c.* 1450–1517 (*Choralis Constantinus* completed by Senfl and published *c.* 1550)		
		Guicciardini, *Storia fiorentina* (written 1509, publ. 1859)
Hofhaimer, 1459–1537		
	Jean Lemaire de Belges, *La Concorde des deux langages* (*c.* 1511)	
Massys, 1466–1530		Erasmus, *Stultitiae laus* (Praise of Folly) (1511)
		Machiavelli, *Il principe* (The Prince) (1513–14)
Arnold van Bruck, *c.* 1470–1554		Budé, *De Asse et partibus eius* (1515)
		Machiavelli, *Discorsi sopra la prima deca di Livio* (*c.* 1515–19)
Dürer, 1471–1528		More, *Utopia* (publ. 1516)
Cranach, 1472–1553		Budé, *Institution du Prince* (written 1516, publ. 1547)
Grünewald, *c.* 1475–1530		
Michelangelo, 1475–1564		
Leonardo da Vinci died, 1519		
	Pierre Fabri, *Grand et Vrai Art de pleine rhétorique* (1521)	Melanchthon, *Loci communes* (1521)

History	French literature	English and Italian literature
Spanish conquest of Mexico, 1521		
Peasants' War, 1524–5		
Emperor Charles V defeats François I at battle of Pavia, 1525		Aretino, *La cortegiana* (1525)
		Tyndale's *Bible* (1525)
Turkish victory at Mohács, 1526		Sannazaro, *De partu virginis* (1526)
Sack of Rome, 1527		Aretino, *Il marescalco* (1527)
Peace of Cambrai between Charles V and François I, 1529		
Collège des Lecteurs Royaux founded, 1530	Lefèvre d'Étaples, *La Sainte Bible* (1530)	Ariosto, *La Lena* (1530)
Inquisition established in Portugal, 1531 Henry VIII supreme head of English Church, 1531	Marguerite de Navarre, *Le Miroir de l'ame pecherresse* (1531)	Alciati, *Emblematum libellus* (Italy 1531 and France 1534)
	Marot, *L'Adolescence Clementine* (1532)	
	Rabelais, *Pantagruel* (1532)	
Spanish conquest of Peru, 1533	Marot, *Suite à l'Adolescence Clementine* (1533)	

Painting and music	Criticism and aesthetic theory	Theology, philosophy, and ideas
		Lord Berners' translation of Froissart's *Chronicles* (1523–5)
Titian, *c.* 1477–1576		Erasmus, *De libero arbitrio* (1524)
		Luther, *De servo arbitrio* (1525)
Hans Baldung Grien, 1480–1545		
Stoltzer died, 1526		
Altdorfer, 1480–1556	Erasmus, *Ciceronianus* (1528)	Tyndale, *The Obedience of a Christen Man and how Christen Rulers ought to governe* (1528)
Lorenzo Lotto, 1480–1556		Castiglione, *Il libro del cortegiano* (The Courtier) (publ. 1528)
		Guicciardini, *Ricordi politici e civili* (1528, 1530)
Raphael, 1483–1520		
	Trissino, *Poetica* (1529–63)	
Andrea del Sarto, 1486–1530		
		Elyot, *The Governour* (1531)
Senfl, *c.* 1490–*c.* 1555		
Claudin de Sermisy, *c.* 1490–1562		
Willaert, *c.* 1490–1562		
Lucas van Leyden, *c.* 1494–1533		
	Marot's preface to *Œuvres* of Villon (1533)	

History	French literature	English and Italian literature
Affaire des Placards, 1534	Rabelais, *Gargantua* (1534)	
Jacques Cartier in Canada, 1534		
Society of Jesus founded by Ignatius Loyola, 1534		
Anabaptists control Munster, 1534–5		
Sir Thomas More beheaded, 1535		Coverdale's *Bible* (1535)
French Alliance with Turks, 1536		
Suppression of the monasteries in England, 1536–40		
Ordonnances de Villers-Cotterêts, 1539		
Emperor Charles V visits France, 1539–40	*Amadis de Gaule* (Bk. I. publ. in French, 1540)	
Cartier's third voyage to Canada, 1541		Giraldi, *Orbecche* (1541)
		Aretino, *Lo ipocrito* (1542)
Cartier's fourth voyage to Canada, 1543		Speroni, *Dialoghi*, 1542
Council of Trent, 1545–63	Scève, *Délie* (1544)	Aretino, *Il filosofo* (1544)
		Rime diverse di molti eccellentiss. auttori nuovamente raccolte (1545–7)
	Rabelais, *Tiers Livre* (1546)	

Painting and music	Criticism and aesthetic theory	Theology, philosophy, and ideas
Correggio, 1494–1534		
Holbein the Younger, 1497–1543	Italian translation of Horace's *Ars Poetica* by Dolce (1535)	
Christopher Tye, *c.* 1500–73	Italian translation of Aristotle's *Poetics* by Pazzi (1536)	Calvin, *Christianae Religionis Institutio* (1536)
Mabuse active, 1503–33		Bonaventure des Périers, *Cymbalum Mundi* (1537)
Parmigianino, 1504–40		
Claude Goudimel, *c.* 1505–72		Vesalius, *De corporis humani fabrica* (1543)
Tallis, 1505–85		Copernicus, *De revolutionibus orbium coelestium* (1543)
School of Fontainebleau (Rosso, Primaticcio, and dell'Abbate)		Ramus, *Aristotelicae animadversiones* (1544)
Jean Goujon, *c.*1510–*c.*1564/9 Philibert de l'Orme, *c.*1510–70 François Clouet, *c.* 1510–72 Bernard Palissy, *c.*1510–*c.*1590	French translation, with preface, of Horace's *Ars poetica* by Jacques Peletier du Mans (1545)	
Jean Clouet (father of François) active, 1516–40		*Ficin sur le Banquet* (trans. Jacques du Bois, 1546)

History	French literature	English and Italian literature
Death of François I and accession of Henri II, 1547 Death of Henry VIII of England, 1547 Charles V's victory at Mühlberg, 1547		Trissino, *L'Italia liberata dai Goti* (1547)
England declares war on France, 1549	Du Bellay, *L'Olive* (1549)	English Book of Common Prayer (1549 and 1552)
Peace of Boulogne, 1550	De Bèze, *Abraham sacrifiant* (1550) Ronsard, *Odes* (1550-1)	
Treaty of Chambord, between Henri II and German Protestants, 1552	Rabelais, *Quart Livre* (1552) Jodelle, *Cléopâtre captive* (1552)	Grazzini, *Le cene* (c. 1552) Udall, *Ralph Roister Doister* (written c. 1553, publ. 1566)
Peace of Augsburg, 1555 Latimer and Ridley burnt at stake, 1555	Louise Labé, *Sonnets* (1555)	
Abdication of Charles V; Phillip II king of Spain, 1556		
English and Spaniards defeat French at St. Quentin, 1557	Ronsard, *Sonnets pour Hélène* (1557)	*Tottel's Miscellany* (1557, comprising songs and sonnets of Wyatt and Surrey)
Calais captured from the English, 1558	Du Bellay, *Les Regrets* (1558) Marguerite de Navarre, *Heptaméron* (1558-9)	

Painting and music	Criticism and aesthetic theory	Theology, philosophy, and ideas
		Les Lois de Platon (trans. Philibert du Val, 1547)
		Adlington translates Aristotle's Ethics (1547)
Cypriano de Rore, c. 1516–65	Thomas Sebillet, Art poétique français (1548)	Hall, Chronicle (1548)
Tintoretto, c. 1518–94	Du Bellay, Deffence et illustration de la langue francoyse (1549)	Cheke, The Heart of Sedition (1549)
	Vasari, Lives of the Artists (1550)	Calvin, Des Scandales (1550)
		More, Utopia (trans. into English, 1551)
		Della Casa, Galateo (1551–5)
Josquin des Prés died, 1521		
(his Missa Pange lingua publ. 1539)	Sir Thomas Wilson, Arte of Rhetorique (1553)	
Andrea Gabrieli, c. 1520–86	Jacques Peletier du Mans, Art poétique (1555)	
		Ramus, Dialectica Libri Duo (1556)
Filippo di Monte, c. 1521–1603		
Brueghel the Elder, c. 1525–69		Knox, The First Blast of the Trumpet against the Monstrous Regiment of Women (1558)

History	French literature	English and Italian literature
Treaty of Cateau-Cambrésis, 1559	Saint-Gelais, *Sophonisbe* (1559)	
Death of Henri II and accession of François II, 1559		
Amboise Conspiracy, 1560	Grévin, *Jules César* (1560)	
Death of François II and accession of Charles IX, 1560		
	Grévin, *Les Esbahis* (1561)	
Wars of Religion waged intermittently, 1562–94		Cellini, *Vita* (*c.* 1562, publ. 1730)
		Sackville and Norton, *Gorboduc* (1562)
		The Mirror for Magistrates (1563)
New Charter for Merchant Adventurers, 1564	Rabelais, *Cinquième Livre* (1564)	
		Giraldi, *Gli ecatommiti* (1565)
	Garnier, *Porcie* (1568)	
Mercator's map of the world, 1569		
Battle of Lepanto, 1571		*Commedia dell'arte* flourishes from 1570s
Massacre of Saint Bartholomew, 1572	Ronsard, *La Franciade* (1572)	
Sea Beggars capture Brill, 1572	Jean de la Taille, *Saül le furieux* (1572)	

Painting and music	Criticism and aesthetic theory	Theology, philosophy, and ideas
	Amyot's preface to *Vies des hommes illustres* (1559)	
Palestrina, *c.* 1526–94 (first book of masses, 1554; *Missa Papae Marcelli*, 1567; *Missa quarta*, 1582)		
Claude le Jeune, *c.* 1527–1600		
Veronese, 1528–88		
Janequin died, *c.* 1560		Pasquier, *Recherches de la France* (Bk. I publ. 1560)
Lassus, *c.* 1530–94 (first book of motets, 1556; *Seven Penitential Psalms* written 1565; *Neue teutsche Liedlein*, 1567)	Scaliger, *Poetices Libri Septem* (1561)	
		Guicciardini, *Storia d'Italia* (first publ. 1561–7)
Germain Pilow, *c.* 1537–90		Sextus Empiricus *Hypotyposes* (publ. 1562)
Byrd, 1543–1623 (*Psalmes, Sonnets and songs of sadness and pietie*, 1588)	Minturno, *Arte poetica* (1563)	Foxe, *Book of Martyrs* (1563)
El Greco, 1545–1614	Ronsard, *Abrégé de l'art poétique français* (1565)	Telesio, *De rerum natura* (1565–86)
Giovanni Gabrieli, 1557–1612 (*Symphoniae sacrae*, 1597 and 1615)	H. Estienne, *Conformité du langage français avec le grec* (1565)	Bodin, *Methodus ad facilem historiarum cognitionem* (1566)
		Les Politiques d'Aristote (trans. Le Roy, 1568)
Morley, 1557–*c.* 1603		
	Castelvetro, *La poetica di Aristotile vulgarizzata* (1570)	Roger Ascham, *The Scholemaster* (1570)
Gesualdo, 1560–1615	Ronsard, first preface to *La Franciade* (1572) (second and third prefaces, 1585 and 1587)	Amyot, *Œuvres morales* (1572)

History	French literature	English and Italian literature
		Tasso, *Aminta* (completed 1573)
Death of Charles IX and accession of Henri III, 1574		
		Gammer Gurton's Needle (1575)
		Tasso, *Gerusalemme liberata* (completed 1575)
		The Paradyse of Daynty Devises (1576)
Drake's circumnavigation of the world, 1577–80	D'Aubigné, *Les Tragiques* (begun 1577, publ. 1616)	
Union of Utrecht, 1579	Garnier, *La Troade* (1579)	Lyly, *Euphues* (1578) Spenser, *The Shepherd's Calendar* (1579)
	Garnier, *Antigone* (1580) Montaigne, *Essais* (Bks. I and II, 1580)	Guarini, *Il pastor fido* (1580–9)
Diet of Augsburg, 1582		Bruno, *Il candelaio* (1582)
	Garnier, *Les Juives* (1583)	
Assassination of William the Silent, 1584 Raleigh discovers Virginia, 1584	Turnèbe, *Les Contens* (1584)	
		Kyd, *The Spanish Tragedie*, (c. 1585) *Arden of Faversham* (1586) Marlowe, *Tamburlane* (1587–8)
Defeat of Spanish Armada, 1588	Montaigne, *Essais* (Bks. I and II revised and Bk. III, 1588)	
Assassination of Henri III and accession of Henri IV, 1589		Marlowe, *Doctor Faustus* (c. 1589) Marlowe, *The Jew of Malta* (1590)

Painting and music	Criticism and aesthetic theory	Theology, philosophy, and ideas
Jacopo Peri, 1561–1633 (*Dafne* performed 1594)		
		Le Roy, *De la vicissitude variété des choses en l'univers* (1576)
Dowland, 1563–1626 (*First Booke of Songes or Ayres*, 1597)		Bodin, *Six livres de la République* (1576)
		Holinshed, *Chronicles* (1578–86)
Hassler, 1564–1612	H. Estienne, *Projet du livre intitulé de la Précellence du langage français* (1579)	North's translation of Plutarch's *Lives* (1579)
	Sir Philip Sidney, *Apologie for Poetrie* (1580)	
Monteverdi, 1567–1643 (first book of madrigals, 1587)		
		Bruno, *La cena de le ceneri* (1584)
	William Webbe, *Discourse of English Poetrie* (1586)	
Wilbye, 1573–1638?	George Puttenham, *Arte of English Poesie* (1589)	Hakluyt, *The Principall Navigations . . . of the English Nation* (1589)
		Bruno, *De immenso et innumerabilibus* (c. 1589)

History	French literature	English and Italian literature
		Sidney, *Arcadia* (1590)
		Spenser, *The Faerie Queene* (Bks. I–III, 1590)
		Sidney, *Astrophel and Stella* (1591)
		Donne, *Satires* (written *c.* 1593), *Songs and Sonnets* (written *c.* 1593–8)
Henri IV enters Paris, 1594		Shakespeare, *Romeo and Juliet* (*c.* 1595)
Henri IV declares war on Spain, 1595		Spenser, *Amoretti* and *Epithalamion* (*c.* 1595)
		Shakespeare, *A Midsummer Night's Dream* (1595), *Richard II* and *The Merchant of Venice* (1597)
		Bacon, *Essays* (first publ. 1597)
Treaty of Vervins (between France and Spain), 1598		Jonson, *Every Man in his Humour* (1598)
Edict of Nantes, 1598		
Death of Philip II, 1598		
		Shakespeare, *Julius Caesar* (1599)

Painting and music	Criticism and aesthetic theory	Theology, philosophy, and ideas
Weelkes, 1575–1623 (*Madrigals*, 1600)		
		Hooker, *The Laws of Ecclesiastical Polity* (1593 onwards)
Elsheimer, 1578–1610		*La Satyre Ménippée* (1594)
Orlando Gibbons born, 1583		
	Pierre de Laudun, *Art poétique français* (1597)	Adlington translates Aristotle's *Politics* (1597)

Index